COUNTRY INNS
OF NEW ENGLAND

PATRICIA BROOKS
Connecticut, Rhode Island
and Western Massachusetts

FRAN JURGA GARVAN
Eastern Massachusetts, Vermont,
New Hampshire and Maine

ROY KILLEEN
Illustrations

101 PRODUCTIONS
San Francisco

COVER DRAWING: Griswold Inn, Essex, Connecticut. Drawing by Roy Killeen; color rendering by Sara Raffetto.

MAPS: Lynne O'Neil

Some of the drawings in this book have been reproduced from the inns' brochure, with permission of the inns, and are credited to the following artists or sources: Silvermine Tavern, page 7; The Elms, page 10; The Hopkins Inn, page 17, Dhris Dunn; The Inn on Lake Waramaug, page 18, Edd Ashe; Under Mountain Inn, page 26, Judy Osborne; Old Riverton Inn, page 28, Hometown Prints; Bishopsgate, page 32, Pat Beveridge; Bee and Thistle, page 40, Virginia Neilson; Old Lyme Inn, page 42, Gigi Horr-Liverant; The Atlantic Inn, page 51, Bruce C. Anderson; The 1661 Inn, page 55; The Queen Anne Inn, page 63; The 1780 Egremont Inn, page 72; The Inn at Stockbridge, page 75, Robert Johnston; The Red Lion Inn, page 77, Doug McGregor; Haus Andreas Inn, page 82, Elyse Carter; The Candlelight Inn, page 85, Bruce McDonald; Yankee Pedlar Inn, page 93, Casey Associates; Whale Inn, page 99, Engler; Colonel Ebenezer Crafts Inn, page 107, John Pearson, Inc.; The Hawthorne Inn, page 118, Gregory Burch; The Colonial Inn, page 119; Addison Choate House, page 127, Brad Sweet; Old Newfane Inn, page 155, Olive Metcalf; Chester Inn, page 159, Henry Crocker; Quechee Inn at Marshland Farm, page 164, Anne Melor; Green Mountain Inn, page 176, Charlotte Ciraldi; The Lyme Inn, page 193, Beth Adams; Follansbee Inn, page 197; Colby Hill Inn, page 201, Olive Metcalf; Monadnok Inn, page 208, Debra McComb-Wright; Captain Lord Mansion, page 219, Stephen M. Perry; The Squire Tarbox Inn, page 222, Olive Metcalf; The Winter's Inn, page 227, Sue Thayer.

Copyright © 1984   101 Productions

All rights reserved. No part of this book may be reproduced in any form without the permission of 101 Productions. Printed and bound in the United States of America.

Distributed to the book trade in the United States by The Scribner Book Companies, New York, and in Canada by John Wiley & Sons Canada Limited, Toronto.

Published by 101 Productions
834 Mission Street
San Francisco, California 94103

Library of Congress Catalog Number 84-42825
ISBN 0-89286-229-7

CONTENTS

Introduction iv
Connecticut 1
Rhode Island 47
Western Massachusetts 67
Eastern Massachusetts 113
Vermont 149
New Hampshire 181
Maine 211
Index 228

INTRODUCTION

You know you're in New England when drug stores become apothecaries, road signs say Dual Carriageway and Thickly Settled, and the bald eagle appears everywhere but in the sky—on wallpaper, bedspreads, over bars, fireplaces and doorways.

You know it most of all by the sudden appearance of inns. New England and inns go together as naturally as baked beans and Boston or johnny cake and Rhode Island. In fact, inns were a way of life for travelers in New England well before our republic began. Wherever a stagecoach stopped, an inn would be on hand for hungry, tired passengers to fuel up and bed down.

To many twentieth-century travelers, the mention of a country inn evokes visions of New England. Time was—and no more than a decade or two ago—when an authentic New England inn had become a rarity, as hard to find as hand-blown glass.

Mercifully, that's in the past. There are now several hundred country and village inns scattered throughout the six New England states. And every time we venture forth still others seem to have sprung up.

Credit the Bicentennial celebrations perhaps. It encouraged the preservation and restoration of our heritage of fine old buildings. At the same time, discerning travelers began to seek accommodations more memorable than a chain motel that was a clone of every other. Fortunately, in New England, a sense of history had never been lost. The old country inns and taverns were still there. Dozens of energetic, newly inspired and dedicated innkeepers opened their doors again.

Today's New England inns are as diverse and eclectic as they were when Longfellow immortalized one of them in his *Tales of a Wayside Inn*. To the traveler it is this individuality that is part of an inn's charm. You'll find it in the building and furnishings of the inn itself and in the innkeeper who has made it so. You'll find it also in the warmth of the greeting to you, the guest. You are welcome here.

Inn-hopping through New England has charms that extend beyond the inns themselves. Many of the splendid vintage houses that were or have been turned into inns are located in villages of special historic interest. Others are in resort, ski or recreation areas that are magnets in themselves. A stay at an inn can measurably expand and enrich one's total vacation experience, and as a result, many travelers have become "inn-ophiles," planning their entire vacations around specific inns—a few days here in an eighteenth-century Georgian house in the woods, a few elsewhere in a rustic farmhouse-cum-inn.

A word or two should be said about the inns included in this book. You won't find every inn in New England—only the best. "Best" means a combination of ambience, sense of history, choice location, exceptional food and geniality of the innkeepers. But "Best" also means high standards of housekeeping, maintenance and service. We included inns we found enchanting, exemplary, unique or remarkable—or all of the above.

Our wanderings through Connecticut, Massachusetts, Rhode Island, New Hampshire, Vermont and Maine during this past year have led to new discoveries and new inn pleasures, a good many of which have not been published before. As veteran critics, we regard it as a matter of professional pride that our visits to every single inn were incognito—many innkeepers will discover we were there only when they read about themselves in this book. This may seem unremarkable to you the reader, but it is not the procedure followed in some other guidebooks. Furthermore, no inn paid to be included in this book. Not every guidebook can make that statement.

We hope that this book will help you chart your course through the New England we love so much and that your stay at each inn will be part of the enriching experience that travel should be. As you go, you may make inn discoveries of your own. If so, let us hear about them. Meanwhile, happy and inn-spired roaming and traveling New England's byways.

RULES OF THE INN

Rates Due to the enormous price fluctuations of these times, we do not quote specific rates, but classify inns as inexpensive, moderate or expensive, based upon the average room rate. Many of the inns, however, have some rooms at a lower or higher rate than indicated.

Reservations, Deposits, Cancellations and Refunds Reservations are advised for all of the inns in this book, especially during peak travel periods. On holidays and weekends, they are often booked for months in advance. Most of the inns require a deposit of at least one night's lodging; many require a minimum stay of two nights on the weekends. In most cases your deposit will not be refunded if you cancel at the last minute; sometimes even a week's notice is required. Call or write in advance to ask about the current requirements, rates and refund policies.

Housekeeping In many of the smaller inns guests share a community bathroom. Be sure to clean out your tub and washbasin, pick up your towels and leave the bathroom in immaculate condition for the next guest. In many of the smaller places, the chambermaid is actually the innkeeper; keep you room as tidy as possible.

Tipping In the larger inns, where you are presented your check at the end of each meal, tip as you would in any hotel or restaurant. In the smaller inns, where the owner does the cooking and serving, you are not required to tip. In fact most innkeepers will not accept tips and some would be insulted. If you wish to express your appreciation, send flowers or leave some wine as you would in a friend's home. You should, however, compensate the innkeeper's helpers. Some inns have a "kitty" and divide the tips among the workers; others expect you to tip individually. We recommend that, at the end of your stay, you ask the innkeeper for advice in handling this.

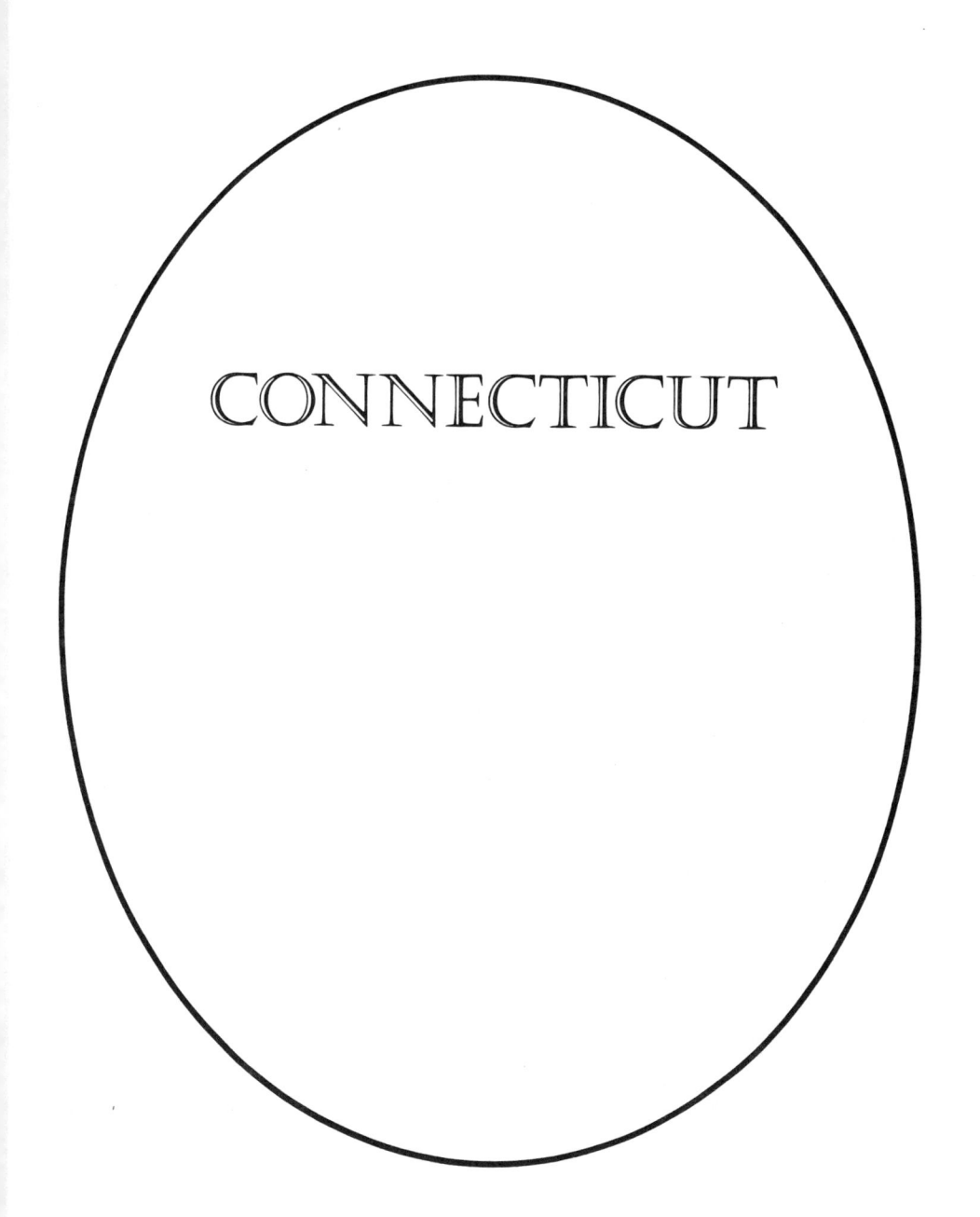

CONNECTICUT

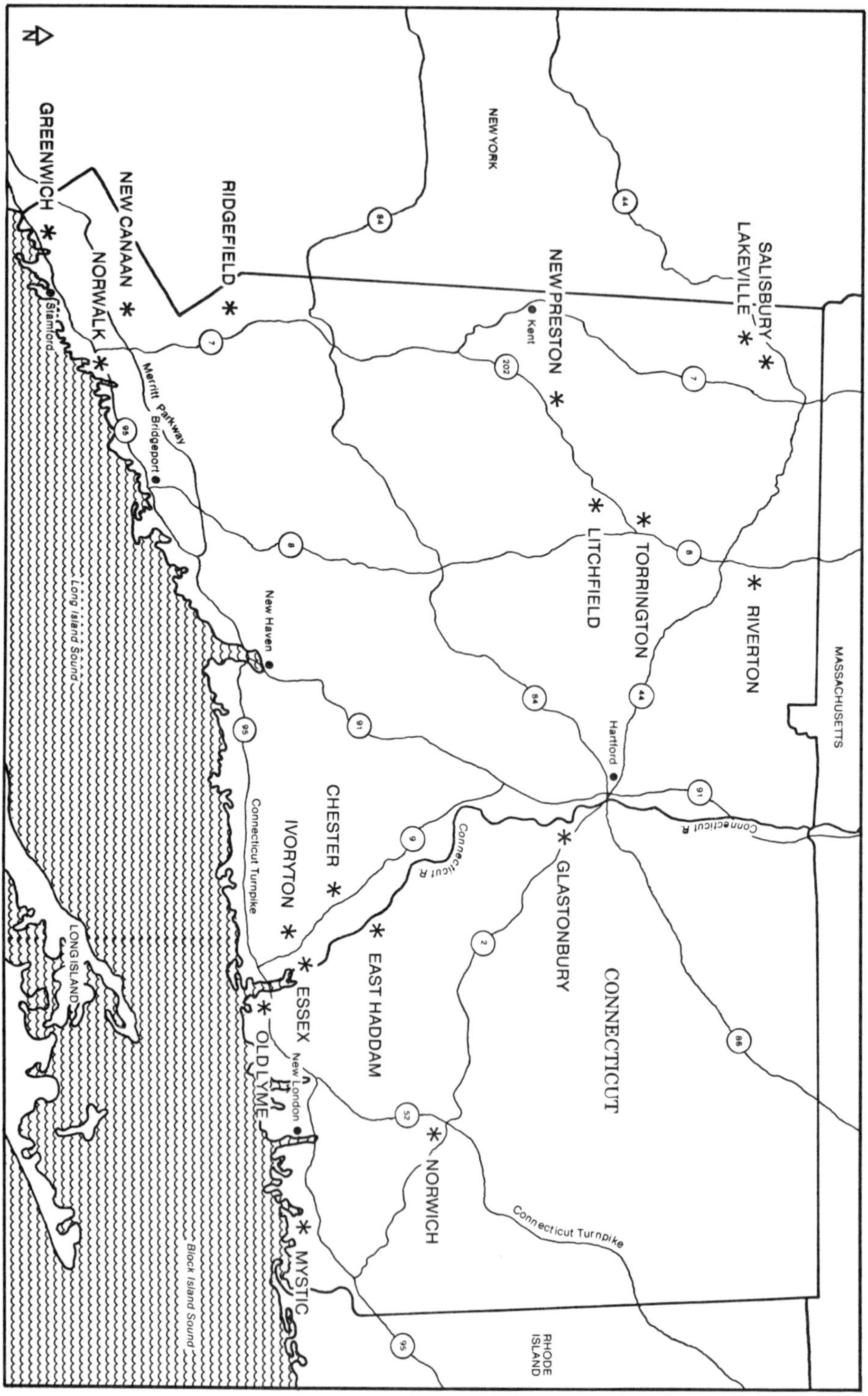
N
NEW YORK
MASSACHUSETTS
RHODE ISLAND
CONNECTICUT
SALISBURY
LAKEVILLE
NEW PRESTON
Kent
RIVERTON
TORRINGTON
LITCHFIELD
RIDGEFIELD
NEW CANAAN
NORWALK
GREENWICH
Stamford
Merritt Parkway
Bridgeport
New Haven
Hartford
GLASTONBURY
Connecticut R.
CHESTER
IVORYTON
ESSEX
EAST HADDAM
OLD LYME
New London
NORWICH
MYSTIC
Connecticut Turnpike
Long Island Sound
LONG ISLAND
Block Island Sound
84
44
7
202
8
95
91
9
2
52
86

FAIRFIELD COUNTY

There are certain areas that take on a mystique of their own, created largely by the kinds of people who live there. Fairfield County, adjacent to New York and bordering Long Island Sound, has long attracted successful New Yorkers—from Broadway, Wall Street, and publishing row—as bedroom, playground and escape hatch from the daily grind of the Big City. Celebrities like Paul Newman, Harry Reasoner, Jack Paar, William Buckley, among hundreds of others, call one or another of Fairfield County's small towns home. Most high-powered people like this part of Connecticut for the anonymity it affords and the chance to live a truly private life while still having instant access and proximity to New York's many attractions.

So come, visitor, but don't expect any bus tour to the home of the stars. This is not Hollywood East, although that's not to say that you might not run into Robert Redford eating an ice cream cone on Main Street in Westport. What this wooded and lovely part of New England offers is a chance to enjoy New York by day and escape to a wooded inn in the country by night. You will also find swimming, sailing and pleasure boat cruising on the sound in warm weather, and cultural pleasures such as the frequently changing exhibitions of New York's Whitney Museum of American Art's handsome Stamford branch and the Aldrich Museum of Contemporary Art in Ridgefield. In addition, the Bruce Museum in Greenwich and Stamford Museum and Nature Center have interesting art and handcraft exhibitions. The latter is especially enjoyable for children, because of the nature trails, planetarium, and numerous domestic and wild animals. Some even roam free, available for feeding, patting and enjoying. You will also find good professional theater at the Hartman in Stamford and, in summer, at the Westport Country Playhouse. Antiques hunters will have a field day along Route 7, stopping at the many shops that dot the highway between Norwalk and Danbury.

High Style, Comfort and Proximity to New York City
HOMESTEAD INN
Greenwich

From the outside, the Homestead looks like an affluent Nutmegger's (as Connecticut residents call themselves) chocolate-colored Victorian manor house. Turreted and rambling, it is set back on property surrounded by other private estates, near Long Island Sound in the sophisticated corporate community of Greenwich.

The Homestead is Victorian to be sure, in what is known as the "carpenter Gothic" style. But its antecedents actually go back even further, to 1799, when it began life as the farmhouse home of Augustus I. Mead, a judge and gentleman farmer. Mead's family went back further still: Some were among the first twenty-seven settlers who, in 1672, bought from the Misehassky Indians the land that later became Greenwich.

The house remained in the Mead family until 1859 when it was sold, remodeled in the present style, and transformed into an inn. After a recent period of decline, the inn changed hands and in 1979 was bought by Nancy K. Smith and Lessie Davison, who updated it. Still retaining its period charm, the Homestead has been repainted and spruced up inside with fresh wallpaper, lovely flower arrangements, handsome fabrics and furnishings, and beautiful antiques. The results are stunning, both in the thirteen individually decorated guest rooms and in the stylish dining rooms, located in the area that was once the attached barn. Huge chestnut posts and exposed beams and wide floorboards remind you of their former role. Note in particular the Bridal Suite with its fishnet canopy bed, hooked rugs, wing chairs and great spaciousness. The lovely Robin Suite is named for the eighteenth-century stenciling discovered under five layers of wallpaper.

Well-located for a restful, woodsy retreat, the inn is also handy for more active excursions. The train station is nearby and it is just a thirty minute ride to New York and its myriad attractions. Greenwich itself is no wasteland, but an interesting small city of sixty thousand with smart boutiques, antiques shops, and numerous good restaurants. Among the current favorites are Tapestries, for elegant French cuisine, and Guy Savoy, the American outpost of a one-star Michelin Parisienne establishment.

More than a word must be said about the Homestead's own restaurant, La Grange, which is a first-rate place to dine. The menu

Homestead Inn

is French, and *specialites de maison* include billi bi soup, veal sweetbreads with chanterelles, duckling with a cassis sauce, chicken in champagne sauce, escargot in a shallot-garlic cream sauce and real escalopes with chestnuts. Chef Jacques Thiebeult was once sous-chef of New York's premier French restaurants, Le Cygne and Le Cirque, and knows exactly what he's doing.

HOMESTEAD INN, 420 Field Point Road, Greenwich, CT 06830. Telephone: (203) 869-7500. Accommodations: thirteen rooms with twin and queen-size beds; private baths with tub/shower; telephones; color television. Rates: expensive, Continental breakfast included. Children welcome. No pets. Cards: AE, MC, VISA. Open all year.

Getting there: Exit 3 from I-95 leads to Horseneck Lane on the left. Make a left onto Field Point Road.

Woods, Waterfalls and an Old Grist Mill
SILVERMINE TAVERN
Norwalk

The area in southwestern Connecticut known as Silvermine was settled as long ago as 1742. Threading its tranquil way along the border between Norwalk and New Canaan is the Silvermine River, and on its banks rests an old inn, the Silvermine Tavern. Parts of the tavern and the adjacent mill date back more than two hundred years and the setting is lovely, at its best in warm weather. You can sit and dine on an open terrace above a millpond, gazing down at the resident ducks and swans which glide past. In winter, three fireplaces keep the dining rooms warm and cosy.

Some inns are acclaimed for their food, others for their rooms. Silvermine Tavern's charms are most evident in the guest rooms—especially the two double rooms with canopy beds and balconies overlooking the river—and in the dining room decor. The American-style food is no match for the Early American accouterments and the setting itself, though Sunday brunch is a popular occasion here, and the fare is hearty and abundant. Notice the unevenness of the old brick floor, and the fine collection of American folk art hung along the dining room walls: antique apothecary signs, old farm implements and household objects. Children love Miss Abigail, a mannequin who stands by the bar, attired in a granny dress and sun bonnet.

A sign states, "Miss Abigail is the only woman who can be served at a bar in Connecticut"—no longer true, of course.

Four buildings comprise the Tavern group: the tavern itself, an old mill, a coach house and a country store. Down the road is the Silvermine Guild of Artists, a good place to view the work of artists who live in this art-conscious corner of Connecticut. The guild has numerous changing exhibitions throughout the year. On the other side of Norwalk, just off I-95, is the Lockwood Mathews Mansion Museum, a palatial Victorian mansion, now a National Historic Landmark. Architecture buffs find its detailing and craftsmanship a joy.

SILVERMINE TAVERN, Silvermine Avenue, Norwalk, CT 06850. Telephone: (203) 847-4558. Accommodations: ten rooms with twin and double beds; private baths with tub/shower; no telephones; no television. Rates: moderate, Continental breakfast included. Children welcome. No pets. Cards: AE, DC, MC, VISA. Open all year, closed Tuesdays.

Getting there: From the Merritt Parkway Exit 38, turn left off the ramp and follow Route 123 (New Canaan Avenue) about two and one-half miles to a firehouse and traffic light. Turn left at this corner onto Silvermine Avenue. Follow this until you see the Tavern on the right, with parking on the left.

Good Food in a Former Minister's House
ROGER SHERMAN INN
New Canaan

Just up a winding road from God's Acre, the church-lined green in this old Connecticut town, sits a rambling clapboard house, a town landmark. The Roger Sherman dates from 1740 and is a prime example, according to the local historical society, of a New England double-breasted house. That means five windows across the second floor with two flanking a center door and a center chimney. The center chimney wasn't as elegant as the later center hall, but it allowed greater interior flexibility.

That flexibility was obvious in the Roger Sherman, which began life as the home of a minister, the Reverend Justus Mitchell, who kept his bible in the cupboard above the fireplace in what is now the inn's taproom. From private home to exclusive prep school for boys, to a New Yorker's weekend retreat, the house underwent many changes and additions until it finally became an inn, the Holmewood, in 1926. Now called the Roger Sherman, the inn has had the same ownership since 1970, providing an even-keeled, steady stewardship, both in the popular dining room and in the inn proper.

The inn's name derives from one of Connecticut's most famous patriots. Sherman was a judge and senator, and the only man to sign all four of the nation's major documents: the Articles of Association, Declaration of Independence, Articles of Confederation and the United States Constitution. He was also the uncle of Reverend Justus Mitchell's wife.

The Roger Sherman's consistency and quality, due largely to owner/maitre d' hotel Stefan Zur's quiet professionalism, have made its five dining rooms magnets for local diners, especially on weekend evenings when the piano in the bar is lively—as are the guests. The culinary emphasis is on Continental specialties, with a slight central European accent. (Calf sweetbreads with ham and mushrooms in a bearnaise sauce, bay scallops garnished with bacon, and scampi Nero in a garlic-butter sauce are delectible trademarks.) In the main dining room, the backdrop is a wall-length Colonial battle scene mural. The small dining room, part of the original house, with Tiffany windows and fireplace lined with blue-and-white Dutch tiles, is particularily charming. In warm weather, it is even more pleasant to dine on the flagstone terrace under towering pines.

You'll see other features of the still-intact original building here and there, such as the twenty-six-inch wide oak floorboards that are found in various parts of the house. According to the local historical society, during one of the inn's renovations the workmen demanded extra compensation because the hardwood used in the original building kept breaking their tools.

The guest rooms—eight in the main house, five in the annex and six apartments—are decorated somewhat eclectically. "Early attic" it's been called. There are comfortable overstuffed chairs, gilded eagle mirrors, and floral patterned wallpaper. The double rooms are more than ample, with extra chairs and tables arranged sitting-room style. Three rooms in the inn and four in the annex have fireplaces. Restful and bucolic, the inn is located across the road from the New Canaan Nature Center, a forested landscape with webs of hiking trails and a pond. On many weekends a number of events, such as sheep shearing and maple tree tapping, are of special interest to children.

ROGER SHERMAN INN, 195 Oenoke Ridge, New Canaan, CT 06840. Telephone: (203) 966-4541. Accommodations: ten rooms with twin and double beds, one triple suite; private baths with tub/shower; telephones; televisions. Rates: moderate. Children welcome. No pets. Cards: AE, CB, DC, MC, VISA. Open all year.

Getting there: Take Exit 38 of the Merritt Parkway and follow Route 123 until the New Canaan turn-off. From New Canaan's town center, follow State Route 124 for a quarter mile north. The inn is on the right side of the road and is well marked.

1775 and All That
THE ELMS
Ridgefield

It's easy to drive right past The Elms on Ridgefield's main thoroughfare and mistake it for just another one of Ridgefield's beautiful Colonial houses, for Main Street is lined with these treasures. The inn is so well known to locals that a small sign in front suffices, especially since it isn't the Elms or the Ridgefield style to be ostentatious—if you've "got it" in this sedate, old-fashioned town, you *don't* flaunt it.

To its devotees, The Elms has "got it," "it" being authentic age in an area that prizes antiquity, charm in the understated furnishings inside the old clapboard building, and serenity for anyone seeking a restful retreat. How ironic that this retreat is on the very site of one of Connecticut's few Revolutionary War engagements, the Battle of Ridgefield.

Though the Elms's dining rooms are busy at lunch and dinner, the tempo is subdued and the pace is leisurely (the same can sometimes be said about the service as well, however). The authentic look of the wood-paneled taproom with its old creaky floorboards is complemented by a small private dining room that looks as it might have when the house was built by cabinetmaker Amos Seymour back in 1760. This room can also be closed off from the other dining areas for small intimate dinners.

Best of all are the four guest rooms with four-poster beds and fireplaces. Seymour's house didn't become an inn until 1799, and it still retains the small rooms, low ceilings and period furnishings that suggest house, not inn. This even means breakfast served in your room, if that's your pleasure.

Robert and Violet Scala have owned The Elms for more than thirty-five years. In 1983 they added an annex with sixteen guest rooms, all nicely furnished in the same Georgian style as the inn proper, but with brand new plumbing and color television, and many rooms have their own fireplaces.

Ridgefield is blessed with good restaurants, both the informal ones such as The Food Chandler and Entrez Vous, and the more elegant ones like Stonehenge, The Inn at Ridgefield, and Le Coq Hardi. If you stay at The Elms more than a single night, you'll enjoy sampling the menus of other places around town.

THE ELMS INN, 500 Main Street, Ridgefield, CT 06877. Telephone: (203) 438-2541. Accommodations: twenty-one twin and queen-size beds; private baths with tub/shower; telephones; color television. Rates: moderate to expensive, Continental breakfast served in rooms included. Children welcome. No pets. Cards: AE, DC, MC, VISA. Open all year.

Getting there: Follow Route 35 from Route 7 right into the center of Ridgefield.

Magnet for Celebrities and Food Fanciers
STONEHENGE
Ridgefield

Long a hideaway for sophisticated New Yorkers and Broadway notables in search of a country setting, Stonehenge made its considerable reputation on the splendid kitchen of the late chef-owner Albert Stockli. Innkeepers David Davis and Douglas Seville have continued the Stockli tradition, and the country French cuisine is generally as delicious as ever.

Dining is exceptionally gracious in the sparkling dining room which faces a well-stocked trout pond. You can watch ducks, geese and swans cavort outside, while dining comfortably inside on the inn's own brook trout, venison and pheasant in season, and suckling pig.

Stonehenge

The inn was built as a farmhouse in 1823. In the inn proper there are two enormous guest rooms with fireplaces—especially cheering on frosty winter evenings. A few steps across the lawn to the annex are six slightly smaller, but still ample rooms tucked quietly into ten acres of wooded surroundings. Breakfast can be brought to your room any day except Tuesday, the staff's day off.

Although the inn seems beautifully insulated from the Real World, Ridgefield is just a few miles away, where you might want to drop by the old Keeler Tavern, which operated as an inn from Colonial times well into the twentieth century. Note the cannonball still lodged in the post, a souvenir of the 1777 Battle of Ridgefield. Antiques aficionados like to make the rounds of the shops along Route 7, going to and from Stonehenge.

STONEHENGE, Route 7, Ridgefield, CT 06877. Telephone: (203) 438-6511. Accommodations: nine rooms with twin, double and king-size beds, four suites will be available by summer of 1984; private baths, each with tub/shower; telephones; color television. Rates: moderate to expensive. Children welcome. No pets. Cards: AE, CB, DC, MC, VISA. Open all year.

Getting there: Follow Route 7 from Norwalk north or Danbury south. The turnoff for Stonehenge is well marked and just a short distance from the road.

A Newcomer to Old Ridgefield
WEST LANE INN
Ridgefield

Ridgefield is a town chock-full of pretty eighteenth- and nineteenth-century homes. The West Lane Inn is ensconced in one of the prettiest. For years the comfortable, rambling building was a private summer home. But in 1978 Maureen Mayer bought the property and, with great taste and flair, turned the big white frame house into an inn. The inn still keeps the spirit of a private home, decorated with floral prints and hunting scenes, wall sconces and thick carpets. The large guest rooms (fourteen in the main house, six in an adjoining cottage) are furnished with style and a few have fireplaces. In the private baths are heated towel racks, European style, along with scales and luxuriously deep, thick towels. Some bathrooms have bidets.

There isn't full dining service in the inn, but Continental breakfast is served, and it is possible to get a snack at lunch time. Not to worry. Just next door is one of Ridgefield's better restaurants, The Inn at Ridgefield, which specializes in elegantly served, well-prepared nouvelle cuisine. In Ridgefield you don't have to travel far to dine well.

WEST LANE INN, 22 West Lane, Ridgefield, CT 06877. Telephone: (203) 438-7323. Accommodations: twenty rooms with queen- and king-size beds; private baths with tub/shower; telephones with 24-hour service; color television. Rates: expensive, Continental breakfast included. Children welcome. No pets. Cards: AE, MC, VISA. Open all year.

Getting there: From Route 7, take Route 35 into Ridgefield proper, and continue on 35 through town. After 35 veers right, the inn is on the right, just beyond The Inn at Ridgefield.

LAKE WARAMAUG
AND THE LITCHFIELD HILLS

Lake Waramaug is one of Connecticut's best kept secrets, a small nine-mile round spring-fed lake nestled into the foothills of the Berkshires in northwestern Connecticut. Waramaug was named after an Indian chief of the Schaghticoke tribe who died in the area in 1736. His tribe put stones on his grave in tribute and later, so they say, other tribes put stones there too, but for another reason—to prevent Waramaug's spirit from escaping. Nowadays, however, no one is quite sure where the grave site is.

Many intriguing excursions can be taken from the Lake Waramaug area. In the pretty little town of Washington is the American Indian Archaeological Institute, with numerous excavated finds. Nearby, in Washington Depot, you might stop for lunch at The Pantry, an informal, popular spot with homemade soups, sandwiches and salads. The Sloane-Stanley Museum of Old Farm Implements at Kent is offbeat and interesting too. Cornwall Bridge is another attractive little town, with a rare New England covered bridge, shops for browsing, and the Cornwall Bridge Pottery, an excellent pottery where you can buy hand-turned pots and casseroles right from the kiln.

Then there is Litchfield, whose wide streets, lined with imposing black-shuttered, white clapboard houses, constitute a rare eighteenth-century legacy. If you chance to be in town for the annual house tour—usually held the second Saturday of July—you will have the added treat of seeing how beautifully maintained the houses are inside as well as out. Otherwise, content yourself with a visit to the Tapping Reeve House and Law School, the first law school in America, founded in 1775. Reeve's brother-in-law and first student was Aaron Burr.

Waramaug itself isn't a total secret, because there are four popular inns nestled into the wooded, sloping hills that surround this picture-perfect setting. Each of the inns is small, with its own particular character and ambience.

Wandering the Woods Around Lake Waramaug
THE BIRCHES INN
New Preston

Newest of Waramaug's four inns is The Birches, a comfortable family-run house with a pleasing hillside view of the lakes and foliage. Innkeepers Heinz and Christa Holl are attempting to bring their Austrian innkeeping know-how to this placid lakeside setting. You'll find unassuming, generously sized guest rooms. There are two in the main house, five in the guest house, and, best of all, three in a cottage directly on the water.

The Birches is the place for leisurely walks through the woods. For more energetic activity, you can golf, play tennis or horseback ride nearby, and the inn has a private beach and boat dock for water sports.

THE BIRCHES INN, New Preston, CT 06777. Telephone: (203) 868-0229. Accommodations: ten rooms with twin and queen-size beds; private baths with tub/shower; some rooms with complete kitchen facilities; no telephones; black-and-white television. Rates: inexpensive, especially the American plan weekend packages. Children welcome. Pets allowed. Cards: AE, MC, VISA. Open all year.

Getting there: From Route 7 in New Milford, go north to Route 202 east to New Preston, then Route 45 to Lake Waramaug. At the lake, turn left and 2.2 miles further is the inn, on the west side of the lake.

Lakeside Peace Where Indians Once Roamed
BOULDERS INN
New Preston

Once a home on 250 hilly acres, the Boulders Inn is still very much a family kind of place, with miles of wooded hiking trails, tennis courts, swimming, boating and canoeing at crystalline Lake Waramaug. In winter, there is cross-country skiing, ice skating and tobogganing.

There's nothing fancy about Boulders. The rustic fieldstone and dark shingle inn sits on a hill facing the lake, and the fourteen guest rooms (five in the inn, nine in cottage units on the well-kept grounds) are simple. Cosy and homelike, the public areas are like a family lodge or camp. All in all, it's a great place to bring the kids. In warm weather you can dine outside on a big terrace sheltered by sweeping branches of ancient pine trees and take in the excellent view of the lake.

BOULDERS INN, New Preston, CT 06777. Telephone: (203) 868-7918. Accommodations: five rooms and eight cottages with twin, double, and queen-size beds; private baths with tub/shower; no telephones; no television. Rates: moderate, with modified American plan (dinner and full breakfast). Children welcome. No pets. Cards: MC, VISA. Open all year.

Getting there: Drive on Route 202 north from New Milford to New Preston, then take Route 45 to the Lake Waramaug turn-off.

Where Fine Food and Lake Views Meet
THE HOPKINS INN
New Preston

If you have any doubt that the best eating on Lake Waramaug can be found at the Hopkins Inn, try to find a parking space on the road leading up to the inn any weekend evening in season. The dining room is plain though lively, but if the weather is accommodating, you might prefer to eat on the tree-shaded terrace that overlooks the lake. A blackboard announces the day's menu. This might include broiled salmon with herb butter, trout meuniere, chicken Cordon Bleu, backhendl, roast pheasant with spaetzle, a rack of lamb or whatever the season's current offerings are. The homemade desserts are memorable too. Portions are bountiful, and chef-owner Franz Schober brings years of culinary experience to his efforts.

Many of the inn's nine guest rooms have sweeping hilltop views of the placid little lake below. The rooms themselves are comfortable although small and cosy with few frills. Guests may swim at a private beach nearby, which is fortunate because, considering how good the food is at the Hopkins Inn, you won't want to stray too far away as dinnertime approaches.

THE HOPKINS INN, New Preston, CT 06777. Telephone: (203) 868-7295. Accommodations: twin and double beds; all but two with private baths; no telephones or television. Rates: inexpensive. Children welcome. No pets. No cards.

Getting there: From New Milford, take Route 202 north to New Preston, then left on Route 45 to Lake Waramaug.

Lakeside Sports in a Rustic Setting
THE INN ON LAKE WARAMAUG
New Preston

Located as it is, right on the lip of the lake, this large and rambling inn has all the earmarks of a lively, active resort property. A large main hilltop house is surrounded by a well-kept, sloping lawn on which two other guest houses are located. At the bottom of the hill is a sandy beach, boat docks, and a showboat dock where you can dine during the summer. There is also a proper dining room and large dining terrace in the inn itself. You can paddle around in an inn rowboat for free, rent a canoe or sailboat, or take a showboat cruise around the lake anytime from May through October. There are also bicycles for rent to circle the lake, and golf and horseback riding facilities are within a short drive. An indoor heated pool, sauna and whirlpool, and clay tennis courts are also among the many sports available here. In winter you can ice skate on the lake, toboggan or sled down the hills, cross-country ski on scenic trails and enjoy a complimentary horse-drawn sleigh ride. The possibilities seem endless.

The Inn's personality is most evident in the old frame house itself. It was built circa 1795, and after several additions and changes came into the Bonynge family. William Henry Bonynge, a lawyer, was one of a group of professional people from New York and New Jersey who recognized Lake Waramaug's potential as a summer resort in the 1890s. Bonynge's grandson, Richard Bonynge Combs, bought the house in 1951, changed its name from Lakeview Inn to the Inn on Lake Waramaug, and began to restore the old building to its present, almost original state. Most rooms have a lake view and nowadays you'll see the old wood-paneled walls, Williamsburg wallpaper, and collections of old maps, silver tea services, and numerous antique cherry and pine cabinets and tables. The dining room fireplace is constructed from bricks that were used as ballast on early eighteenth-century English sailing vessels.

The Inn's strong point is its wide range of sports and recreation facilities, as well as its gregarious, clubby atmosphere. The food is basic but plentiful fare.

THE INN ON LAKE WARAMAUG, New Preston, CT 06777. Telephone: (203) 868-0563. Accommodations: twenty-five rooms with twin, double, queen-size beds; private baths with tub/shower; some rooms with working fireplaces; no telephones; color television. Rates: moderate, includes modified American plan (breakfast and dinner), discount for stays of seven days or longer; weekend packages. Children welcome. No pets (there are kennels nearby). Cards: AE, DC, MC, VISA. Open all year, except Christmas Day.

Getting there: Take Route 7 through New Milford, then turn off to Route 202 east to New Preston, and then Route 45 to Lake Waramaug.

Handy Location in an Eighteenth-Century Town
THE LITCHFIELD INN
Litchfield

Litchfield, located midst the Litchfield Hills and Housatonic Valley, has often been called the loveliest town in New England. You probably won't quarrel with that. Wide streets lined with trees that form a canopy with their branches overhead, well-maintained Colonial houses, and a unity of architecture combine to make this an altogether pleasing town.

Until recently however, there wasn't really any compelling place to stay. Fortunately, in 1981, the Litchfield Inn opened just at the edge of town. The expansive eighteenth-century-style inn—a white clapboard building with black shutters—is as spacious inside as it is out and has all of the twentieth-century comforts. Lounges, a large bar and a dining room which serves well-prepared Continental dishes invite crowds to congregate, and the inn is becoming a gathering place for small conferences. Fires burn in the inn's various fireplaces on brisk days—though unfortunately the fires burn behind protective glass which masks the good, rich smell of wood smoke.

A winding stairway leads past a huge, hanging Colonial-style brass chandelier up to twelve ample bedrooms that are furnished with dark wood reproductions of period pieces. A newly built annex has made twenty more rooms available as well.

THE LITCHFIELD INN, Route 202, Litchfield, CT 06759. Telephone: (203) 567-4503. Accommodations: thirty-two rooms with queen-size beds; private baths with tub/shower; telephones; color television. Rates: moderate. Children welcome. No pets. Cards: AE, MC, VISA. Open all year.

Getting there: Located on Route 202.

Where Wooded Serenity and Good Food Meet
TOLL GATE HILL INN
Litchfield

From having no proper accommodations for years, the serene little town of Litchfield has suddenly blossomed with two new inns. Newest is the Toll Gate Hill Inn, which opened in July, 1983. This charmer is located just two and one-half miles from the town center in a beautiful old barn-red Colonial house. It was built in 1745 and is now listed on the National Register of Historic Places. The fresh individuality of the guest rooms, the feel of the building, and the fine food are all enchanting.

Each of the six guest rooms is furnished in a different color scheme, with fluffy handmade comforters on the canopy beds that coordinate the color of the walls and draperies. Early American prints and pictures enliven the walls. Given your "druthers," especially on chilly evenings, you might prefer one of the three second-floor guest rooms, because each has a well-used wood-burning fireplace. The sitting room on the second floor, with its table full of current magazines, is also a welcome spot to linger.

There are two small, cosy dining rooms on the ground floor, and a third larger one for special parties on the second floor. Each room has a personality, as well as fireplace, of its own. The furnishings of the large upstairs room convey a light airiness while one ground-floor room is softly lighted and lined with dark wood-paneled walls. The other has a wood-paneled fireplace wall, Pompei-red painted woodwork and Early American primitive portraits on the walls. The food served in all three rooms is first-rate nouvelle cuisine adapted to the bounteous harvest of the local market. There are many commendable offerings, such as a creamy, succulent seafood chowder, tomato bisque with crabmeat, crisp Tollgate puff pastry enveloping a number of different fillings (a lunch special), duck with apple brandy sauce, pan-fried yellowtail flounder, hot and spicy penne laced with vodka, and pork medallions paired with white wine, shallots and capers. The list could go on and on. Desserts, also, are out of this world. Have an aperitif or perhaps a nightcap in the comfortable taproom, which also has a large, hearthed fireplace.

TOLL GATE HILL INN, Route 202, Litchfield, CT 06759. Phone: (203) 482-6116. Accommodations: six rooms with double beds; private baths with tub or shower; no telephones; no television. Rates: moderate to expensive, Continental breakfast included. Children welcome. Pets permitted. Cards: AE, MC, VISA. Open all year.

Getting there: Follow Route 202 north of Litchfield. Just two and one-half miles north of town, watch for the inn on the left.

Handy Center Town Locale for Old Hostelry
YANKEE PEDLAR INN
Torrington

Right in the center of the bustling little town of Torrington is the Yankee Pedlar, a handy springboard for exploring this interesting part of Connecticut. The inn's saffron facade with white trim has been a beacon to travelers since 1890. The building is large, encompassing a roomy Colonial-style dining room, a more inviting private dining room, the Pedlars Pub and a hotel-like lobby in which locals tend to gather. Inn guests breakfast in the Pedlars Pub which is also the lunch spot for the Torrington Club. A friendly, accommodating front desk staff contributes to an enjoyable stay. Guest rooms are adequate, some are even quite roomy, furnished with Hitchcock rockers and other period furniture. One especially large room sports a fireplace and sofa bed. Nothing fancy here, mind you, just seventy-five neat, clean and comfortable rooms with an old-fashioned look.

YANKEE PEDLAR INN, 93 Main Street, Torrington, CT 06790. Telephone: (203) 489-9226. Accommodations: seventy-five rooms with twin and double beds; private baths with tub/shower; telephones; color television. Rates: inexpensive. Children welcome. No pets. Cards: AE, CB, DC, MC, VISA. Open all year.

Getting there: From Route 84, take Route 8 north straight into Torrington.

NORTHWESTERN CONNECTICUT

The lower Berkshire hills are a haven for hikers, skiers, winter sports addicts, and escapees who love the laziness and away-from-it-all pleasures that these wooded hills engender. Of late, Manhattan fashion designers and other trendy types have discovered this area and have been snapping up fine old houses as their weekend retreats. However, artists such as Robert Osborn and the late Alexander Calder, as well as writers like Arthur Miller and William Styron had already made this discovery years ago. Dedicated antiques buffs like to roam the hills and village shops for bargains and handcraft enthusiasts find local weaving and pottery a special delight. In summer, the Sharon Playhouse in Sharon and the Yale Concerts, held on the lawn of the vast Stoeckel Estate in Norfolk, spike the sheer physical beauty of the landscape with cultural life.

In autumn, the incendiary foliage attracts almost anyone with wheels, for the displays of color are truly nature's own Fourth of July fireworks. Fall is probably the most popular season in these parts, so unless you reserve well in advance, you're likely to find no room at the inn, any inn. Winter, too, has its devotees, and not just downhill and cross-country skiers, but anyone who thrives on the Currier and Ives scenes that are part of each small town's village green.

Where James Thurber Once Slept—and Played
WAKE ROBIN INN
Lakeville

The Wake Robin Inn, built in 1898 and located in the middle of the attractive town of Lakeville, has changed a lot in the last fifteen years or so, when the innkeeper used to proudly show the room "where author George Thurber used to write when he visited here." *George* Thurber? "You mean James?" "Yes. No matter, he and his wife came here many summers." This ground floor room was spacious, high-ceilinged and graced by a handsome white brick fireplace.

Today's Wake Robin has been brightly redecorated, in what might be called a New Yorker's theatrical version of a New England country inn. Nobody on the present staff seems to have heard of James (or George) Thurber, and the "Thurber Room" has been swallowed by the reconstruction.

Wake Robin Inn

Neverthless, you will still find the same stately colonnaded Georgian Revival mansion dominating a small hilltop, with hill and valley vistas that are especially spectacular during the fall foliage season. An outdoor swimming pool makes summer a pleasing time to visit too. Inside, the focal point of the public areas is the large bar. Guest rooms are generous and decorated in vibrant, lively color combinations, with lots of greens and yellows. There are twenty-three guest rooms in the house, with seventeen more in the adjacent motel.

Lakeville itself is a lively little town which was settled in 1741. It has a classic village green, a splendid Colonial church, and is the home of the prestigious Hotchkiss School. While you're in the neighborhood, look in at the handsomely furnished Holley-Williams House, which was built in 1808. Across the road from the inn is Gallery Import, a shop specializing in Japanese antiquities and prints. The antiques are beautifully accented by the subtly restored Victorian home of art dealers William and Elizabeth Spurgeon.

WAKE ROBIN INN, Route 41, Lakeville, CT 06039. Telephone: (203) 435-2515. Accommodations: forty rooms with twin and double beds; private baths with tub/shower; no room telephones or television; cable television in lounge and taproom. Rates: moderate to expensive. Children welcome. Pets allowed in motel, but not the inn. Cards: AE, MC, VISA. Open May through October.

Getting there: Situated on Route 41, just one-half mile south of Lakeville center.

Swiss Food and Know-How in Scenic Connecticut Village
RAGAMONT INN
Salisbury

The Salisbury Antiques Fair, held in late September or early October, is this small New England town's major annual event. That's not to say that Salisbury has no other claims to fame. During the American Revolutionary War, this most northwesterly town in Connecticut was called "the arsenal of democracy" because so many swords, sabers, muskets and cannons were produced in the local furnaces. Bear Mountain, the state's highest peak at 2,355 feet, is also in Salisbury.

The small one-street town contains three inns, two of which are recommended in these pages. Ragamont Inn is located right in the town center. Imposing white columns in the front signal the inn's presence, but chances are the line-up of cars any evening will tip you off as well.

The Ragamont is one of those inns where food is a primary consideration, rooms secondary. Not that there's anything the matter with the rooms. There are thirteen in the inn above the dining rooms, three in an annex. Most of the rooms are ample, simply decorated, with handsome, stripped-down wooden floors, and attractive Colonial-style wallpaper. Many rooms have huge bathrooms.

But in truth, it is the dining rooms that are the inn's *raison d'etre*. In summer, the most pleasant place to eat is outside on the flagstone terrace which is screened from the road by a hedge. Wherever you sit, you'll enjoy the well-prepared Swiss dishes of chef-owner Rolf Schenkel, who has been indulging guests at the Ragamont since 1969. The menu changes, but look for such specialties as jaeger schnitzel, sweetbreads, geschnepzeltels (veal scallops sauced with brandy, cream and tarragon), and super desserts like almond torte, linzer torte, peach custard pie, and fresh blueberry puff.

RAGAMONT INN, Main Street, Salisbury, CT 06068. Telephone: (203) 435-2372. Accommodations: fourteen rooms with twin, double or king-size beds; some private baths, some shared, with tub/shower; Rates: inexpensive. Children welcome. No pets. No cards. Open May 1 to November 1.

Getting there: Located right on Route 44 in Salisbury.

Seclusion at the Berkshires Border
UNDER MOUNTAIN INN
Salisbury

Hikers, skiers, antiques and handcraft devotees, and other visitors to the Berkshire hills will be delighted to find this charming inn located on the very northwestern tip of Connecticut, almost at the Massachusetts line.

Under Mountain Inn is the stereotypical New England inn: an authentic Colonial house, circa 1740, painted white with dark green shutters and situated on a quiet country road opposite an old farmhouse with a pond across the way. The seven guest rooms are individually decorated with antiques and the public rooms have low-key furnishings, which give a lived-in atmosphere. Books and magazines are on the table in the cosy parlor and on Sunday *The New York Times* is on hand for the inn's many weekenders from the city.

Especially nice is Room 2 which faces the road. Circular area rugs cover the beautiful old wood floorboards, plush soft blue wing chairs accent the blue and rose-red wallpaper pattern, and there is a full length freestanding mirror. Those who like to read in bed will appreciate the extra-strong bed lights too.

Flames licking at the logs in the fireplace on chilly days, the exposed beamed ceiling and center posts, wide-planked floorboards, and glasses sparkling on neatly set tables make the main dining room, the Blue Room, especially welcoming. The room price includes a full breakfast, which is usually a choice of five different items, and might include pan-fried trout with chives and eggs scrambled with smoked salmon.

Under Mountain was the seventy-seventh inn that Lorraine and Al Bard looked at in 1977 when they decided to become innkeepers. The inn spoke to them. It will probably speak to you as well. Spend a weekend or just a night here, and it will be easy to understand why the Bards looked no further.

UNDER MOUNTAIN INN, Under Mountain Road (Route 41), Salisbury, CT 06068. Telephone: (203) 435-0242. Accommodations: seven rooms with twin and double beds; private baths; no room telephones or television. Rates: expensive, full breakfast included. Children welcome. No pets. Open all year.

Getting there: Follow Route 41 (Under Mountain Road) north from the center of Salisbury. The inn is on the left side of the road four miles from town.

Hitchcock Chairs and a Moment in History
OLD RIVERTON INN
Riverton

One of Connecticut's oldest inns, Old Riverton was built in 1796 and served for a time as a stop on the Albany-Hartford-Boston stagecoach run. Now it seems to be on the Hartford-Litchfield antiques hunting run, judging by the number of antiques shops in the immediate area. Focal point of much activity is the Hitchcock Chair Factory, the original 1826 factory where Lambert Hitchcock made his famous stenciled chairs. In fact, Riverton was once called Hitchcockville. These days, the old factory is busy churning out replicas of the old Hitchcocks. For a glimpse of many fine originals—Hitchcock, Sheraton, Hepplewhite and others—drop by the Hitchcock Museum, located in a delightful early nineteenth-century stone church, which Hitchock and a friend built in 1829.

Hitchcock's friend, Jesse Ives, was responsible for the Old Riverton Inn, which he called Ives Tavern when he opened its doors in 1796. Since then, there have been many owners and several changes and additions, including a new wing. The Grindstone Terrace, with a floor made of stones quarried in Nova Scotia and a brick fireplace at the far end, was enclosed years ago as an additional dining room. Much of the original flavor of an old inn remains—in the vintage fireplaces, low ceilings and old hemlock exposed beams, and antiques scattered throughout.

If you have the option, ask for the largest guest room on the second floor, which has a fireplace. (Unfortunately, however, it is no longer used because of the fire hazard in this old frame building.) All third-floor front rooms have a river view and all ten of the inn's rooms are simply but nicely furnished, many with Hitchcock stenciled reproductions, some with oriental rugs. The settling of the building over the centuries has given all of the wooden bedroom floors a slight slant. On the second floor, a pleasantly decorated sitting room is equipped with comfortable chairs, current news magazines, decent reading lamps and attractive paisley wallpaper.

The Continental menu of the dining room is popular with locals at dinnertime and with antiques-hunters at lunch, when the decibel level can get quite high from all the good-humored chattering.

OLD RIVERTON INN, Route 20, Riverton, CT 06065. Telephone: (203) 379-8678. Accommodations: ten rooms with twin, double, and queen-size beds; private baths with tub/shower; no telephones; no television. Rates: inexpensive to moderate, full breakfast included. Children and well-behaved pets welcome. Cards: AE, CB, DC, MC, VISA. Open all year except Christmas Day, the first week of January and every Monday.

Getting there: Route 8 north, turn right onto Route 20, right into Riverton.

HARTFORD AND THE CONNECTICUT RIVER

Don't underestimate the attractions of Connecticut's capital. Hartford in the past ten years or so has had a facelift that is more than just cosmetic—there has been a spirit-lift as well in this old insurance headquarters town. Mark Twain may have had the right idea all along when he said Hartford was, "The handsomest town I have ever seen." Although that was in the 1880s, Hartford's renaissance has brought dramatic modern buildings, a new Civic Center with auditoriums, restaurants and shops, and a refurbishing of the Old State House, a handsome Bullfinch structure that is the oldest statehouse in the United States. There is also a lively night life that didn't exist a few years ago—with music, coffeehouses and the exciting Hartford Stage Company, a professional theatre where many plays that later appear on Broadway are first produced.

First on any sightseeing list should be the Mark Twain house, a steamboat Gothic wonder, which is fascinating for its history, its many charming architectural idiosyncracies, and most of all, its personal evocation of the man himself. The well-trained guides who take you through the house regale you with witty and delightful anecdotes about Twain and his twenty years in Hartford and in this house. Next door is the Harriet Beecher Stowe cottage—intriguing in its own right and decorated quite imaginatively for that gloomy Victorian era. Visit Hartford's State Capitol, another nineteenth-century Gothic gem, and do save time for the Wadsworth Atheneum, a splendid museum with a permanent collection that ranges from the fifteenth through the twentieth centuries, with paintings, sculpture, and some excellent Early American furniture. There's a pleasant restaurant in the Atheneum, called Jonathan's, a handy and attractive lunch stop.

Just south of Hartford is Wethersfield, one of the oldest towns in the state, with some 150 seventeenth- and eighteenth-century houses. Several of the most historic are the Webb, Deane and Stevens houses, all open to view. The Webb House is a special delight, an elegantly furnished Georgian mansion where George Washington and the French commander, Count Rochambeau, planned the strategy that eventually led to victory over the British at the Battle of Yorktown. One can easily spend a day exploring Old Wethersfield—indoors and out.

You may also want to wend your way along the Connecticut River. In balmy weather, you can rent canoes and paddle along the turns beneath the wooded bluffs or take a riverboat cruise from Deep River Landing. Then cross to the other side and picnic in the heights above the river at Gillette State Park, explore actor William Gillette's castle or attend a performance of the latest musical comedy at the Goodspeed Opera House in East Haddam. The Goodspeed, a refurbished Victorian "wedding cake" of a building is a joy to look at as it sits defiantly above the river. But the Goodspeed is far more than just an architectural caprice. The productions staged there are so good that many later move along to Broadway. "Man of La Mancha," "Annie" and "Shenandoah" are just a few of the memorable Goodspeed productions that later made the leap to 42nd Street.

If you have children in tow, consider taking a short ride on the Valley Railroad, a vintage steam train that makes a one hour loop through the woods from Essex to Chester and back. It is a quick, nostalgic trip into the past.

Antiques Galore and Pet Goats Too
BUTTERNUT FARM
Glastonbury

Settled in 1650, Glastonbury today is a quiet suburb of nearby Hartford. Fortunately, many of Glastonbury's handsome eighteenth-century houses have recently been snapped up and rejuvenated by Hartford's new suburbanites. One such old house is Butternut Farm, located on two acres along the town's single long main thoroughfare, shielded from the street by a fence, a discreet sign, and towering trees. Jonathan Hale built the farmhouse in 1720 and lived there until he and his son died at the battle of Bunker Hill fifty-five years later. It remained in the Hale family until 1840 when a Hale descendant bought the whaling vessel *Alert*. Luck was not with him, however, for a mutiny cost him his ship along with his house.

Antiquarian Donald B. Reid bought the old house some years ago and painstakingly restored the building, uncovering the original wide pumpkin pine floorboards and brick fireplaces. Reid then filled the four bedrooms and public rooms of what may be Connnecticut's tiniest inn with his own collection of superb antiques. The prize is a cherry highboy with a scalloped center and transitional Queen Anne/Chippendale legs. It keeps company with an Early American gaming table, Bokara rugs, and a glass painting of George Washington over the sofa in the green wood-paneled parlor. The dining room, formerly the kitchen, boasts a beautiful long wood-paneled fireplace, a collection of English Delft, and eighteenth-century bannister-back chairs.

The choice room has a pencil-post cherry four-poster bed with a fishnet canopy over it, candle sconces on the white walls, a 1790 wing chair, an antique blanket chest at the foot of the bed, oriental rugs spread over the planked wood floor, and a finely proportioned six-drawer cherry chest. There are electric blankets to insure winter snugness, and on one wall you'll see an amusing old sign with "Rules of this tavern" posted. Among the rules: "No more than five to sleep in one bed; no boots to be worn in bed; no razor grinders or tinkers taken in; organ grinders to sleep in the wash house; and no dogs allowed upstairs." There are still no dogs upstairs, although you may find Lilac or Sister, Reid's two Burmese cats, curled up by the fireplace. Near the fireplace chocolates and a glass decanter of sherry with two stem glasses await your evening return. You'll share a bath with the adjoining twin bedroom—inviting with its saffron-painted wood walls, naive paintings, hook rugs, ball-footed twin "hired man" beds, and antique jigsaw puzzles. Note the many old books in the bookcases, such as Benjamin Franklin's *On The Choice of a Mistress and Other Satires and Hoaxes*. Even the bathrooms are full of treasures: an antique map of *Le Bresil*, clipper ship prints framed over the tub, and a hand-colored print of *A Dutch Cupid Reposing After the Fatigues of Planting*.

Breakfast, the only meal served at Butternut Farm, includes tea or coffee, freshly squeezed orange juice or apple cider from an old mill down the road, and muffins with homemade elderberry, peach or zucchini preserves, all served on English Adams ironstone with family heirloom silver and a silver teapot. Linger a few moments in the keeping room, where herbs and yarrow are drying before the wide walk-in fireplace and the scent of rose potpourri floats through the air.

On the large green behind the house, Hildegarde and seven other goats graze happily under a willow tree and the sheltering leaves of a sugar maple which is over 110 years old. Dogwood and lilacs make springtime especially appealing here.

While Glastonbury has no shortage of places to dine, a greater variety of restaurants—Italian, French, nouvelle American, Chinese and others—can be found in Hartford, a mere five miles away. Especially notable are L'Americain, for French and nouvelle American dishes, Gaetano's in the Hartford Civic Center, Carbone's for northern Italian, and Jonathan's at the Atheneum for lunch or Sunday brunch.

BUTTERNUT FARM, 1654 Main Street, Glastonbury, CT 06033. Telephone: (203) 633-7197. Accommodations: two rooms with twin and double beds; shared baths with tub/shower; one room with telephone; portable television available. Rates: inexpensive, Continental breakfast included. Children welcome. No pets. Smoking discouraged. No cards. Open all year.

Getting there: You can reach Glastonbury via Route 2 south from Hartford.

Goodspeed Opera and A Vintage Village
BISHOPSGATE
East Haddam

Julie Bishop's gate has moved—from a few miles outside East Haddam several years ago to a handier location in the center of the village that she now has. The breakfast-only inn couldn't be more ideally situated for theatre devotees, for it is just a block or so from the popular Goodspeed Opera House. Both theatre and town sit high on a cliff above the Connecticut River.

Ms. Bishop has shown a dramatic flair in decorating her comfortable Colonial house, built in 1818, where Goodspeed performers often stay. The single suite, complete with sauna, dressing room and private deck, is attractively furnished with marquetry furniture. Other rooms have *chinois* elements and an eclectic yet stylish mix of periods. Guests have a way of becoming fast friends and repeat visitors, probably from chatting and lingering over coffee, pancakes or hot apple crisps at the more than generous "Continental breakfast," which is often served in front of the glowing logs of the kitchen fireplace. The cosy house has no shortage of fireplaces, with one in the living room and in four of the six bedrooms, all burning brightly on crisp winter evenings.

BISHOPSGATE, Goodspeed Landing, East Haddam, CT 06423. Telephone: (203) 873-1677. Accommodations: six rooms with twin, double, queen- or king-size beds, including one suite; private baths; no room telephones; no television. Rates: moderate. Children over six years welcome. No pets. No cards. Open all year.

Getting there: Take Route 9 north from Exit 6 off I-95. Take Exit 7 to East Haddam. Over the drawbridge, bear left up Route 149. Bishop's Gate is the third driveway on the right.

Americana Where the Woods Are
THE INN AT CHESTER
Chester

What magic turns a sleepy New England town into a chic retreat for city dwellers in search of country quiet? Real estate entrepreneurs would be rich if they could predict such a metamorphosis. In the space of just a few years, this is just what has happened to Chester, a little backwater near the banks of the Connecticut River.

Much of the credit belongs to David Joslow, who was one of the first to discover Chester, and has since been active in preserving and restoring some of the town's fine old buildings. His first was an old broom factory which he turned into a popular restaurant, the Chart House. His newest venture is his own house, a vintage (1776-1778) chimney cape, which, through careful additions, blossomed into The Inn at Chester in 1983. It is a charming, well-situated hostelry, surrounded by apple and maple trees and shaded by a copper beech. The inn sits on twelve acres that adjoin the Cockaponsett State Forest.

The inn, set deep in the woods, makes an idyllic spot for a weekend getaway. You can hike the nature trails, play tennis, swim in a nearby lake, use the inn's joggercise course, ice skate in winter on the pond, or just laze in the congenial ambience. If you're feeling more active, the innkeepers will pack a picnic and send you on your way to any number of sightseeing excursions in the Connecticut River area. Collectors of original handcrafts gravitate to Middletown and the Wesleyan Potters Shop, to the Connecticut River Artisans' in East Haddam, and to crafts shops in Chester itself.

The Inn at Chester has a low-key way of making guests feel welcome. An assortment of daily newspapers (*The New York Times, The Wall Street Journal* and others) and new magazines await as you pass through the small lobby on the way to breakfast. Notice the original print by Rafael Tamayo in the entrance, part of the Joslow collection scattered throughout the inn. There's also an exercise room where a sauna and massages are available as well.

And exercise is called for, especially after some of the bounteous fare served in the inn's attractive dining room, called the John B. Parmelee House after the building's original owner. The dining room is actually an old barn, with high ceilings, a loft and barn siding walls. A big walk-in fieldstone hearth at one end, old prints and a greenhouse attached to one side for light and airiness all make for a graceful dining environment. Chefs Charles and Sally Lewis-LaMonica have composed a menu of truly scrumptious New England and other regional specialties which changes with each season. But don't expect plain old-fashioned food. These talented two have a touch, based on their culinary service at the Park Hotel in Vitznau, Switzerland, and The Breakers in Palm Beach, Florida. You may find fresh wild rabbit in a rich dark wine sauce, Cornish game hen stuffed with a heavenly ground sausage and spinach dressing, or skewered lamb roasted with cumin and fresh lime juice.

Both new and vintage guest rooms are available. Four rooms, furnished with antiques, old chests and bureaus of the late eighteenth and early nineteenth centuries, are bedded down in the old eighteenth-century part of the house. Nineteen new rooms—each different, some dormered, all with a tranquil view—are in the new wing of the avocado-green clapboard house.

THE INN AT CHESTER, 318 West Main Street, Chester, CT 06412. Telephone: (203) 526-9541. Accommodations: twenty-two rooms with twin and double beds; private baths with tub/shower; telephones; color television. Rates: moderate. Children welcome. No pets. Cards: AE, MC, VISA.

Getting there: From I-95 (from New York or Boston), turn off at Exit 69, then follow Route 9 north to Exit 6. Turn left on Route 148. The inn is three miles farther, on the right hand side.

Sparkling Crystal and Elegant Dining
THE COPPER BEECH INN
Ivoryton

This might be the most famous dining room in the state, but few people realize that the Copper Beech Inn is truly an *inn* in the hostelry sense of the word. There are a mere five rooms, but each is a romantic, impeccably decorated treasure, furnished with Queen Anne, Chippendale and Empire pieces, canopy and four-poster beds, and several even have fireplaces. Number 5 is usually the favorite, with its love seat and comb-back Boston rocker. The inn is named for the magnificent beech tree in the front yard, whose burnished copper-leaved branches shelter the path leading to the 1898 Victorian clapboard building.

Ivoryton's major claim to fame has long been its summer theatre, the Ivoryton Playhouse. Though the tiny town is not a cynosure for tourists, it is handy to the Connecticut River. The inn has bicycles, so you can pedal over to Essex and Chester, two towns near the river with special character.

Special emphasis at the Copper Beech is on the table. A large menu encompasses such dishes as clams roasted with a hazelnut dressing, pheasant braised in a cassis sauce, and tarte tatin. Service is attentive and impeccable.

COPPER BEECH INN, Main Street, Ivoryton, CT 06442. Telephone: (203) 767-0330. Accommodations: five rooms with twin, queen- and king-size beds; private baths with tub/shower; air-conditioning; no telephones; no television. Rates: moderate to expensive, Continental breakfast included. Children welcome. No pets. Cards: AE, CB, DC, MC, VISA. Open all year.

Getting there: From I-95, take Exit 68, then Route 9 north. Turn off at Exit 3 west.

An 1812 Overture and Twentieth-Century Fun
GRISWOLD INN
Essex

A popular yacht haven on the Connecticut River, the postcard-pretty town of Essex boasts one of the loveliest waterfronts in the state. The main street, free of neon signs and other twentieth-century distractions, has a decided other-century air. All in all, this is one of the most agreeable places in Connecticut in almost any season.

If you find yourself in Essex, you'll most likely gravitate to the "Gris," as the old inn on Main Street is affectionately known. Most anything happening in town happens at the Gris. The white clapboard inn, a few steps from the old steamboat dock, is one of the oldest and most historic inns in Connecticut, and has been owned by only five families. Longtime owner-innkeeper William Winterer has turned a sleepy backwater hostelry into one of the liveliest and best-run establishments in New England.

British troops occupied the inn during the War of 1812 after they had destroyed the small Essex fleet. (It's no coincidence that the last four digits of the inn's phone number are 1812.) A sign at the end of Main Street notes "British marines landed here and burned twenty-eight local ships April 8, 1814." When the commanding officer left, he supposedly said the Gris was "long on charm but short on plumbing."

The charm is still abundant, especially in the dining rooms, such as the book-lined, wood-paneled Library where you'll have a help-yourself Continental breakfast, and the Steamboat room, which resembles the dining salon of an old-fashioned steamboat, complete with binacles and bells. The unusual Covered Bridge dining room was constructed from an authentic New Hampshire covered bridge and moved to Essex. Its large well-used fireplace plays second fiddle to the many fine Currier and Ives steamboat prints and temperance banners hung along the walls. Gun aficionados will find lots to admire in the musket-laden Gun Room, with its library of firearms dating back to the fifteenth century. In fact, everywhere you turn in the Gris you'll see prints, vintage signs and interesting memorabilia.

At night the Tap Room, with its steamboat Gothic bar and antique popcorn machine (still working beautifully), is the place to be. On cool evenings a fire crackles in the wood-burning fireplace, and there's always music in the air—live piano, banjo, robust singing of sea chanteys, Irish ballads and anything else that comes to mind. You may even see Walter Cronkite, a veteran yachtsman, at a nearby

Griswold Inn

table. Frank Sinatra, Andy Devine, Richard Arlen and Edward Everett Horton are among the list of notables who were guests at one time or another at the Gris. Even Nathan Hale stopped at the Gris, but that was some time ago.

The Sunday Hunt breakfast has been a Gris institution since the British occupation—and with good reason. It's a gargantuan buffet, and from noon to 2:30 p.m. you can eat yourself foolish on unlimited helpings of eggs, grits, kippered herring, lamb kidneys, creamed chipped beef, sweet rolls and breads, and sundry other goodies.

The Gris pays attention to the calendar, and you'll find a special menu and festivity for Valentine's Day, St. Patrick's Day, even Ground Hog Day. At Halloween there's a costume parade in nearby Griswold Square, followed by a popcorn, cider and beer party at the inn. Christmas caroling is concluded with hot cider for all the carolers. In 1983 the Gris introduced a new custom: "A 1776 Country Inn Christmas" with game dinners, the Colonial Brass Quintet, the Trinity Boys Choir, and Baroque musical evenings scheduled throughout December.

The inn's twenty-one guest rooms are simple and comfortable. Many are furnished with old brass beds, hooked rugs, and other Americana. And yes, the plumbing has improved since 1812. Prize quarters, might be the General Trumbull Suite, with a spacious book-lined sitting room, comfortable couch and chairs, and exposed wood beamed ceilings.

GRISWOLD INN, Main Street, Essex, CT 06426. Telephone: (203) 767-1812. Accommodations: twenty-one rooms with twin and double beds; private baths, some with tubs, some showers; no telephones or television. Rates: moderate, Continental breakfast included. Children welcome. No pets. Cards: AE, CB, DC, MC, VISA. Open all year, but closed December 24 to 25.

Getting there: Take Exit 69 off I-95, onto Route 9 north. Continue on Route 9 to Exit 3 into Essex. Follow signs to the waterfront.

ALONG THE EASTERN SHORE

A favorite target for tourists, and with good reason, this northeastern section of the state has many sights of interest. Mystic Seaport Museum, a beautifully re-created nineteenth-century seaport and whaling village, stages many special events in every season, even winter, and it is the largest maritime museum in the United States. If you are a sailor at heart, you'll love the chance to roam aboard the 1841 whaleship *Charles W. Morgan* and the square-rigged *Joseph Conrad,* among others. You can even take a short ride in the coal-fired steamboat *Sabino* that cruises the Mystic River harbor. If you are old enough to recall the movie *Moby Dick*, you may remember the early seaport scenes, which were filmed in Mystic. There is also the Mystic Marinelife Aquarium where you'll see dolphins, seals, sea lions and the only whales in New England. Mystic's attractions also include a one hundred-foot windjammer schooner, the *Mystic Whaler,* on which you can cruise Long Island Sound for one to five days. It is also fun to stroll the modern town of Mystic, browsing in the shops, watching the modern sailboats glide by.

In nearby New London you can visit Monte Cristo, Eugene O'Neill's boyhood home, the schoolhouse where Nathan Hale taught, and several restored whaling captains' homes. Groton is home to the U.S. Naval Submarine Base. Kids (and their parents) love to climb aboard the World War II submarine, *USS Croaker*, which is open to the public. You might also like to explore the coast. Following the coastal route will lead you past dozens of scenic coves, inlets and picnic spots.

Along the shore to the south, you'll first come to Guilford, with a splendid wide green and the Henry Whitfield House, believed to be the oldest stone house in New England. Branford, with its delightful Trolley Museum, where children love to ride the old-fashioned trolleys, is next. Then soon you're in New Haven, which has more than its share of sightseeing attractions. Yale University has three prize museums: Yale Art Gallery, Peabody Museum of Natural History, and the dramatic new Yale Center for British Art. It is pleasant just to stroll the Yale campus or drop into one of the college pubs. In the evening, you might catch a performance at the Long Wharf or at the Yale Repertory Theatre, which are both professional companies. Not to worry, New Haven can keep you busy day after day.

Artists, Artists Everywhere—and Fine Food Too
BEE AND THISTLE
Old Lyme

Staying overnight at the Bee and Thistle is as pleasing and comfortable as a visit to a friend's home. That is, if the friend is an antiques collector. Bob and Penny Nelson bought the inn in 1982 and have been busily turning its modest atmosphere into a more authentic showplace of Americana. Fresh period wallpapering and fishnet canopy or four-poster beds add a new individual charm to each of the ten medium-sized bedrooms. There is a commendable dining room with true home cooking, and Friday night after dinner you can enjoy folk singing. Saturday evening the entertainment is classical harp. It is a treat to sip pre- or post-dinner drinks in either of the two homey lounges. In winter a fire burns merrily in both rooms' hearths.

Old Lyme has much to offer. It is no accident that turn-of-the-century painters discovered the charm of this little coastal town, with its scenic sea and marsh views. Just down the road from the inn is the Florence Griswold Museum. This late Georgian house was once a boarding house and the magnet for those painters who escaped New York for the quiet of Old Lyme to paint the summer away. On the wood paneling of the Griswold dining room you'll see small pictures by Childe Hassam, Willard Metcalfe and others. One erstwhile painter was Woodrow Wilson's wife, and chances are you'll hear stories of Wilson's visit to "Miss Florence's" and how the uninhibited bohemian artists dealt with his stuffiness—they served him sawdust instead of his usual shredded wheat for breakfast.

Old Lyme still attracts artists, and near the Griswold Museum on Lyme Street is the Lyme Art Association, which presents five major art shows each summer.

BEE AND THISTLE INN, 100 Lyme Street, Old Lyme, CT 06371. Telephone: (203) 434-1667. Accommodations: eleven rooms with twin or double beds; private baths (in all but two rooms) with tub/shower; no room telephones; no televison. Rates: moderate. Children over five welcome. No pets. Cards: AE, MC, VISA. Open all year.

Getting there: Exit 70 on the New England Thruway (I-95) leads you right off the ramp to Lyme Street and the inn.

Style and Substance along the Shore
OLD LYME INN
Old Lyme

The first thing that comes to mind at the mention of the Old Lyme Inn is the dining room. Its imaginative nouvelle cuisine and beautiful presentation make this one of the best restaurants in an area in which good restaurants thrive. Such dishes as a prawn and artichoke salad dressed with raspberry vinegar and walnut oil, duck pate with black currants, and braised fresh salmon in a delicate wine sauce linger fondly in the memory.

Other Old Lyme Inn memories: the sight of Sassafras, the multicolored cat and mascot waiting on the front porch; front steps framed in lilacs, violets, rhododendron and laurel; the one perfect apricot rose gracing each table in the elegant, high-ceilinged Victorian dining room; a quiet breakfast in the Rose Room, named for the yellow roses in the wallpaper, with freshly made blueberry coffeecake accompanied by coffee poured from a silver pot; and the charming pastel mural of Old Lyme that covers the entrance wall and winds its way to the top of the stairs—the work of a Colchester painter.

The Old Lyme Inn seems as if it's been around forever, but the old white frame house became an inn only in 1977 after a stint as a tavern of questionable reputation. The house was built in 1850 as part of a working farm, the first in the state to raise race horses. Another claim to fame is that it was the first house in Old Lyme to have an iron bathtub.

An antiques buff, innkeeper Diana Field Atwood cleaned and restored the Old Lyme, then decorated it with the imposing Empire pieces (note the handsome gilt-framed mirror in one parlor) that accentuate the house's architecture. A standout is the ornate 1890s stained oak bar that was acquired from a Pittsburgh tavern and which fits into one long wall as though it were built in. Of the five individually furnished guest rooms upstairs, a favorite is number 4 with its double exposure, velveteen settee and Japanese prints lining the walls. Number 2 is a close second with its imposing brass-fixtured Empire bureau and tranquility. Try to avoid Number 3, which faces the turnpike and in summer is noisy.

OLD LYME INN, 85 Lyme Street, Old Lyme, CT 06371. Telephone: (203) 434-2600. Accommodations: five rooms with twin and queen-size beds; private baths with tub/shower; no room telephones or television. Rates: moderate, Continental breakfast included. Children welcome. Pets permitted, but not left alone in the guest rooms. Cards: AE, MC, VISA. Closed Mondays and Christmas week.

Getting there: Take Exit 70 off the Connecticut Turnpike (I-95).

Bogart & Bacall Slept Here—with a Sound View
THE INN AT MYSTIC
Mystic

From the busy road, you'd never know that behind the modern motel and restaurant sits an imposing, white-columned neo-classical mansion, perched high on a rocky ledge overlooking Fisher's Island Sound and the Atlantic Ocean beyond.

The Inn at Mystic has been a hostelry only since 1981. The beautiful building began life at the end of the last century, built by the widow of the owner of New York's Fulton Fish Market. Sparing no expense, she hoped to make the house a showcase for her daughter. The girl was paraded through the salons of Europe, as many eligible nouveau riche American girls were at the time, in the hope she would snare a titled European husband. Alas, Mama showed off daughter and pictures of the family manor, Grecian columns and all, to no avail. No impoverished nobleman nibbled on the bait. The girl finally returned home and married a local boy.

That wasn't the end of the tales of this intriguing house. One later owner, a wealthy *bon vivant* lent his home to newly married Humphrey Bogart and Lauren Bacall as a honeymoon retreat. Guests today can speculate as to which of the ten elegant guest rooms was the hideaway. A likely candidate would be Room 5, with its magnificent view of the water and of Pequoit Sepois Cove.

Innkeeper Jody Dyer has beautifully furnished each room differently, although only five in the inn are open so far, along with four more in the gate house. In one (Room 1) a French door leads to a private sunning deck that overlooks the Sound. Another (Room 2) has an 1820 four-poster canopy bed from Texas, a view of both the water and Mystic, and gold-plated fittings in the bathroom. In Room 4 there is a fireplace, pine-paneled walls, and a bath with a demi-Jacuzzi and sauna. A favorite is room 5, the ultimate in comfort. From the Jacuzzi in the bathroom, you can roll up a wall panel and peer into the large bedroom to watch television or the logs burning in your private fireplace. Small wonder that Robert Redford, Harvey Korman and others seeking privacy and comfort have found their way here.

Every detail is perfect, from the fresh flowers on a sideboard that complement the oriental prints on the fabric-covered walls to the Chickering baby grand piano in the parlor, which guests are invited to play. English seventeenth-century pine paneling from a ducal

The Inn at Mystic

estate, discovered in an outbuilding, now graces the walls of the spacious parlor—a restful place for the complimentary tea served each afternoon. The full breakfast, available below the hill in the inn-owned Flood Tide restaurant, includes fresh-squeezed orange juice, French toast, eggs or pancakes—enough to fortify you for a day's sightseeing.

THE INN AT MYSTIC, Junction Routes 1 and 27, Mystic, CT 06355. Telephone: (203) 536-9604. Accommodations: sixty-eight rooms with queen-size canopy beds; private baths, some with whirlpools; bath scales; telephones; color cable television; outdoor swimming pool. Rates: expensive. No children. No pets. Cards: AE, MC, VISA. Open all year.

Getting there: Take I-95 to Mystic turn-off at Route 27. The inn is located where Routes 27 and 1 meet.

A Polished Gateway to Northeastern Connecticut
NORWICH INN
Norwich

Thank goodness for the newly re-opened (1983) Norwich Inn, a much needed hostelry in this northeastern part of Connecticut. There is much to investigate in the area, and some wonderful restaurants as well (Cavey's in Manchester, Chez Pierre in Stafford Springs, The Golden Lamb Buttery in Brooklyn, My Pantry in Putnam), but until 1983 there was a dearth of interesting places to stay.

No more. Edward J. Safdie, owner of the Sonoma Mission Inn and Spa in Sonoma, California, spent a small fortune renovating the old stone Norwich Inn. Centerpiece of the celadon-cool lobby is an elongated white birdcage in which two beautiful white Mexican fantail doves coo and carry on, oblivious of the passersby. In three thoughtfully decorated and understated dining rooms, a subtle form of nouvelle cuisine is served. There is also a breezy, sunny terrace which overlooks the huge outdoor swimming pool where guests dine on balmy days. Guests on the terrace one recent summer day may have heard fellow guest Placido Domingo practicing his scales in his bedroom upstairs.

The seventy-five guest rooms are as handsomely furnished as the rest of the inn, in soft shades of blues and cinnamon, enlivened by country print wallpaper, chintz-covered sofas and armchairs, hand-woven rag rugs, Chippendale mirrors, and four-poster beds, some with step stools.

There's so much to do on the two hundred secluded acres surrounding the inn that you may not want to leave the grounds: swimming in the Olympic-size pool, golfing at adjacent Norwich Golf Course, jogging the special jogging trails and, in winter, cross-country skiing. By the time you read this, there promises to be a spa and full health facility available as well.

Yet there are marvelous excursions nearby, including Caprilands, a delightful herb farm and gardens in Coventry, where you can have lunch, stroll in the gardens and hear a lecture on herbs; the Nathan Hale Family Homestead, also in Coventry; Roseland Cottage in Woodstock, a rare and delightful nineteenth-century Gothic Revival house, visited by many U.S. Presidents; and in Canterbury, the Prudence Crandall House, site of the first school for black girls in the U.S. Not to mention the proximity of all the pretty coastal sights and the historic Leffingwell Inn, a seventeenth-century saltbox in Norwich itself.

NORWICH INN, Route 32, Norwich, CT 06360. Telephone: (203) 886-2401. Accommodations: seventy-five rooms with twin, double, queen- and king-size beds; private and shared baths with tub/shower; some suites; telephones; color cable television. Rates: expensive. Children welcome. No pets. Cards: AE, CB, DC, MC, VISA. Open all year.

Getting there: From I-95 take Route 52 (Interstate 395), to Exit 79A. The inn is 2.7 miles from the exit.

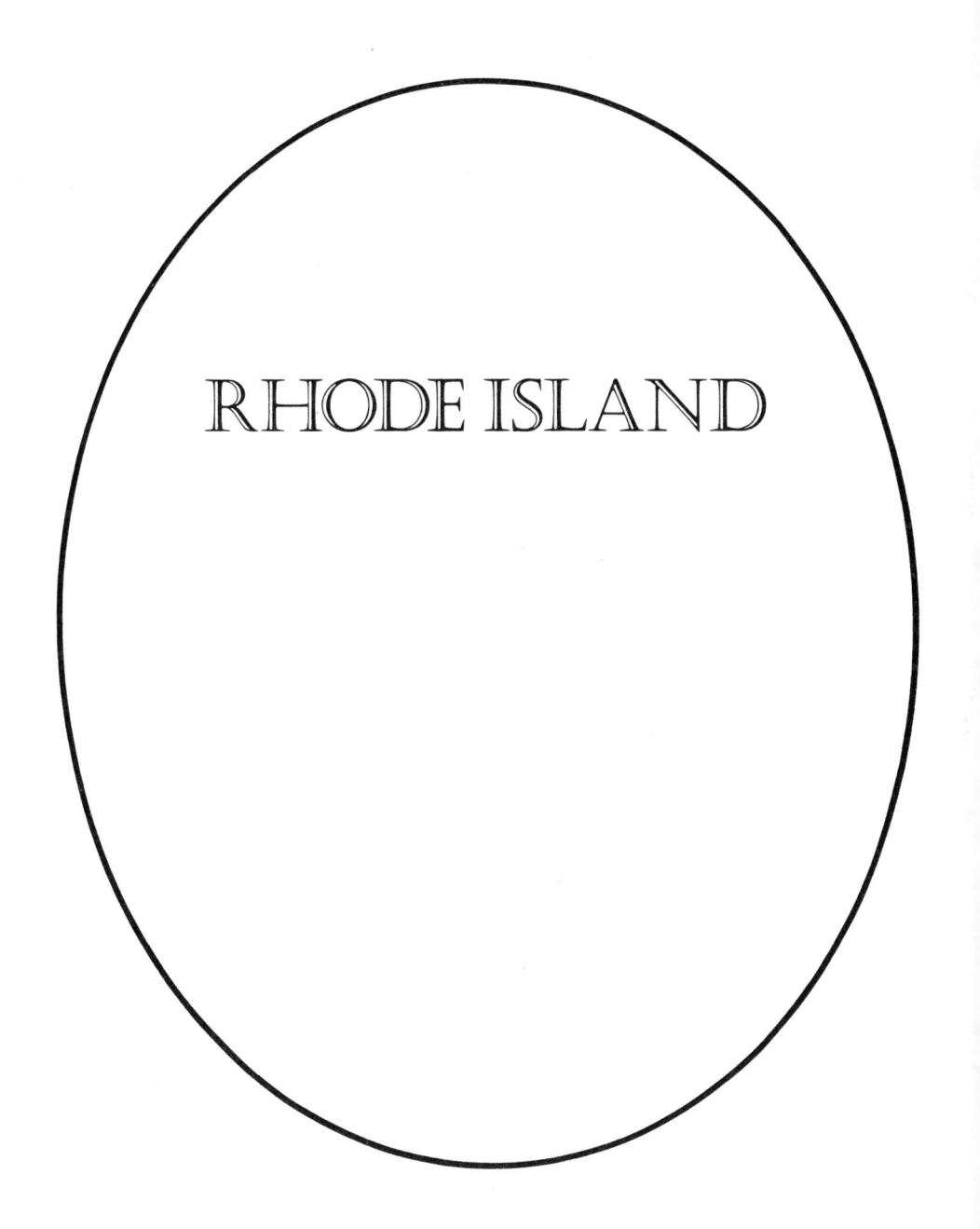

RHODE ISLAND

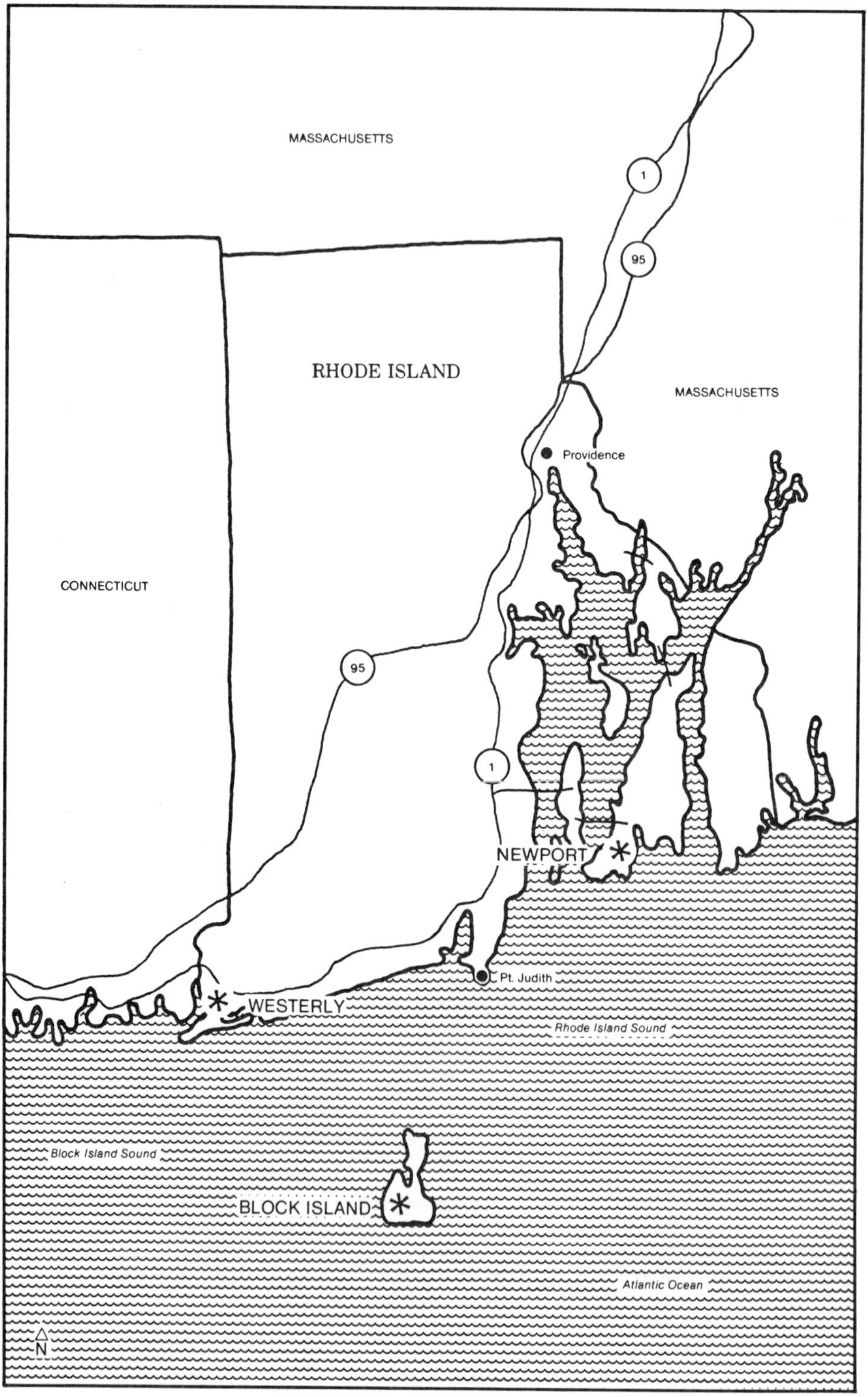
MASSACHUSETTS
1
95
RHODE ISLAND
MASSACHUSETTS
Providence
CONNECTICUT
95
1
NEWPORT
Pt. Judith
WESTERLY
Rhode Island Sound
Block Island Sound
BLOCK ISLAND
Atlantic Ocean
N

THE COASTAL ROUTE

Considering its size, our smallest state, Rhode Island, packs a lot of history, fun and good eating inside its limited borders. Much of Rhode Island's vacation action is offshore, in its islands or along the coast. Beginning at Westerly on the Connecticut border facing Block Island Sound, the coast then winds and curves up past Narragansett Bay northeast to Providence, the state's civic, political and cultural core.

In just the twenty or so miles between casually chic, old-monied Watch Hill near Westerly and the fishing center, Point Judith, there are secluded inlets and coves, ocean beaches with surging surf, four golf courses, eighteen marinas, wildlife sanctuaries, picnic grounds, beaches where surf-casting is at its best, and hiking and biking trails. Rhode Island is a cyclist's dream, it is so flat and even. For those who care, there is even a nudist beach, Moonstone, near Galilee.

In addition, the area is studded with antiques shops, art galleries, handcraft shops, a summer theatre (Theater-by-the-Sea near Matunuck), restaurants and casual clam shacks where the local specialties are Block Island swordfish, clams and lobster. This coast is very much a family place to be. And given Rhode Island's size, virtually everything in the state is easily accessible.

Old-Fashioned Familial Cosiness near the Water
SHELTER HARBOR INN
Westerly

The inn's name is appropriate, for you do feel sheltered and protected here. The water is visible from several second-story bedroom windows and a quiet beach is just a short drive away. The inn itself has the weathered look that old frame farmhouses near the coast tend to have in new England. Yet the big house only dates back to 1911.

Comfort is the name of the Shelter Harbor game, from the easy-to-roam, slightly unstructured grounds with two paddle tennis courts, tennis and basketball courts, to the pleasantly, casually furnished inn itself. The two dining rooms are a case in point. The larger is a low-ceilinged room with wood posts and a fieldstone fireplace which seats forty-four, but seems smaller and cosier than that. The smaller adjoining room, with pine bar, potbellied cast-iron stove, and rush-seated Hitchcock-Nichols-Stone chairs, makes an even cosier place for a light lunch of steaming oyster stew or creamy corn chowder. The salt air almost guarantees an appetite for the inn's largely marine fare, such as scallops, broiled scrod, smoked bluefish with horseradish Chantilly or crab-stuffed shrimp. Homemade muffins, genuine Rhode Island johnnycake, French toast at breakfast, and other goodies reflect the inn's homey stance.

Shelter Harbor's eighteen guest rooms (eight in the inn proper, the others in the barn) are not luxurious, but they are sizeable and one even has its own fireplace. Light quilts cover the beds, and you don't have to worry about the kids breaking the proprietor's treasured antiques. It's a place to relax and enjoy.

SHELTER HARBOR INN, Route 1, Shelter Harbor, Westerly, RI 02891. Telephone: (401) 322-8883. Accommodations: seventeen rooms with twin, double and king-size beds; private baths with tub/shower; no telephones; color television in twelve bedrooms. Rates: moderate, full breakfast included. Children welcome. Some pets allowed, depending on circumstances. Cards: AE, MC, VISA. Open all year.

Getting there: Follow Route 1 south of Westerly. The inn is about five and one-half miles from downtown Westerly on the right side of Route 1.

BLOCK ISLAND

Shaped more like a pear than a block, Block Island was actually named for a a Dutch navigator named Adrian Block who discovered the seven by three-and-one-half mile island in the early seventeenth century. A few settlers and a lot of pirates and smugglers recognized this small island's charms and advantages early on, but it was not until the late 1800s that tourists discovered the salt air, sea breezes, good bathing and deep-sea fishing possibilities here, just ten miles or so off the Rhode Island shore. This is a part of the ocean where tuna, bluefish, striped bass and swordfish play.

Block Island is accessible by ferry from Point Judith (seventy-five minutes), Providence (three and one-half hours), Newport (two hours), and New London, Connecticut (two and one-fourth hours), and by air from Westerly. The tourist onslaught peaks during July and August, with most inns, restaurants and shops closing in winter. Wind-blessed, wild and rugged, with a scruffy, rocky, almost Greek terrain, Block Island prides itself on attracting a certain type of tourist, the kind content to savor the cool air, swim, fish, bicycle or sail. Dress is casual, lifestyle the same. Night owls, jet setters, nightclub fanciers and party goers need not apply.

Spectacular Sunsets and Good Food
THE ATLANTIC INN
Block Island

A favorite spectator sport on Block Island is sunset watching, an indication of the island's fast-paced life. A favorite gathering place for sunset and harbor-viewing is the front porch of the large hilltop Atlantic Inn. Cocktail in hand, you have a sweeping vista of delightful boat-jammed Old Harbor from the hilltop and then, when the last radiant ray fades, you can move slowly into the glassed-in porch or one of the other two small dining rooms for dinner.

The focus at the Atlantic Inn is food, an ingenious coupling of nouvelle cuisine techniques with the island's nautical bounty and garden-fresh herbs and vegetables grown by the inn. Swordfish, broiled and served with a hollandaise sauce or grilled with a garlic sauce, stuffed baked native lobster, fillet of sole en beurre blanc, or striped bass en chemise (steamed in a lettuce blanket with a creamy mushroom sauce) are a few of the chef's specialties. In addition, you'll find fresh, hot rolls and breads, homemade cakes, like a special chocolate walnut torte, and pies made with island-grown peaches and fresh berries. After dinner, sip your coffee on the porch and watch the stars light up the sky.

The big white frame inn with cardinal shutters began life as the Norwich Inn in 1880. Hard times turned the inn into a rooming house, but things are looking up again. In 1981 a new owner, Vin Ryan, began massive renovations to turn the comfortable old house back into an inn. The lobby/lounge is small, as most of the ground-floor space has been turned over to the highly successful restaurant. There are twenty-seven bedrooms on the second and third floors, many with even more spectacular views of the harbor than from the porch. Old oak chests and headboards augment new wallpaper in the inn's simply furnished rooms.

THE ATLANTIC INN, High Street, Block Island, RI 02807. Telephone: (401) 466-2006 or 466-7727. Accommodations: twenty-seven rooms with twin and queen-size beds; thirteen private baths, others share, with tub/shower; no telephones; no television. Rates: inexpensive to moderate. Children welcome, but not babies. No pets. Cards: AE, MC, VISA. Open all year, but only three heated bedrooms are available in the off season; restaurant open May 31 to September 30.

Getting there: By air on New England Airlines from Westerly, or ferry from the towns listed above. The inn is just a five minute walk or taxi drive from Old Harbor.

Romantic Victorian Charm with the Comforts of Home
HOTEL MANISSES
Block Island

Once upon a time—1870 to be exact—there was a big and beautiful resort hotel, known as one of the best in the East, where summer visitors to Block Island wined, dined and slept.

Once upon another time—1972—the same once-beautiful hotel, now decrepit, deserted and abandoned, was about to be torn down. Then Joan and Justin Abrams, Providence residents and owners of another Block Island property, The 1661 Inn, bought the hotel and proceeded to "shore it up." This involved building a new foundation, massive structural work, gutting the interior and tearing down a badly deteriorated rear wing with fifty rooms. Two old rooms became one large one, private baths were installed, and Jacuzzis were added to four of the rooms.

Now, Hotel Manisses is once again wining, dining and sleeping Block Island visitors—but with a difference. The landmark building

Hotel Manisses

is now a freshly painted grey with white trim, highlighted in front with vibrant flower beds. The original moldings from the old hotel are visible in the lobby's arches, which you can admire while having tea in the stylish lobby any afternoon. Handsome Victorian antiques are visible throughout the inn-hotel. Some of the original double beds—now used as singles for today's larger bodies—are still in evidence. And where authentic antiques are missing, the proprietors have taken great pains to reproduce near-perfect reproductions such as the custom-made Victorian-style carpeting, the headboards for the new queen and king-size beds that replicate the oak designs of the original doubles, and the floral wallpaper in keeping with the period mood of the entire hotel. Each of the seventeen guest rooms is furnished differently, with antique prints and accouterments. Each is named after a ship wrecked off the island before 1870 and some have their own private decks for sunning. A special delight is the third floor bridal suite with cathedral ceiling and an expansive Jacuzzi.

The glass-enclosed dining room, which faces the lawn and another outdoor dining terrace, opened before the hotel did in 1978. Now it is a magnet for diners from all over the island. Note especially the variety available at the raw bar—fresh smoked cod, smoked octopus, smoked mussels, fresh oysters and little neck clams, king prawn, and smoked mackerel are a few of the offerings. The dinner menu tilts toward seafood, as you'd expect here, with treats such as scallops with herbs, baked flounder stuffed with oysters and walnuts, and bouillabaisse. The Abrams are justifyably proud of their carefully chosen wine list.

The name Manisses means "Island of the Little God," which is what the Indians originally called Block Island.

HOTEL MANISSES, Spring Street, Block Island, RI 02807. Telephone: (401) 466-2836. Accommodations: seventeen rooms with twin, double, queen- and king-size beds; private and shared baths with tub/shower, four with Jacuzzis; some kitchenettes; no telephone; no television. Rates: moderate to expensive, mini-buffet breakfast and complimentary wine hour included. Children over ten years welcome. No pets. Cards: AE, MC, VISA. Open April to January 1.

Getting there: Hotel personnel will meet guests at the ferry in season if notified ahead of time.

All This Privacy and Block Island Too
THE 1661 INN
Block Island

Where this inn's sister hostelry down the road, Hotel Manisses, is properly Victorian, The 1661 Inn has the look and decor of a Colonial dwelling. And that is just what it was. In 1661 the first settlers straggled over the water to the island from New England. Once a small hotel called Florida House, it was renamed as well as totally refurbished by Joan and Justin Abrams when they bought the property in 1969. In keeping with the Colonial theme, each of the sixteen guest rooms is named after one of those brave settlers. There's the Samuel Deering room, for instance, with its handsome inlaid wood Empire bed and a view that sweeps over Old Harbor. The John Ackurs room boasts two brass-ornamented beds and a private sun-dappled deck. All the rooms are individualized by their special Colonial furnishings and Early American portraits. Some rooms have mini-bars.

Even the light and airy lobby is special, furnished in white wicker chairs and couches. The only meal served at 1661 Inn is breakfast, so most guests simply amble down to Hotel Manisses for lunch and/or dinner. Breakfast is a gargantuan buffet, featuring fish, quiche, eggs, bacon, sausage, fresh fruits and many other delights. Having walked through the buffet, you have a choice of eating it in the dining room with its ocean view or outside under an umbrella on the terrace.

THE 1661 INN, Spring Street, Block Island, RI 02807. Telephone: (401) 466-2421 or 466-2063. Accommodations: twenty-five rooms with twin, double, queen- and king-size beds; some private baths, some shared, with tub/shower; no telephones; no television. Rates:

moderate to expensive (higher in summer), buffet breakfast and complimentary wine hour included. Children over ten years welcome. No pets. Cards: AE, MC, VISA. Open April to January 1, adjacent guest house is open all year.

Getting there: With advance notice, you will be met at the ferry, in season.

NEWPORT

Newport is many things to many people, which is why it is always, any time of year, an exciting place to be. Of course summer is *the* season. That's when yachting pennants and flags are unfurled, and the city's scenic harbor becomes a hub for small crafts.

But that's one side of Newport. Another is the Colonial town that has been carefully restored over the past dozen years. A classic example from this period is the Hunter House, an eighteenth-century gem, furnished with first-rate examples of Newport furniture of the period. The house is open to the public, as is another treasure from the same period—Touro Synagogue, the first synagogue to be built in America.

Then there's the famous Newport of Bellevue Avenue and Ocean Drive, where the late nineteenth-century nouveau riche one-upped each other building their monumental summer "cottages"—one European-style chateau, hunting lodge and turreted "castle" after another. Many are open to tourists. Don't miss Cornelius Vanderbilt II's seventy-room "cottage," The Breakers; Rosecliff, designed by Stanford White after the Grand Trianon at Versailles; The Elms; and Chateau-sur-Mer, once known as the most expensive residence in Newport. Hammersmith Farm, where Jacqueline and John F. Kennedy were married, is farther along on Ocean Drive.

There is also the Newport of the Music Festival, smart shops, art galleries and boutiques, and Bannister's and Bowen's Wharf, studded with good restaurants and snackeries. Among the better restaurants, try Le Bistro for creative food with a French accent, both the Black Pearl and the Clarke Cooke House for American and French dishes, and Frick's for a Continental menu with Austrian panache. Visitors don't run out of things to do in Newport. They just run out of time.

Admiral Benbow Inn

A Handy Central Location in a Sea Captain's House
ADMIRAL BENBOW INN
Newport

Once the home of a prosperous local resident, this grey clapboard house on a tree-shaded street near the center of Newport was built in 1855 by a retired sea captain from Block Island and was the home of Captain Augustus N. Littlefield until he died in 1878. (There is a rubbing from his gravestone in the back hall of the house now.) Captain Littlefield's main claim to fame seems to have been that he was the rare and lucky ship captain who never had to file an insurance claim.

Restored and refurbished, the house was opened as an inn in 1982. Each of the fifteen guest rooms is unique, furnished with brass beds and antiques. Some rooms have views of the harbor a few blocks away, one has its own sundeck and two others are efficiency units. Room 2 is especially roomy, cheerful and inviting, with two double brass beds.

Breakfast is the only meal served, and on Sunday the day's newspapers appear along with it. The breakfast lounge is in the basement in a relaxed setting with comfortable yellow chairs and a wood-burning stove, which gets full use on chilly mornings or evenings. There is a television in the lounge as well.

And why is the inn named Admiral Benbow instead of Augustus N. Littlefield? Because, said innkeeper Arlene McKenna, "Those of us involved in the inn liked Robert Louis Stevenson's book, *Treasure Island*. You may remember that everything began at the Admiral Benbow Inn."

ADMIRAL BENBOW INN, 93 Pelham Street, Newport, RI 02840. Telephone: (401) 846-4256. Accommodations: fifteen rooms with twin, double and queen-size beds; private baths with shower; no telephones; no television. Rates: moderate, higher mid-May through October, Continental breakfast included. Children welcome. No pets. Cards: AE, MC, VISA. Open all year.

Getting there: Located two blocks from the harbor in the center of the old part of Newport. Coming over the Newport Bridge turn right, continue to the second traffic light, then turn right onto Americas Cup Avenue. Follow it along the harbor to the first traffic light in front of the U.S. Post Office. Make a U-turn there to the left and follow the cobblestone road (Thames Street) two or three blocks to Pelham. Take a right onto Pelham, continue up the hill two blocks. The inn is on the corner on the right.

Sweeping Ocean Views Along with a Touch of Victoriana
THE INN AT CASTLE HILL
Newport

One can understand why a naturalist like Alexander Agassiz would build his summer home where he did. And, in fact, Agassiz used his new house as a springboard for his studies of marine biology. The dark brown shingle house, with its turrets, dormers and porches, commandeers a hilltop on Ocean Drive, with a wide-angle view overlooking both the Atlantic Ocean and the entrance to Narragansett Bay, the channel to the Atlantic. Windswept and dramatic, the location could hardly be improved on, as Thornton Wilder once noted. The author, a frequent visitor, wrote in *Theophilus North* about the view from one turreted room: "From that magical room I could see at night the beacons of six light houses and hear the booming and chiming of as many sea buoys."

Inside, innkeeper Paul McEnroe has kept the Victorian style of the 1870s house intact. In fact, many of the original furnishings are here as well. Note the Arabic design in the inlaid wood facade of the parlor fireplace, the finely polished wood paneling throughout, and the rich color of the old oriental rugs. Guest rooms are as ample and idiosyncratic as the public areas and have equally breathtaking ocean views. Seven of the ten rooms have baths, most of which are as large as modern-day bedrooms.

Piece de resistance is the kitchen, from which emanate such delicacies as lobster bisque, tournedos Rossini, steak bearnaise and other dishes which vary daily. Wide windows in the inn's four dining rooms provide panoramas as spectacular as the ones visible from most of the other rooms throughout the inn.

A rocky coastline gives way below the inn's hillside to three private beaches, one sandy, one pebbly, one rocky. The small, secluded one is dubbed the "Grace Kelly Beach," so named because it was the one favored for its privacy by the late Princess Grace when she was a guest here. The beach can be reached by stairs built especially for her behind the inn's Harbour House, an annex with an additional six guest rooms. For greater privacy, the inn has eighteen beach cottages staggered along the thirty-two acre property. Princess

The Inn at Castle Hill

Grace wasn't the only one who liked the inn's serenity—Sir Laurence Olivier, Paul Newman and Joanne Woodward are among the many notables who have visited.

THE INN AT CASTLE HILL, Ocean Drive, Newport, RI 02840. Telephone: (401) 849-3800. Accommodations: ten rooms with twin, double, queen- and king-size beds; private and shared baths with tub/shower; no telephones; no television. Rates: moderate to expensive. Children 12 years and older welcome. No pets. Cards: MC, VISA. Open all year, but dining room closed December to March (except for Continental breakfast for inn guests).

Getting there: From Newport, follow the signs to Ocean Drive. The inn is four and one-half miles from town, past the U.S. Coast Guard station.

A Convenient Central Location with Colonial Ambience
THE INNETOWNE
Newport

Paul and Betty McEnroe have shown the same taste and flair in decorating this hostelry, set in the center of town, as in refurbishing their beautiful Inn at Castle Hill. But in the case of The Innetowne, the grey clapboard building was Colonial, not Victorian, in style, and was totally rebuilt in 1980, after a serious fire had destroyed most of it. Stylish accouterments are a congenial blend of high quality reproductions, such as delicate patterned wallpaper to match the coverings on the comfortable wing chairs and white chenille bedspreads, and originals like the "family" ancestor portraits on the walls, authentic old washstands, chests and mirrors in many of the guest rooms.

The lobby is especially welcoming, decorated as comfortably as a family living room, although better maintained than most, with its couches and chairs all covered in a pleasing bachelor's-button blue and Chinese red and white pattern, handsome carpeting and accessories. Continental breakfast, the inn's only meal, is served on fine china and with silver tea and coffee pots in a small, attractive breakfast room that is furnished with antiques, many of which are for sale to guests. Afternoon tea and cookies are served between 4 and 5 p.m. each day. And there is no need to worry about dining, as the inn is within a short walk of most of Newport's best restaurants.

There are twenty-five guest rooms in all, both in the inn and in a separate turn-of-the-century house called Restoration Building a few steps up Mary Street. This too is furnished in Americana, with each of the guest rooms decorated differently. A great family favorite is the Rathskeller Suite, in the lower floor of the annex. The suite consists of a charming bedroom, cosy parlor with an oriental area rug on a flagstone floor, and a kitchen with plenty of room for a pine table and chairs. Both buildings are in a prime location for walking to the harbor, sightseeing the old Colonial part of town, or shopping at the Brick Marketplace and along busy Thames Street.

THE INNETOWNE INN, Thames Street, Newport, RI 02840. Telephone: (401) 846-9200. Accommodations: twenty-six rooms with twin, double, queen- and king-size beds; private baths with tub/shower; no telephones; no television. Rates: moderate to expensive. Children welcome. No pets. Cards: MC, VISA. Open all year, except December 25.

Getting there: Take the first exit over Newport Bridge, turn right onto Farewell Street. At the second traffic light bear left onto Thames Street. The inn is six blocks farther on Thames on the left side.

Cheerful Victoriana and Newport at Your Doorstep
THE QUEEN ANNE INN
Newport

It would be difficult to get closer to the spirit of Old Newport than this small inn which is located on one of the oldest streets in town. The street itself is a charmer, with gaslights and many handsomely restored old houses. Diagonally across from this rose-colored 1890 Victorian house is the armory of the Artillery Company of Newport, with a splendid bas relief plaque on its facade. The Artillary Company's lineage is long, stretching from early Colonial days through World War I. Inside this old Greek Revival building, which now serves as a military museum, military buffs will find memorabilia of General Dwight Eisenhower, King Hussein of Jordan, Britain's Field Marshall Montgomery, and other American and foreign soldiers.

Clarke Street, once symptomatic of downtown Newport's slow, long-time decay, is now a testament to the city's architectural revival and preservationist spirit. Take the Queen Anne as an example.

Proprietor Peg McCabe has transformed what had over the years become a somewhat seedy boarding house, turning it back into a fine example of Victoriana, just as it might have been in its late nineteenth-century prime. Each of the twelve pretty, moderately sized guest rooms is decorated individually. One is a frothy rose and white, another is an arresting combination of light blue and deep turqouise, featuring a neoclassical arched headboard. Each of the seven shared baths, too, has been thoughtfully decorated and the lounge is done in delicate pastels. Breakfast, the only meal provided at the Queen Anne, is often served in a quiet flower-filled garden behind the house.

THE QUEEN ANNE INN, 16 Clarke Street, Newport, RI 02840. Telephone: (401) 846-5676. Accommodations: twelve rooms with twin and double beds; shared baths with tub/shower; no telephones; no television. Rates: inexpensive, Continental breakfast included. Children welcome. No pets. No cards. Open April to Thanksgiving, but sometimes open later—call in advance.

Getting there: Coming off the Newport Bridge, bear left at the second traffic light. Turn left at the third light, Washington Square. Turn right on Clarke Street, the second right.

Greek Revival Charm in the Center of Newport
THE YANKEE PEDDLER INN OF NEWPORT
Newport

One of the delights of Newport is its variety. Just a few steps away from its dazzling seafront, its modern pubs and cafes and its wharfside shopping areas is another Newport, an old-time sleepy city that peacefully coexists with the modern trends and happenings. Tree-dotted Touro Street takes the visitor back to the nineteenth century, the time when the Yankee Peddler Inn of Newport was built.

The Yankee Peddler, an austerely handsome Greek Revival house, looks today just as it must have when it was a privately owned

The Yankee Peddler Inn of Newport

mansion. Inside, however, there have been changes. The house went through a boarding house phase, but a recent face-lift has made it into a bright and pleasant inn. A blend of antiques and comfortable modern furniture in light and airy rooms together create a friendly ambience, suggesting a quality European pension. Continental breakfast is served each morning in a cheerful basement lounge where you can relax, borrow books from the large bookcase and feel at home. Or you can take a book or newspaper up to the third floor deck to sun yourself and enjoy the view of the water at the same time. Most of the fifteen guest rooms, as well as the five in the carriage house next door, are large and have high ceilings and simple but agreeable furnishings such as pine rockers, flowered draperies, baskets of flowers and ferns, and comfortable beds.

THE YANKEE PEDDLER INN OF NEWPORT, 113 Touro Street, Newport, RI 02840. Telephone: (401) 846-1323. Accommodations: twenty rooms with queen-size beds; private and shared baths with tub/shower; no telephones; no television. Rates: moderate, Continental breakfast included. Children welcome. No pets. Cards: AE, MC, VISA. Open all year, except January.

Getting there: Once over the Newport Bridge, bear left at the second traffic light. At the third light, Washington Square, turn left, then continue until square leads into Touro Street.

Tree-Shaded Elegance on Stately Bellevue Avenue
WAYSIDE
Newport

Driving up to this enormous, black-shuttered, beige brick mansion shaded by a towering beech tree, you might fantasize about what it might have been like in the days, back in 1896, when New Yorker Elisha Dyer and his family drove up in their horse-drawn carriage to the portico of this, their palatial summer home. The house was certainly in the center of the Newport social action, for it is just down the street from the "cottages" of the Astors and Vanderbilts and across from The Elms. The wide avenue itself is a beauty, shaded by beeches and giant ancient oaks.

Actually, as Newport "cottages" went, Wayside, with its twenty rooms, was on the smallish side. But it proved large enough to become a girl's dormitory for Salve Regina College later. Since 1975 Wayside has been a spacious and handsome inn, handily located for sightseeing around Newport, but still giving a great sense of privacy. A swimming pool on the grounds makes a wonderful escape on muggy summer days, but what makes Wayside so special is its sense of past grandeur. Step inside the door and revel in the oak parquet floor of the high-ceilinged entrance hall, an area big enough to encompass two bedrooms. This is the area where breakfast coffee and pastry are served each morning. Adjacent to the entrance is a lounge area with mirrored fireplace and cascades of floral arrangements.

Rich architectural detailing, embellished cornices and fine woodwork are evident throughout the house. A sweeping staircase leads upstairs to most of the guest rooms. One of the most splendid of the seven guest rooms, which range from large to super-large, is an enormous high-ceilinged room, called The Library, on the ground floor. It has an unusually high fireplace with a delicately ornamented Florentine mantel. In addition to the rooms in the house itself, there is a carriage house on the grounds with two bedrooms, a living room, a galley kitchen and bath—perfect for a family or two couples traveling together.

WAYSIDE, Bellevue Avenue, Newport, RI 02840. Telephone: (401) 847-0302. Accommodations: seven rooms with twin, double, queen- and king-size beds; private baths with tub/shower; no telephones; no television. Rates: low moderate, Continental breakfast included. Children welcome. No pets. No cards. Open all year.

Getting there: Once in Newport, follow signs to Bellevue Avenue. The inn is on the left side of the street between Parker and Narragansett, two doors diagonally across the street from The Elms.

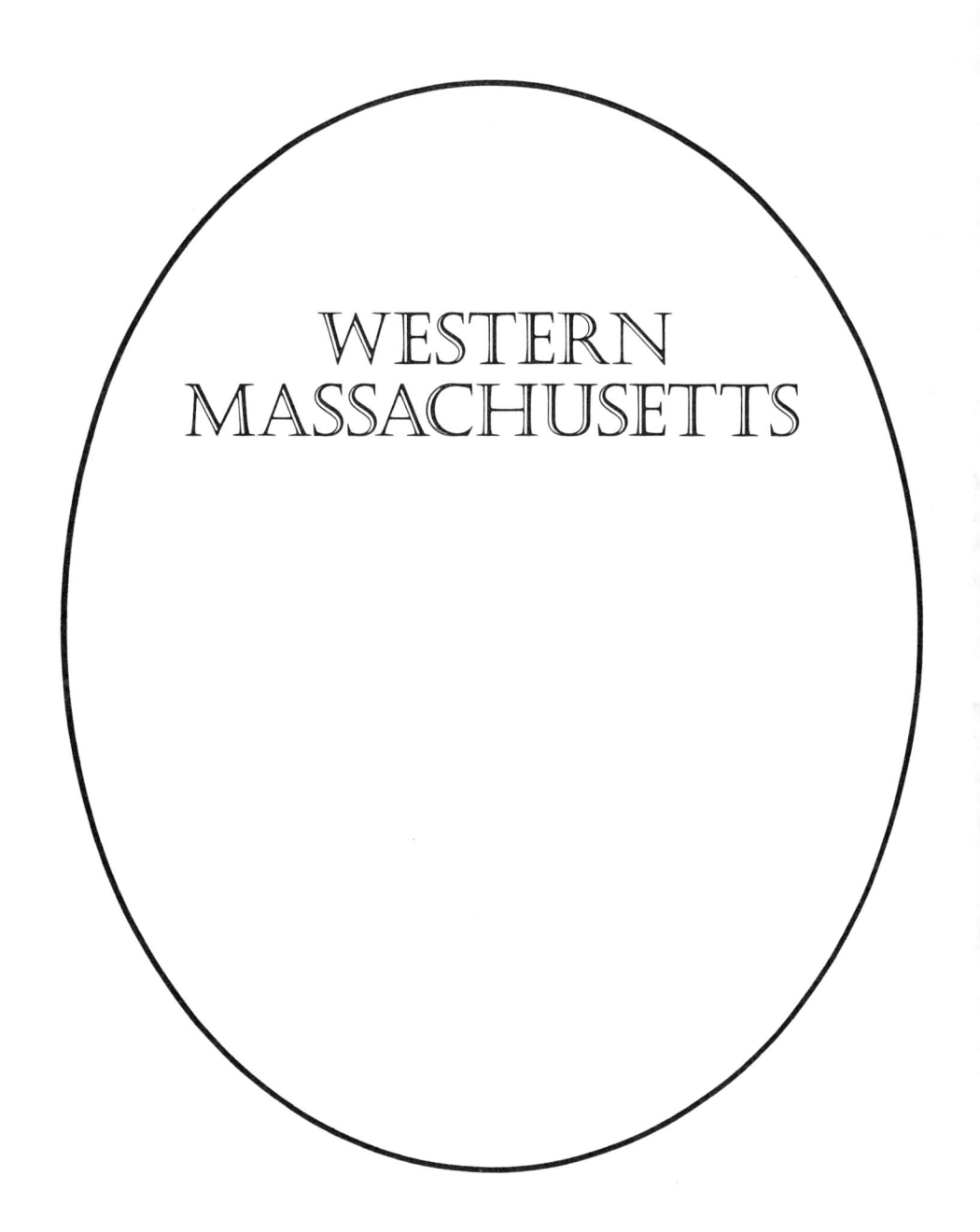

WESTERN MASSACHUSETTS

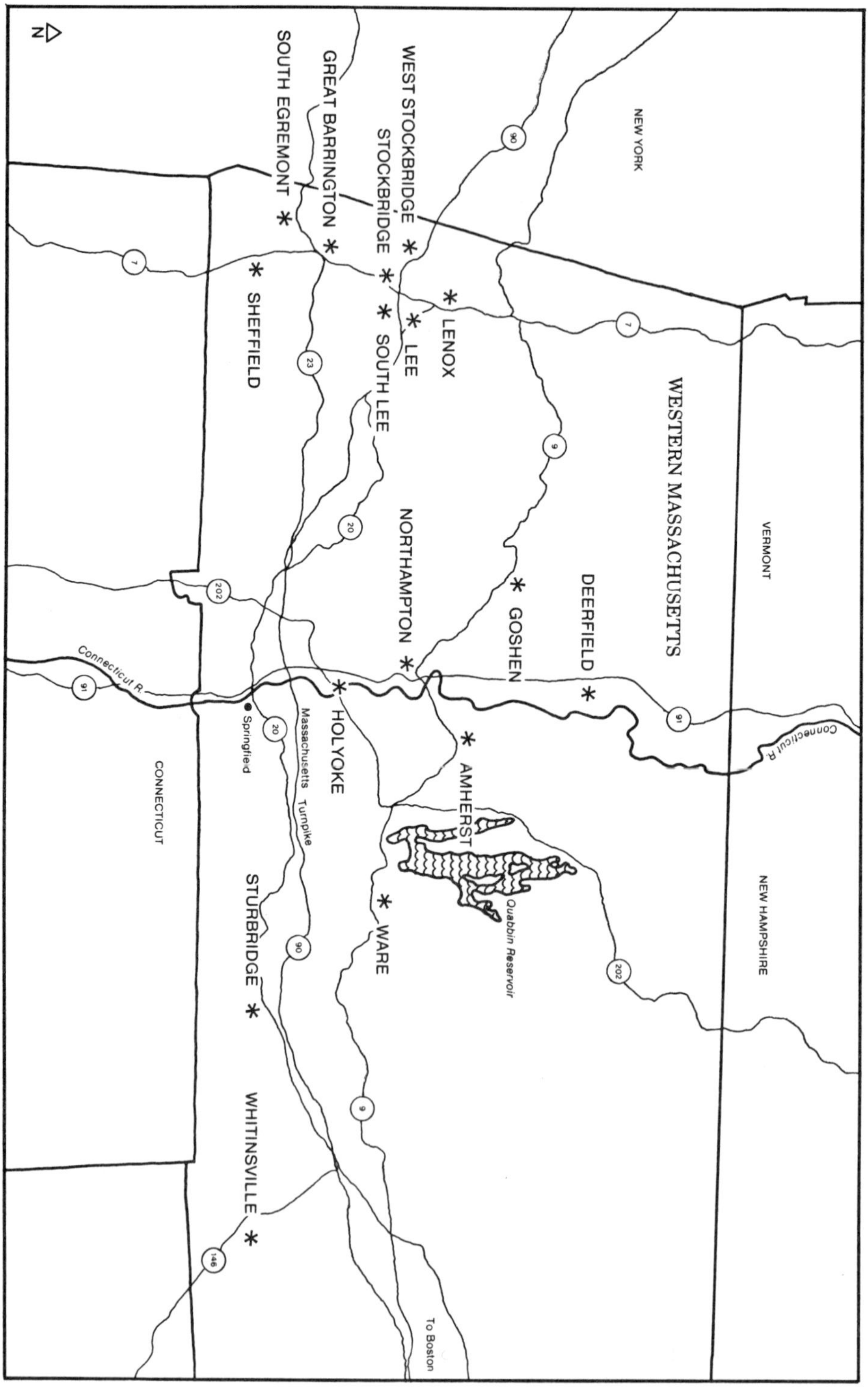
WESTERN MASSACHUSETTS
N
NEW YORK
VERMONT
NEW HAMPSHIRE
CONNECTICUT
WEST STOCKBRIDGE
STOCKBRIDGE
GREAT BARRINGTON
SOUTH EGREMONT
SHEFFIELD
LENOX
LEE
SOUTH LEE
NORTHAMPTON
GOSHEN
DEERFIELD
HOLYOKE
AMHERST
WARE
STURBRIDGE
WHITINSVILLE
Springfield
Connecticut R.
Quabbin Reservoir
Massachusetts Turnpike
To Boston
90
7
23
9
20
202
91
146

A Magnet for Artists and Craftsmen
THE BERKSHIRES

To skiers, hikers, artists, music lovers and vacationers, the Berkshires have long had a magical aura. These beautiful mountains, foothills and valleys, dotted with fascinating attractions, follow the route of the Housatonic River through the western part of Massachusetts. Artists and craftsmen have long gravitated here and each summer musicians fill the hills surrounding Tanglewood with music. Writers such as Edith Wharton, Herman Melville and Nathaniel Hawthorne summered in the Berkshires, as did scores of wealthy nineteenth-century New Yorkers and Bostonians—and you can too.

Among the Berkshires' many sights, are Arrowhead, just outside Pittsfield, where Melville wrote *Moby Dick,* and the Berkshire Athenaeum in Pittsfield, with its collection of Melville memorabilia, including his writing desk. Just three miles or so west of Pittsfield on Route 20 is the Hancock Shaker Village, where you can visit twenty restored buildings, herb gardens and a shop selling Shaker reproductions and other crafts. You might opt to climb Mount Greylock, the highest point in the state (3,491 feet) or hike, picnic or fish at the Greylock State Reservation, just west of North Adams.

In Lenox, you'll find Tanglewood, site of New England's most famous summer music festival, where there is a replica of the cottage where Hawthorne wrote *The House of Seven Gables.* On Laurel Lane is The Mount, the summer home of Edith Wharton. Further north in Williamstown is the superb Sterling and Francine Clark Art Institute with its impressive collections of nineteenth-century French and American art, including splendid works by Renoir, Corot, Monet and Degas.

A Touch of England in the Berkshire Hills
STAGECOACH HILL INN
Sheffield

A little bit of Old Britannia in the Berkshire hills is the way a friend described this fine old inn. You will, in fact, see the Union Jack flying below the Stars and Stripes from the flagpole when you arrive. It might seem a far cry from the early 1800s when the inn, which was built in 1829, served as a stagecoach stop, for the old place actually has the look and feel of an English inn. Hard to believe it now, but the inn once had a phase when it served as the local poorhouse.

Inside the old frame building you will find yourself in a small darkened taproom with a free-standing fireplace, mugs lined up convivially above the bar, a poster of the English highwayman Dick Turpin and a sign proclaiming this to be the English pub of the Berkshires. Old hunting prints and photographs of Lady Diana, Prince Charles and other members of the Royal Family decorate the walls of two cosy, low-ceilinged dining rooms. Floral curtains, barn-red walls and crystal wall sconces all give an inviting tone to the place. Owner John Pedretti's English-born wife, Ann, has seen to it that steak and kidney pie and steak and mushroom pie are on the otherwise Continental menu. Roast beef with Yorkshire pudding is a Saturday specialty.

Three guest bedrooms in the main house reflect, with a Colonial flair, the same cosiness so evident downstairs. There are thirteen additional guest rooms in a cottage, barn and two chalets in the rear. All in all, the Stagecoach Hill Inn is a comfortable place to use as a springboard to exploring both lower Massachusetts and northwestern Connecticut. There's a lot to see and do, with three ski resorts (Otis Ridge, Butternut Basin and Catamount) only minutes away, along with the other Berkshire sights.

STAGECOACH HILL INN, Under Mountain Road (Route 41), Sheffield, MA 01257. Telephone: (413) 229-8585. Accommodations: seventeen rooms with twin and double beds; private baths with tub/shower; no telephones; color television except in rooms in the inn. Rates: inexpensive. Children welcome. Pets accepted. Cards: AE, CB, DC, MC, VISA. Open all year.

Getting there: Located on Route 41 coming north from Salisbury, Connecticut, or south from Stockbridge, Massachusetts.

Stagecoach Hill Inn

A Stop on the Old Albany-Boston-Hartford Stagecoach Trail
THE 1780 EGREMONT INN
South Egremont

Sitting in one of the two cosy candlelit dining rooms or the more casual Francis Hare Tavern is an easy reminder that the old 1780 Egremont Inn is no hostelry-come-lately. In fact, the handsome old frame building dates back almost to the founding of the small village of South Egremont itself—give or take fifty years. The village's major claim to fame in the early days was that it cost thirty quarts of rum and three barrels of cider to buy it from the Indians in 1722.

Some time after Revolutionary War soldier Francis Hare (whose military service lasted just sixteen days) built the inn in 1780, it became a prime stopover on the Albany-Hartford-Boston stagecoach run. Its handy location at the very edge of Massachusetts, with New York and Connecticut borders within shouting distance, made the old inn a natural rest stop.

It is the same today, a restful and handy stepping stone to all the Berkshire fun. But now the somewhat expanded inn has extras such as a swimming pool, all-weather tennis courts and central air-conditioning. The old stable has been absorbed by the inn proper and is now the comfortable Common Room, complete with a curved brick fireplace which was formerly a forge. Antiques, mostly from the nineteenth century, adorn the inviting living room.

A modern touch is evident only on the menu. It is small and French and emphasizes fresh local game. But of course, private baths and modern bedding in the twenty-three guest rooms are reminders that this is the twentieth, not the eighteenth century after all.

THE 1780 EGREMONT INN, Old Sheffield Road, South Egremont, MA 01258. Telephone: (413) 528-2111. Accommodations: twenty-three rooms with twin and double beds; private baths with tub/shower; no telephones; no television; air conditioning. Rates: moderate, modified American plan on weekends, Continental breakfast included on weekdays; three-day minimum stay during July-August. Children over four years welcome. No pets. Cards: AE, MC, VISA. Open all year.

Getting there: From New York State, take Route 23 east from the Hillsdale Exit on the Taconic Parkway. From Massachusetts, follow the Massachusetts Turnpike to the West Stockbridge Exit, then take Route 41 south to South Egremont.

A Family-Run Inn with Familial Flair
WINDFLOWER
Great Barrington

Entering Windflower is just like entering the living room of a nineteenth-century farmhouse, which is indeed what the inn is. It has actually been through several metamorphoses, and has only been an inn since 1981.

Centerpiece of the inn is the extremely comfortable sitting room-lounge, with a white brick fireplace and blue and red couches grouped around a big coffee table covered with magazines. Beyond the main sitting room is a second one, a bit more rustic, like a game room. Many of the twelve bedrooms, including some on the ground floor, are big and roomy, with a mix of comfortable, no frills furnishings and some attractive antique pieces. Adjoining baths are also roomy, as befits a rambling old house.

An attractive, wood paneled dining room, with *its* own white brick fireplace, a swimming pool and nearby tennis and golf facilities make Windflower something of a one-stop, all-purpose inn. The inn is owned by Barbara and Gerald Liebert and their daughter and son-in-law, Claudia and John Ryan. Barbara and Claudia form a talented mother-daughter team in the kitchen, keeping guests supplied with home-baked breads and desserts and a menu which changes daily.

You'll want to browse in nearby Great Barrington, a marvelous resort town settled in the eighteenth century. A hotbed of Toryism during the American Revolution, the town was home in the mid-nineteenth century to poet William Cullen Bryant.

WINDFLOWER INN, Route 23, Great Barrington, MA 01230. Telephone: (413) 528-2720. Accommodations: thirteen rooms with twin and double beds; private baths with tub/shower; no telephones; some rooms with color television. Rates: moderate, modified American plan. Children welcome. No pets. No cards. Open all year.

Getting there: Located on Route 23, three miles west of Great Barrington.

Where Artists and Sportsmen Meet
STOCKBRIDGE

Although a charming contemporary resort town with a lovely wide, tree-shaded main street and a variety of crafts shops and eateries, Stockbridge has had its share of history too. The town was settled in 1736 as a mission for the Algonquin Indians, who were later pushed off their land. The first missionary, Reverend John Sergeant, built Mission House in 1739, a very imposing structure for its time. Later, Jonathan Edwards preached here and wrote *An Inquiry into Freedom of The Will* in the house. Today The Mission House is a museum of Colonial life, with antiques, an Indian Room, Weaving Room and fine displays of Early Americana (closed in winter).

Artist Norman Rockwell was a local resident and many of his paintings are now displayed in Old Corner House, a nicely restored eighteenth-century Georgian house on Main Street. A few miles northwest of town on Route 183 is Chesterwood, the nineteenth-century home and studio of Daniel Chester French, who sculpted the statue of Lincoln in the Washington D.C. Memorial, the Minuteman statue in Concord, Massachusetts and many other public monuments. From May through October, the estate is open for viewing.

Country Home Living away from Home
THE INN AT STOCKBRIDGE
Stockbridge

The Inn at Stockbridge may remind you of one of those glamorous movies of the late 1930s and 1940s in which the hero pursued the heroine from New York to her family's luxurious country home in New England. Although its role as an inn is new (1982), the stately white frame house, with its massive front columns and porches at either end, dates back to 1906. A Boston attorney built it as a summer home and it stayed in his family for seventy years.

As inns go, this is a small one, with just seven guest rooms. Innkeepers Lee and Don Weitz have furnished the place with great style and comfort. You feel you have been invited for a weekend to a friend's luxurious country home—and the warm welcome you receive reinforces that impression. The large main living room is beautifully decorated in a slightly formal manner with wing chairs and comfortable groupings around the fireplace. The second living room is large too, although slightly cosier, with chintz-covered couches and chairs. It too boasts a fireplace, a wonderful spot to cosy up to with a book on a crisp fall or winter evening. In summer, however, you will very likely spend more time around the outdoor swimming pool. The handsome dining room, with a silver tea service sitting on an antique sideboard, cabinets displaying heirloom silver and a large oblong table, is the setting for the inn's only meal—a large breakfast served gratis to each guest.

The guest rooms are as spacious and well-decorated as the downstairs public areas. The largest is truly splendid, with a king-size bed and chess game set up by a couch, ready for play.

THE INN AT STOCKBRIDGE, Route 7, Stockbridge, MA 01262. Telephone: (413) 298-3337. Accommodations: seven rooms with double and king-size beds; five private baths, others share, with tub/shower; no telephones; no television. Rates: inexpensive to moderate, full breakfast included. Children over eight welcome. No pets. No cards. Open all year, but only on weekends January to March with advance reservations.

Getting there: After passing under the Massachusetts Turnpike one mile north of Stockbridge on Route 7, look for the inn's small sign on the right side of the road. Take the Lee exit, turn onto the road to Stockbridge, then turn right on Route 7; proceed north for one mile.

Gathering Place of Presidents
THE RED LION INN
Stockbridge

The Red Lion Inn, dating from 1773 when it was built as a stagecoach stop on the Albany-Boston route, is one of the oldest continuously operating inns in the states. Daniel Webster was one of the first guests, and later guest books record such illustrious names as Nathaniel Hawthorne, William Cullen Bryant, Henry Wadsworth Longfellow and a number of presidents including Martin Van Buren, Grover Cleveland, William McKinley, Teddy Roosevelt, Calvin Coolidge and Franklin Roosevelt.

Once you arrive in Stockbridge, you won't be able to miss the four-storied Red Lion Inn, as it covers most of a block smack in the center of town. It is no wonder that the inn is such a popular local meeting place. Afternoon tea, served in the main parlor, is also a favorite gathering time.

The original building was seriously damaged by a fire in 1896. The rebuilt inn has seen the addition of a motor lodge and a recreation complex, complete with a swimming pool. Since 1968, when present owner John Fitzpatrick bought it, there have been other additions and the kitchen and dining rooms have both been renovated. There are now 115 guest rooms, but more than the spirit of the old inn lives on. Uneven floorboards, ample guest rooms furnished in antiques and old-fashioned chairs, desks, rockers, four-poster beds and carpeting all contribute to the feeling of another era.

THE RED LION INN, Main Street, Stockbridge, MA 01262. Telephone: (413) 298-5545. Accommodations: 115 rooms with twin, double, and queen-size beds, some suites; private and shared baths with tub/shower; telephones; thirty rooms with television, some color; elevator. Rates: inexpensive to expensive, depending on season, time of week and type of accommodations. Children welcome. Pets subject to surcharge. Cards: AE, CB, DC, MC, VISA. Open all year.

Getting there: From Boston, follow the Massachusetts Turnpike to Exit 2 and go south a few miles to Stockbridge. From Connecticut, follow Route 7 north into town.

A Romantic Hideaway—A Delightful Lovers' Retreat
FEDERAL HOUSE INN
South Lee

Small, choice and well-known in the Stockbridge area for its first-rate cuisine, Federal House is not as well-known for its overnight accommodations. There are ten newly decorated guest rooms, all with fluffy quilts and pretty as valentines. Not a bad idea for a lovely weekend or retreat.

The inn, a red brick period house with four white columns built in 1824, is as handsome outside as it is in. It was a private home built by Thomas Hurlbut for his wife, right across the road from his Hurlbut Paper Company. A carriage barn and tack room were attached in 1850 and in 1979 Robin Slocum Almgren and Ken Almgren took the house over and refurbished it as an inn.

The food here, elegantly served in two small, stylish dining rooms, is the *tour de force*. Though innkeeping is a new experience for them, the young Almgrens both have strong food backgrounds. Robin worked at La Caravelle in New York City and Ken at Stonehenge in Ridgefield, Connecticut. Fresh flowers in cut glass bowls, a silver candlestick on each beautifully set table and, on crisp fall and winter evenings, a fire in each room's fireplace all set the stage for superlative dining a la nouvelle cuisine. Beautiful servings of delights such as pike quenelles lavished in nantua sauce, roast quail with foie gras and a robust Madeira sauce, pork medallions with apples and chestnuts and a piquant bearnaise sauce appear on the tables. Meander into the large, comfortable tap room for coffee or after-dinner drinks before heading upstairs to dream away dinner in the folds of your luxurious bed.

FEDERAL HOUSE INN, Route 102, Main Street, South Lee, MA 01260. Telephone: (413) 243-1824. Accommodations: seven rooms with twin, double and king-size beds; some private and some shared baths with tub/shower; no telephone; no television. Rates: inexpensive to moderate. Children over 12 welcome. No pets. Cards: MC, VISA. Open all year, except for one month for refurbishing each spring after ski season; check for current dates.

Getting there: Take Exit 2 off the Massachusetts Turnpike at Lee. Follow Route 102 toward Stockbridge. The inn is located on the town's main street.

Federal House Inn

At Home in the Eighteenth Century
MERRELL TAVERN INN
South Lee

In 1981, Charles and Faith Reynolds, retired school teachers with an interest in history, bought an historic red brick building on the main thoroughfare in the tiny town of South Lee. However, there were strings attached when they bought. The seller, the Society for the Preservation of New England Antiquities, was relinquishing a late eighteenth-century tavern on the condition that it be restored with historic accuracy. "We had twenty-five pages of specifications we had to adhere to," innkeeper Reynolds recalls.

Built circa 1794 by General Joseph Whiton (though some books say the building dates back to 1760), the sturdy three-story structure was bought in 1817 by William Merrell, who gave it his name and turned it into a stop on the Boston-Albany Pike. After the decline of the stagecoach, the inn stood empty for one hundred years, but in 1970 took a place in the National Register of Historic Places.

True to their word, the Reynolds precisely restored the graceful structure. Now, its colonaded and porched facade intact, the inn's interior manages to surpass the beautifully restored exterior. Each of the nine bedrooms is a gem of the Colonial period. Furnishings have been chosen for accuracy, from the antique canopied four-posters to the candle wall sconces to the pastel reproduction wainscoting. The two bedrooms with their own fireplaces are especially charming, although every room is furnished to please the antiques-loving purist who would be hard put to choose a favorite. (The past is so present here that one guest insisted her room had a ghost, although this has not been corroborated by anyone else.) You can't help the feeling of stepping directly into the past in the Old Tavern Room lounge. A full breakfast is the only meal served—and in summer you can have your waffles or omelet and sweet rolls on the front porch. With so many restaurants in the Stockbridge area, the inn's limitation is not a serious problem.

MERRELL TAVERN INN, Route 102, Main Street, South Lee, MA 01260. Telephone: (413) 243-1794. Accommodations: nine rooms with twin and double beds; seven private and two shared baths with tub/shower; no telephones; no television. Rates: inexpensive to moderate, higher on summer weekends; full breakfast included. Children accepted. No pets. No cards. Open all year, except December 24 & 25.

Merrell Tavern Inn

Getting there: Take Exit 2 at Lee off the Massachusetts Turnpike. Follow Route 102 toward Stockbridge. The inn is on the main street in the center of South Lee.

Continental Perfection in the Berkshire Hills
HAUS ANDREAS INN
Lee

An impeccable cream-colored Colonial house with blue trim, the Haus Andreas was built by a Revolutionary War soldier and modernized in the early 1900s for George Westinghouse, Jr. In 1930 still more renovations and additions were made and in 1942 Queen Wilhelmina of the Netherlands, her daughter, Princess Juliana, and two granddaughters spent the summer here.

Now owned by Gerhard and Lilliane Schmid, who made the Gateways Inn in Lenox such a success, Haus Andreas has been an inn only since 1981. The Schmids named the inn for their son, Andreas. It is exquisitely furnished, beginning with the imposing living room with a fireplace, baby grand piano, library for the guests and a stereo. The bright and cheery dining room is where Continental breakfast is served. Although breakfast is the only meal offered by Haus Andreas, a guest pantry is available too. Each of the seven guest rooms is furnished differently—one has a dark, heavy Victorian bedstead, three have their own fireplaces. A favorite room is Number 1, an end bedroom with an alcove, fishnet canopy over the old bed and pretty old-fashioned wallpaper. The grounds are as well maintained as the house. You'll find a heated pool, tennis courts, golf course across the road and complimentary bicycles to wheel you to Tanglewood a few miles away.

HAUS ANDREAS, Stockbridge Road, Lee, MA 01238. Telephone: (413) 243-3298. Accommodations: six rooms with double, queen- and king-size beds; two with shared baths, others have private baths with tub/shower; color television in lounge. Rates: moderate to expensive, Continental breakfast included. Children over ten welcome. No pets. Cards: MC, VISA. Open all year.

Getting there: From Massachusetts Turnpike, take Exit 2. After toll, bear right toward Route 20 and the town of Lee. Haus Andreas is on the left side of the road, almost a mile after the first stop sign in town.

Civilized Charm Tucked into the Woods
THE WILLIAMSVILLE INN
West Stockbridge

One of the most comfortable and civilized country inns in the Berkshires, the Williamsville Inn began as a farmhouse in 1797. Its isolation is exactly what makes the Williamsville Inn so appealing to city escapees. Conveniences such as a swimming pool, clay tennis court, and a fishing pond combine with wooded trails, ten acres of graceful lawns, gardens and woods to make the inn a one-stop vacation.

Add to all this a highly acclaimed country French kitchen, fireplaces scattered here and there throughout the old house, fifteen antiques-adorned guest rooms, nine rooms in the main house, two in a separate unit and four more in a converted barn, including one with its own fireplace, and you may never want to leave. When you aren't dining on paupiette of chicken smothered in artichokes, mushrooms and melted Gruyere or coquille St. Jacques provencale, you might find yourself napping by one of the glowing fires or curled up with a book in a comfortable chair in one of the various sitting rooms.

There is antiqueing along the back roads and skiing in winter—almost anything is possible here in the Berkshires—if you can pull yourself away from the comforts of the Williamsville Inn itself. Aficionados of pottery and things Japanese like to follow Route 41 to the Great Barrington Pottery at Housatonic, where Richard Bennett's showroom displays pots made in his Japanese wood-burning kiln. In summer, the Japanese tea ceremony is performed periodically in a traditional tea house with formal Japanese gardens on the grounds.

THE WILLIAMSVILLE INN, Route 41, West Stockbridge, MA 01266. Telephone: (413) 274-6580. Accommodations: fifteen rooms, including one suite with twin, double and queen-size beds, the six rooms in separate units unavailable in winter; private baths with tub/shower; no telephones; no television. Rates: moderate to expensive. Children over ten welcome. No pets. Cards: MC, VISA. Open all year, except the first three weeks in November and three weeks after Easter.

Getting there: Take Massachusetts Turnpike to Exit 1 (Route 41). Turn left toward Great Barrington. Continue four miles south of Turnpike to inn.

Tanglewood and Tangled Skis in Nearby Hills
LENOX

For many visitors to the Berkshires, Lenox is the very epitome of an affluent nineteenth-century New England village. Take time to wander the village streets, to admire the handsome old churches and splendid homes built by summertime escapees from urban life. Andrew Carnegie was just one (and the richest) of the tycoons to discover the peacefulness of this lovely town.

Visitors are still "discovering" Lenox and its proximity to good ski slopes, historic sightseeing, and recreation possibilities. The village itself complements the surrounding countryside with a plethora of intriguing shops, good restaurants and attractive inns.

While Lenox is an all-seasons town, it is at its busiest during July and August. That's the time when the Berkshire Music Festival is held on the 210-acre Tanglewood estate. Some 250 thousand people attend these concerts, which are highlighted by the Boston Symphony Orchestra. The Music Shed, designed by the late Eero Saarinen, seats six thousand, but part of the fun of Tanglewood concerts is to take a picnic lunch and blanket and listen to the open-air concerts on the well-kept grounds.

Old-Fashioned Comfort in an Old New England Town
THE CANDLELIGHT INN
Lenox

Like the other two Lenox inns cited below, the Candlelight is smack in the center of this resort town's action. Visitors come in droves in the summer to browse the local galleries and craft shops, listen to the music at Tanglewood or watch the dance performances at Jacob's Pillow.

Aside from its convenient location, the Candlelight has an excellent reputation locally for its hearty meals prepared by chef and owner Jimmy De Mayo. Both lunch and dinner are busy, drawing crowds to the sunny glass-enclosed porch and dining room which is lit by candles at night. These two dining areas have the look of an earlier era—dark wood wainscoting, lace curtains at the rounded windows and antiqued wallpaper in cream and red. The menu complements the decor, with such hearty classics as beefsteak and kidney pie, roast beef hash, baked Boston scrod and chicken pot pie. The chef has surprises as well, however, creating specialties such as crepes stuffed with chicken and artichokes with a hollandaise sauce, coquilles St. Jacques, veal Marengo en casserole and veal Oscar. Summertime you can dine in the open courtyard, while in winter you can count on a toasty fire in the grate.

There are just five bedrooms in the black shuttered, white clapboard *fin de siecle* building, but they are roomy, simply but comfortably furnished and immaculately maintained. Note the marble counters in some of the bathrooms—one of many old-fashioned touches you'll find throughout the rambling old inn.

THE CANDLELIGHT INN, 53 Walker Street, Lenox, MA 01240. Telephone: (413) 637-1555. Accommodations: five rooms with twin and double beds; private baths with tub/shower; no telephones; no television. Rates: moderate, with minimum three night stay during July and August. Children welcome. No pets. Cards: AE, DC, MC, VISA. Open all year except December 24 to 25.

Getting there: From the Massachusetts Turnpike, take Exit 2 at Lee, and then follow Route 20 through Lee to intersection of Route 183. Left on 183 leads you right into Lenox and the inn. From Connecticut follow Route 7 north into Lenox.

Prize-Winning Continental Cuisine
GATEWAYS INN
Lenox

Chef-owner Gerhard Schmid and his wife Lilliane have turned the former 1912 summer home of Harley Proctor (of Proctor and Gamble) into an imposing hostelry in the Berkshires. (Local tradition holds that the house, with its rectangular shape and flat, squared-off roof looks like a bar of Ivory soap.) Even if you don't overnight at the inn (its nine bedrooms are booked up far in advance during the busy summer and fall foliage seasons), plan to dine here. The smaller dining room, the Rockwell Room, is named after the artist, Norman Rockwell, who used to frequent the place.

Chef Gerhard, a gold medal winner at two Culinary Olympics, was the chef at a 1976 Bicentennial dinner for Queen Elizabeth of England. His prowess shows in such specialties as shrimp Andreas (stuffed with veal, crabmeat and mushrooms), medallions of veal Lucullus, squab chicken Veronique and roast duckling Gateways (with apple rings and a mandarin Napoleon sauce). Save room for one of the special house desserts—Viennese apple strudel, perhaps, or

Gateways Inn

sabayon torte, linzer torte or pecan pie chantilly. Overnight guests delight in the Victorian charm of the inn, from the high-ceilinged entry hall and wide, graceful staircase to the spacious, individually decorated guest rooms. The largest room, Number 2, is the Victorian Room, a corner room facing the street, with a majestic two-tone wood ensemble of double bed with chest to match, pleasing period wallpaper and a huge bathroom. The Fiedler Suite, where Arthur Fiedler often stayed when he was conducting at Tanglewood, is a dream, decorated in soft colors with floral wallpaper, a comfortable couch and two fireplaces. Leaving is difficult.

GATEWAYS INN, 71 Walker Street, Lenox, MA 01240. Telephone: (413) 637-2532. Accommodations: nine rooms with double, queen- and king-size beds; private and shared baths with tub/shower; no telephones; television in TV room. Rates: expensive, higher on weekends during July-August, a three-night minimum stay during July-August, Continental breakfast included. Children over ten welcome. No pets. Cards: MC, VISA. Open all year.

Getting there: From Exit 2 off the Massachusetts Turnpike, follow Route 20 through Lee, then onto Route 183 at intersection outside Lee. Gateways is one mile further on the right.

Afternoon Tea and Sympathetic Innkeeping
VILLAGE INN
Lenox

This large, rambling L-shaped clapboard house dates back to 1771, making it one of the oldest houses in Lenox. An inn since the 1800s, it is currently run by a friendly twosome, Clifford Rudisill and Ray Wilson, whose chief goal in life—or so it seems—is to make their guests satisfied, answering questions about local sights, suggesting sightseeing itineraries in the area and recommending shops and restaurants of interest.

Its twenty-seven ample guest rooms (and one suite) have a bright, cheerful look, making the Village Inn a homey resting spot. Room 23 is especially delightful, with blue and yellow wallpaper and pretty bedspreads and couch cover. Four of the guest rooms have fireplaces, as do the lounges and large dining room. The cellar taproom, known as the Village Tavern, has a wood-burning stove, stained-glass windows and church pews which double as seats. Coun-

Village Inn

try antiques are placed throughout the inn and the proprietors have a wonderful collection of Early American paintings.

After shopping or strolling through town, treat yourself to an old-fashioned English tea with scones, jam and Devonshire cream back at the inn. Breakfast, Sunday brunch and dinner—Thursday, Friday and Saturday evenings only—are also good times to be in this comfortable place. The chef, trained at the Culinary Institute of America, makes dinner especially pleasant, with a five-course American-accented menu that includes Shaker chicken with tarragon, broiled bluefish and scrumptious homemade desserts like banana custard tart and chocolate chip pie. For late night snacks, just descend to the Village Tavern for treats such as nachos or killer chili with cornbread.

THE VILLAGE INN, 16 Church Street, Lenox, MA 01240. Telephone: (413) 637-0020. Accommodations: twenty-six roms with twin, double and queen-size beds; private and shared baths, with tub/shower; no telephones; no television. Rates: inexpensive to moderate, higher in July-August. Children welcome. No pets. Cards: MC, VISA. Open all year.

Getting there: Take Exit 2 from the Massachusetts Turnpike, then follow Route 20 north to Lee. Just beyond Lee turn onto Route 138 to Lenox. From Connecticut, follow Route 7 north to Lenox.

A Romantic Estate within a Hop-Skip of Tanglewood
WHEATLEIGH
Lenox

When New York industrialist H. H. Cook decided to build a summer house as a wedding present for his daughter in 1893, he decided to do it right. No modest honeymoon cottage for the new Countess de Heredia and her Count. Cook imported and set to work a veritable army of Italian artisans—masons, carpenters and the like—in order to recreate a sixteenth-century Italian *palazzo* on the crest of a small hill in the summer-cool Berkshires.

More than one million dollars and a considerable time later, Wheatleigh was born. Named for Cook's ancestral home in England, the estate, on twenty-two beautifully landscaped acres, was a model of Mediterranean grace, somewhat contradictorily ensconced in the middle of New England. Liberally embellished with ornamented cornices with Renaissance designs, colonnades, ballustrades and porticos, the elegant beige brick house and its satellite wings, terraces and covered walkways was known in its heyday as "the showplace of the Berkshires."

Frederick Law Olmstead, the landscape architect responsible for New York's Central Park, created a wonderland of sculptural driveways, grape arbors and cedar-shaded pool, rolling lawns and marble statues and fountains. Wheatleigh is as splendid inside as the outside promises. The Great Hall, with stained-glass windows, a grand staircase made for dramatic entrances, ornate mantels faced with bas relief cupids and flowers and a romantic Victorian dining room hung with Impressionist and post-Impressionist paintings, all make for the perfect romantic weekend getaway. The food of Wheatleigh's Swiss chef, Paul Eugster, is so special you'll probably find yourself arriving early at the dining room.

Nine of the fifteen guest rooms have fireplaces, some have balconies and all have sweeping Berkshire views and individualized furnishings, such as canopied four-poster beds. Though the beautiful Wheatleigh grounds are virtually self-contained, providing tennis courts, a swimming pool, hiking and cross-country skiiing trails, Tanglewood is within easy walking distance.

WHEATLEIGH, West Hawthorne Road, Lenox, MA 01240. Telephone: (413) 637-0610. Accommodations: seventeen rooms with twin, double and king-size beds; private baths with tub/shower; no telephones; no television. Rates: expensive. Children over eight welcome. No pets. Cards: AE, CB, DC, MC, VISA. Open all year.

Getting there: From Massachusetts Turnpike, take Lee Exit and follow signs to Lenox. In Lenox center at Curtis Hotel corner, take Route 183 to fork, then bear left of fork 1/10 mile. Turn left on West Hawthorne Road and one mile further is Wheatleigh entrance.

THE CENTRAL COLLEGE BELT

Cut a wide swath north to south through the middle of Massachusetts and you will include some of the nation's finest schools. You will also find yourself in Pioneer Valley, which in the seventeenth century was the western frontier for settlers from the Massachusetts Bay Colony. This is a majestic area of dramatic basalt ridges, rock formations, fertile fields along the Connecticut River and sedimentary rocks imprinted with dinosaur tracks—some of which can be seen at the Pratt Museum at Amherst College and at the Granby Dinosaur Museum. There is skiing at Mount Tom, hiking and fishing at the Quabbin Reservoir, a great deal of early American history to be seen, as well as more than a little cultural activity in this area.

Farthest south is Springfield, an industrial center which is going through a rapid renewal. The Museum Center, a grouping of several fine museums, includes the George Walter Vincent Smith Art Museum, with oriental and European decorative arts; the Museum of Fine Arts, with many Dutch, French and Italian paintings, American nineteenth-century primitives, and works by Winslow Homer and John Singer Sargent; and the Connecticut Valley Historical Society Museum, with period rooms and fine examples of local crafts, antique furniture and artifacts. In West Springfield is Storrowton Village, a grouping of Colonial buildings, such as the country store, schoolhouse, private homes and blacksmith shop. The Old Storrowton Tavern in the village is an excellent lunch or dinner spot.

The college circuit begins at South Hadley with Mount Holyoke. North of it is bustling Northampton, home of Smith College and its splendid Museum of Art. Calvin Coolidge once lived in town and a C.C. Memorial Room is ensconced in the Forbes Library. The town also boasts several fine old houses that are open to the public (Parsons, Damon and Pomeroy-Shepherd houses), along with the Arcadia Nature Center and Wildlife Sanctuary, a 475-acre preserve on a migratory bird flyway. Amherst, home of Amherst and Hampshire colleges and the University of Massachusetts, is the quintessence of a peaceful New England college town. It was also the home of Emily Dickinson and her house is open to the public—and fascinating. Other notables who once called Amherst home were poets Robert Frost and Eugene Field, along with Noah Webster of dictionary fame.

As college towns, both Amherst and Northampton have their share of small and interesting restaurants. In Amherst, you might look in on La Raclette or Judie's. In Northampton, there's a good

Chinese restaurant, Sze's Chinese Cuisine, as well as excellent little places like Beardley's, Greenstreets, Paul and Elizabeth's, and the lively, pub-like Fitzwilly's.

The Liveliest "Inn" Place in Town
YANKEE PEDLAR INN
Holyoke

Just like the original Yankee peddler spreading a variety of goods with which to tempt his customers, this Yankee Pedlar seems to have attractions for everyone. There are lounges for quiet conversations and tete a tetes. There is the lively Oyster Bar with brass lamps, wood paneling, popcorn machine and a variety of fresh bivalves to tempt you from 7 a.m. till midnight. The ornate, wood-paneled Gilded Cage Lounge jumps with live music at night. The wood-lined walls of the Tavern are adorned with Currier and Ives prints and the room's cosiness is conducive to leisurely imbibing. A completely different, exuberant feeling is in the air each Sunday morning when an elaborate New England-style brunch is served in the Opera House, a gala complex adorned with a crystal chandelier, a balcony and a polished bar.

And all this is accessory. Locally, it is the inn's large dining room that is the Yankee Pedlar's primary magnet. Exposed beamed ceilings, rough-hewn wood posts and barn-red wide wall paneling create a Colonial atmosphere that accents a menu that features American, New England and some Continental dishes perfectly. Saddle of lamb carved at tableside, broiled fresh bluefish and stuffed fillet of sole in a lobster sauce are but a few of the specialties.

Waitresses decked out in blue with ruffled white pinafores and lacy caps complement such accouterments as tin "pie pan" wall sconces, pine tables, and shelves displaying copper and pewter pitchers and brass pots and bed warmers. A second dining room beyond the first large one has a mix of weathered barn siding and aged brick walls. There is a huge walk-in kitchen with hanging copper pots gleaming along the walls. Yankee Pedlar innkeepers Frank and Claire Banks were trained at the Culinary Institute of America so their attention to and interest in food is natural. In addition, Frank brings twenty-five years of hotel experience to this new labor of love.

That attention extends below stairs too, to a low-ceilinged taproom which holds a country-style French restaurant, Simone's. At lunch, light crepe and quiche meals are served here, and at dinner, there is a more formal six course prix fixe menu.

Although much is going on in the public areas, the forty-eight guest rooms located in five different adjacent buildings are not to be forgotten. The seven rooms in the inn itself have the most ambience. Most have a Victorian look, some with fishnet canopy or ornate four-poster walnut beds, upholstered furniture, period wallpaper and antique artifacts, such as old wall clocks and marble counter tops. The original building of the inn dates back to 1875. The Banks bought it in 1977, and it has been improving ever since.

YANKEE PEDLAR INN, 1866 Northampton Street, Holyoke, MA 01040. Telephone: (413) 532-9494. Accommodations: forty-seven rooms with twin, double and queen-size beds; private baths with tub/shower; telephones; color television; air-conditioning. Rates: inexpensive. Children welcome. No pets. Cards: AE, CB, DC, MC, VISA. Open all year, but no dinner served Christmas Day.

Getting there: Take I-90 to Exit 4, north on I-91 to Exit 16. Then turn right on Route 202 to Route 5. The inn is at the junction of Routes 5 and 202.

Where the "Smithies" (and Others) Hang Out
HOTEL NORTHAMPTON
Northampton

Stepping down into Wiggins Tavern, the incredibly cosy, basement-level taproom/dining room of the Hotel Northampton, is like dropping back into the eighteenth century. Lewis Wiggins achieved this effect by taking a wall from an old Northampton building here, a brick fireplace built with bricks from an old kiln there, adding black wood overhead beams and posts, and then decorating the weathered walls with his original Currier and Ives and other old prints. Voila! Though it is a twentieth-century re-creation of the 1786 tavern that Lewis's uncle, Ben Wiggens, owned in a small New Hampshire town, Wiggins Tavern is made up of authentically aged elements. Behind the hotel is a Country Store, vintage 1797, which was moved from North New Salem.

A favorite dining area is the cosy Tavern Kitchen, one of three small dining areas in the tavern. Here a stone Colonial fireplace, carried from its original home elsewhere, was installed. Adding to the illusion of centuries past are waitresses in long patterned skirts and ruffled blouses and waiters in white shirts and brown leather Paul Revere aprons. The menu, too, echoes other times, with dishes such as clam chowder, scallop and oyster pie, steak and mushroom pie, Yankee pot roast and roast prime ribs of beef.

Not all is old at the Northampton, however. In fact the hotel, which is more like a comfortably old-fashioned town inn, had a facelift in 1981. Freshly papered walls, new carpeting and paint have all done wonders with this old standby, a place where Smith College students, their friends and parents have stayed for generations. The slightly formal lobby, with a crackling fire in cold weather and groups of chairs and couches, is spacious enough to make the grand piano inconspicuous on one side of the room. An addition to the hotel is the Wine Bar Cafe installed on the corner of the ground floor. It features a Cruvinet wine machine, which enables the bar to dispense wine by the taste or glass while keeping the remainder of the bottle virtually unopened. What this means is the wine bar can offer a broad selection of interesting wines, such as boutique California estate wines and fine Bordeaux and Burgundies for sampling. The hotel even features a number of weekend wine-and-dine packages.

As part of the refurbishing, the eighty-four guest rooms have been enlarged and are nicely furnished with traditional pieces, desks for writing and gilt-framed mirrors. There are even a few suites. A nice extra touch is the way each floor has a welcoming arrangement to greet you as you leave the elevator. (With five floors, an elevator is appreciated.) For example, on the second floor, a beautiful hand-woven rug is hung on the wall and in front of it is a grouping of elegant antique furniture.

Located smack in the center of town, it is no wonder that the Northampton has played host over the years to such celebrated visitors as Dwight and Mamie Eisenhower, the Franklin Roosevelts, John F. Kennedy, his brother Ted and various other Kennedys, the Barrymores, Elizabeth Taylor and Richard Burton, not to mention Calvin Coolidge.

HOTEL NORTHAMPTON, 36 King Street, Northampton, MA 01060. Telephone: (413) 584-3100. Accommodations: eighty-four rooms with twin, double and queen-size beds; private bath with tub/shower; telephones; color cable television; individual room thermostats; room service. Rates: inexpensive to moderate. Children welcome. No pets. Cards: AE, CB, DC, MC, VISA. Open all year.

Getting there: From the north, take Exit 20 off I-91, follow Route 5 one mile to the hotel. From the north, take Exit 18 off I-91, go left onto Route 5, then one mile into town.

Village Inn with a Citified Flair
THE LORD JEFFERY INN
Amherst

For the runner, jogger or stroller, the Lord Jeffery Inn couldn't be better located. It is right on the common in the center of Amherst, next to and almost part of Amherst College, within a block of most of the intriguing little shops, eateries and movies in town.

The sprawling inn with its whitened brick facade fits into Amherst's aged brick look perfectly. It owes its name to Lord Jeffery Amherst, a hero of the French-Indian War. The inn is actually a twentieth-century version of a Colonial inn, but the book-lined library with walk-in fireplace, wing chairs, huge couches and the elegant portrait of Lord Jeff himself, and the large lobby with fresh flower arrangements and its fire blazing in cool weather, all fit the image of an authentic old hostelry. Wisteria-covered walls, a Colonial garden where you can lunch or sip cocktails in warm weather under

The Lord Jeffery Inn

the shade of flowering apple trees, and the prospect of afternoon tea served in the library on bleak wintry days, these too are part of the inn's considerable charm.

Recent renovations have provided facilities for small conferences, sales meetings and seminars. But the leisurely village pace is still evident, as is the Colonial look, especially in the sparkling dining room, with its knotty pine beamed ceiling, fireplace, Windsor chairs and brass chandeliers. The menu undergoes periodic revision and is now more Continental than New England, symptomatic perhaps of the changing tastes of the inn's guests. Beef Wellington, rack of lamb, and veal Oscar are a few of the choices.

Guest rooms now number forty-nine. For the most part, they are ample, furnished with old maple chests, bright quilted floral bedspreads, comfortable chairs and prints on the walls, an attractive mix of antiques and period reproductions. A few rooms have balconies that open to the Colonial garden, an especially pleasant place to be in springtime or summer.

THE LORD JEFFERY INN, 30 Boltwood Avenue, Amherst, MA 01002. Telephone: (413) 253-2576. Accommodations: fifty rooms with twin and double beds; forty-three private baths, others share, tub/shower; telephones; color television. Rates: moderate. Children welcome. Pets accepted. Cards: AE, DC, MC, VISA. Open all year.

Getting there: Coming from the south, take I-91 to Exit 19, then go eight miles east on Route 9 to Amherst. From Boston, take I-90 (Massachusetts Turnpike) west to Exit 4, turn north on I-91 to Amherst exit (Exit 19), then follow Route 9 eight miles to Amherst.

A Berkshire Hideaway
WHALE INN
Goshen

You know you've arrived at Kenneth Walden's Whale Inn when you see the big black metal cutout of a whale over the front and back doors of the large pale gold frame building accented by hunter green shutters. Located inland on winding, twisty Route 9 between Northampton and Pittsfield, the inn is in the midst of a pleasing woodsy area, with the D.A.R. State Forest almost next door. Less than ten miles east is Williamsburg, a small, charming village with a nifty General Store selling homemade breads and pies. The name Whale

Inn, a surprise for this inland locale, derives from the quote: "The whale he swam around the ocean and landed Jonah up in Goshen."

Whale Inn began life in 1799. Its age shows in the creaky and uneven floors leading to some of the five upstairs guest rooms. There's nothing pretentious about this old inn, the bedrooms possessing a homey rather than decorator appeal. Each is furnished differently, most with old four-poster beds and several with fireplaces. In certain rooms you'll find delightful old glass paintings, wicker rocking chairs or dormer windows. Rag rug carpeting covers the hall floors throughout. While the large dining room caters to a loyal clientele—offering fish and chips, finnan haddie, prime ribs and fresh seafood—it is the bedrooms that capture the true old-time spirit of the place.

WHALE INN, Route 9, Goshen, MA 01032. Telephone: (413) 268-7246. Accommodations: six rooms with twin and double beds; private baths with tub/shower; no telephones; no television. Rates: inexpensive. Children and pets welcome. No cards. Open all year.

Getting there: Follow Route 9 west from Northampton twelve miles; from Pittsfield thirty-one miles east.

DEERFIELD

You don't have to have a child studying at one of the town's three preparatory schools (Deerfield Academy, Bement School, Eaglebrook) to have an excuse to visit this seventeenth-century town. One of the oldest in New England, Deerfield was first settled in 1660. History buffs love to explore the town's ignominious past, site of not one, but two Indian massacres. The first, Bloody Brook Massacre, took place in 1675, and it was seven years before Deerfield was resettled. Then in 1704 half the resettled town was burned, many settlers were killed, and over one hundred were marched to Canada as captives. The town was not resettled again until 1735. Over the next century it became a thriving farm community, one of the most prosperous in the entire valley.

The town's mile-long Old Deerfield Street is considered one of the loveliest streets in the United States, shaded by ancient elms and lined with imposing frame houses, many with intricately carved entrance portals—characteristic of this area. A combination ticket, available at the Hall Tavern Information Center, across from the Deerfield Inn, entitles you to see a number of the twelve historical buildings along the street. Of special interest is the Frary House, with portions dating back to 1689. Its owner, Samuel Frary, was massacred by Indians. His house later became a tavern in which Benedict Arnold supposedly negotiated the sale of fifteen thousand pounds of beef for his troops during the American Revolution. Some of the houses are veritable museums of decorative arts, showing the art, furniture and artifacts of eighteenth- and nineteenth-century rural New England life. The first of the restored historic villages, Old Deerfield, has been designated a National Historic Site—small wonder!

Where History, Indian Sagas and Preppies Meet
DEERFIELD INN
Deerfield

Though this beautiful inn dates back to 1884, its third floor was severely damaged by fire in 1979. Careful renovations have restored the old cream-colored, pillared inn to better than new, however, and the look is still old, thanks to a scattering of fine antique furnishings and the care taken in matching reproductions, such as the finely

Deerfield Inn

stenciled wallpaper in the bar and the Beehive Parlor, to the authentic period pieces.

Many delights await guests here. One might be an after-dinner coffee or a cordial before the fire in the comfortably formal Beehive Parlor, furnished in soft gold and blue with a beehive wallpaper pattern. Another might be dinner by candlelight in a room that sparkles with crystal, silver, antiques and four handsome bay windows. The menu blends sophisticated fare like escargots with a Pernod-accented lobster sauce or lemon sole a la dijonaise with hearty New England Indian pudding, maple-walnut pie or bread pudding with apricot melba. Still another delight is breakfast downstairs in the large sunny coffee shop, where you can watch yellow finches hopping in and out of the flowering crab apple tree outside the window. Your special moment might be teatime, a lazy afternoon's respite in the Beehive Parlor. Or it might be the inn's willingness to pack a box lunch for you to take on a day of exploration in the area.

There are eleven guest rooms in the inn proper and another twelve in a new attached addition. Each room is named for an early or prominent Deerfield resident and a small printed card in the room tells you in detail about the person your room is named for. It could be Consider Dickenson, the town character back in the mid-ninteenth century, or perhaps Cora Carlisle, who ran Deerfield Inn when it was a summer hotel in the early part of this century. The Horatio Alger room honors the "rags to riches" author, who spent one term as principal at Deerfield Academy in 1856. If you stay in the Martin Kellogg room you'll learn about the eighteen-year-old boy who was captured by Indians during the 1704 massacre and marched one hundred miles through snowy wilderness to Montreal. Later he became a wilderness scout, a founder of many small New England towns, and a teacher of Indian boys in Newington, Connecticut. The Parson Ashley room recalls the Tory minister of Deerfield, whose irate parishioners denied him firewood and locked him out of his pulpit one Sunday during the Revolutionary War. In the Jeremiah Dummer room, you'll learn about the first native-born silversmith in America—you can also see some of his work in Old Deerfield. The Allen Sisters room commemorates Frances and Mary Allen, avant garde photographers who lived and worked in Deerfield early this century. Their house in town is open to the public. You can learn quite a lot about Deerfield itself from the details on these cards!

Each room is furnished with considerable panache, from the nicely patterned Greff draperies and matching bedspreads, to the colored sheets and abundance of thick, fluffy towels. Four-poster canopied beds with steps, good lighting in both bed and bathrooms, and extra chairs and reading lamps all make for considerable comfort. No wonder the likes of Jacqueline Onassis, Happy Rockefeller, and Ted Williams have found their way here at one time or another.

DEERFIELD INN, Main Street, Deerfield, MA 01342. Telephone: (413) 774-5587. Accommodations: twenty-three rooms with twin and queen-size beds; private baths with tub/shower; telephones; no television (color television in two parlors); air-conditioning. Rates: moderate. Children welcome. Pets, if checked in advance. Cards: AE, DC, MC, VISA. Open all year, except December 24 to 25.

Getting there: Take I-91 north to Exit 24. The inn is just off Route 5 and 10. Watch for signs to Historic Deerfield.

THE QUABBIN RESERVOIR AND EAST CENTRAL MASSACHUSETTS

Almost smack dab in the middle of the state, covering 128 square miles, is the Quabbin Reservoir. The Indian name, *Quabbin,* signifies "much water"—and that it is. To build the vast reservoir, which serves the entire Boston area, the Swift River Valley and four entire valley towns were flooded in the 1930s. The result is like a small fjord, with misty views of water, islands, hills and woods. Some fifty islands in the watery reserve were once hilltops and many are visible from the observation tower on Quabbin Hill. On a clear day you may not see forever, but you will have a glimpse of Mount Monadnock in the far distance. Views aren't the only pleasures at Quabbin. You can hike the scenic trails (the fall foliage season is especially rewarding here), bicycle along the water's edge, picnic, canoe and fish. The only no-nos are hunting and swimming. Birds love the area as much as people do. In fact, Quabbin is now the winter residence of the bald eagle.

A Winning Trio: Antiques, Good Food, a Genial Innkeeper
THE WILDWOOD INN
Ware

This imposing cocoa-colored, turreted Victorian house has more going for it than its proximity to Quabbin Reservoir—though that can be diversion enough for a weekend visit. Nestled into two acres of apple and chestnut tree-dappled land at the edge of a tiny Currier and Ives town, with the Ware River crisscrossing the property, the inn has views from almost every window that change with each season.

The inn's assets are almost too many to mention. One of these is innkeeper Margaret Lobenstine herself, an enthusiastic hostess, cook, craftsperson and naturalist. Margaret is a "people-person," which makes her a natural innkeeper, though she's the first to admit her training has been "on the job." In 1978 Margaret and her husband, Geoffrey, who had been living with their twins in Berkeley, California, came east for a family reunion. A wrong turn off the Massachusetts Turnpike at Exit 8 led the Lobenstines into the woodsy little town of Ware, which Margaret still jokingly calls "Where?"

Discovering the turreted old house near the end of a quiet street stirred all Margaret's childhood fantasies of living in a big house in the country. "It seemed to me the only way we could afford to do it was to open the house as an inn," she recalled. "Little did we know what was involved." First step was a visit to the Board of Selectmen to get a license. This took time, for no one had ever had an inn in Ware before. Geoffrey then had to arrange a transfer in his job in the U.S. Postal Service. Finally everything fell together and in 1979 the Wildwood opened, just in the nick of time for the fall foliage season. Now, watching Margaret greet strangers and quickly turn them into friends, you'd think she had been an innkeeper her entire life.

Her love of nature and antiques and her own inventiveness spill over into the inn's decor: hooked and braided throw rugs, homespun curtains and a huge spinning wheel called a walking wheel (you walk it to make it spin); rare Benjamin Franklin tiles at the edge of the parlor fireplace; Early American pine and maple chests in various guest rooms; an antique cradle in the parlor, full of books on handicrafts and on the Quabbin area for guests to peruse; an old-fashioned wringer washing machine used as a luggage rack in one of the five guest rooms, a wicker cradle in another; and homemade quilts on

The Wildwood Inn

guest beds, good for snuggling under on lazy days, though there are electric blankets as well. Each antiques-adorned guest room bears the name of its quilt design—Patchwork Quilt Room, Flower Garden Quilt Room (a large corner room that seems surrounded with maple trees), Cranberry-Center Afghan Room (a treasure with four bay windows), Corner Room, and Old Embroidery Quilt Room. This last, the spacious master guest room, is perhaps the prize, with its four bay windows that frame apple and chestnut trees, a heady sight visible from the room's queen-size four-poster bed.

The inn serves only Continental breakfast, but what an interesting variation it is! Rush-seated chairs around pine tables with tile inserts afford sunny morning views of the wisteria and apple trees outside the window. Each morning's fare is different. "I like to surprise our many repeat guests," Margaret explains. One day it might be an old Finnish recipe, puff pancakes. Another time it could be peach point muffins, popovers, captain's delight, lemon twist ("an old New England recipe, a distant cousin of Yorkshire pudding"), pecan puffs, maple cheese squares made from syrup from the inn's own maple trees, country yummies, or maybe the universal favorite, chipmunk pie (made with apples and spices). Accompanying the homemade sweet is Margaret's own peach butter, along with juice and coffee or an herb tea (drawn from a selection held in a fine old chest kept nearby). "Magic really happens at breakfast," says the ebullient innkeeper. Guests are relaxed and discuss their day's plans. Margaret provides them with a list of nearby attractions such as Sturbridge Village and the superb Worcester Art Museum, along with recommended restaurants. It's a quiet, friendly time when guests become acquainted with each other and with the inn. If the day is rainy, or a guest merely wants to unwind around the inn, there are books, an antique carpenter's chest full of games and puzzles, a glowing fire and, of course, all those beautiful views. More energetic guests may use the inn's canoe to paddle along the Ware River on the grounds behind the inn, swim in a brook-fed swimming hole or play tennis on the property courts. In winter, take to the inn's sleds and toboggans for a romp over nearby hills or ice skate the frozen river.

THE WILDWOOD INN, 121 Church Street, Ware, MA 01082. Telephone: (413) 967-7798. Accommodations: five rooms with twin, double and queen-size beds; shared baths with tub/shower; no telephones; no television. Rates: inexpensive, Continental breakfast included. No children under six. No pets, but a heated kennel in town. No cards. Open all year.

Getting there: From the Massachusetts Turnpike, take Exit 8 (Palmer-Ware), then go left on Route 32 eight miles. Route 32 bears right and becomes Ware's Main Street. At the second traffic light, turn left on Church Street. The inn is 3/4 of a mile up the hill on the right. From Sturbridge Village, drive west from Exit 9 on the Massachusetts Turnpike to Exit 8, then follow the directions above.

Where the Pastoral Nineteenth Century Lives On
STURBRIDGE

Old Sturbridge Village, one of New England's major attractions, couldn't be better located. Two major highways (Massachusetts Turnpike and I-84) meet at this old farm village, which recaptures and preserves the period from 1790 to 1840, and might be dubbed New England's response to Colonial Williamsburg. But there's nothing elegant about Old Sturbridge. In painstaking authenticity it shows—with numerous craft, artisan, cooking and other demonstrations—the simplicity and austerity of New England country life at the time. Old Sturbridge Village never actually existed per se, but its buildings did. They were acquired and moved into a village setting to form a museum of the past. Every tool, implement and artifact is genuine.

So, after a day spent exploring the Common, Quaker and village meetinghouses, the parsonage, school, printing office, Pliny Freeman farm, the three mills, the shops and numerous houses, continue your visit to the past with a stay in an inn that evokes the same spirit.

Colonel Ebenezer Crafts Inn

Country Comfort and a Sense of History
COLONEL EBENEZER CRAFTS INN
Sturbridge

In 1786, when David Fiske built his impressive clapboard house on a hilltop named for his grandfather, he probably never would have dreamed that his treasured home would one day, almost two hundred years later, be turned into an inn and named, of all things, not for him but for the Revolutionary War officer who founded the local tavern, Ebenezer Crafts. Vagaries of time! But what's in a name? After all, it's the ambience and comfort that count. Fortunately, the Colonel Ebenezer Crafts Inn has an abundance of both.

Eight ample rooms, some with views of the gently rolling hills beyond, are furnished with an agreeable mix of antiques and tasteful reproductions. There is also a small swimming pool on the well-landscaped grounds. The Colonel Ebenezer Inn is a more peaceful adjunct of the immensely popular Publick House a mile or two down the road, which is where you'll go first to check in, then later for lunch or dinner. Expect a generous Continental breakfast at the Crafts Inn, accompanied by the morning newspaper. And in mid-afternoon, you'll be served tea and goodies. Much later, there'll be fruit and cookies waiting on your night table for a late night snack.

THE COLONEL EBENEZER CRAFTS INN, Fiske Hill, Sturbridge, MA 01566. Telephone: (617) 347-3313. Accommodations: nine rooms with twin, double and queen-size beds; private baths with tub/shower; telephones; no television; air-conditioning. Rates: moderate, with Continental breakfast, afternoon tea, and nighttime sweets included. Children welcome. No pets. Cards: AE, CB, DC, MC, VISA. Open all year.

Getting there: From the Massachusetts Turnpike, take Exit 9, then onto Route 131. From Hartford, take I-84, which becomes I-86, then take Exit 3 to Sturbridge and the Publick House. When you register there, get directions to Fiske Hill.

Fun for the Kids Next Door to Old Sturbridge Village
PUBLICK HOUSE
Sturbridge

A replica broadside announcing the many upcoming activities at the Publick House (and the list is always a long one) notes that during the Revolutionary War, "Colonel Ebenezer Crafts equipped and drilled a cavalry company on the Sturbridge Common in front of the Publick House—of interest because the Publick House was started by Colonel Crafts in 1771. General Lafayette and his son, George Washington Lafayette, passed through Sturbridge in 1824 and spent time in the inn's taproom. Long a popular stagecoach stop, the inn's real heyday is now, however. Proximity to Old Sturbridge Village one mile away makes the Publick House a magnet for visitors.

The inn's nineteen guest rooms are comfortably and attractively furnished, with fine reproductions and a sprinkling of genuine Early American antiques. Uneven, wide, planked floor boards and low, exposed wood-beamed ceilings add to the Colonial atmosphere.

Yet the greatest delight at Publick House is in the public areas. Five cosy partitioned dining rooms—with wood paneling, Colonial chandeliers, glowing fires and ancient, squeaky floors—provide the perfect settings for a cuisine that blends modern culinary know-how with old-fashioned American, especially New England, dishes. The Publick House's bakery yields delicious fresh breads and flat molasses cookies called Joe Froggers and onion popovers along with flaky crusts for favorites such as lobster pie, French Canadian meat pie (tourtiere) and southern pecan tart. Breakfast, featuring home-baked muffins and rolls is served in front of the glowing embers of the open hearth of the Tap Room.

Something always seems to be going on at the Publick House. Even bleakest winter offers the fun of sleigh rides and "sugaring off," part of a special Yankee Winter Weekend package. Innkeeper Buddy Adler has all kinds of surprise packages up his sleeve to bring visitors back again and again. There's a "Twelve Days of Christmas" celebration, complete with a boar's head procession with suckling pig, roast goose and plum pudding. And at Easter, the bunny comes with eggs and chocolates for the kids. No question, with Old Sturbridge as a neighbor, Publick House is a fun place for kids—of any age. If there's no room at the inn, you can always try the Country Motor Lodge, which is part of the property, built in the style of a New

England village. And adjacent to Publick House is Chamberlain House, also a venerable building, with four formal, handsomely furnished suites and one bedroom.

PUBLICK HOUSE, On The Common, Sturbridge, MA 01566. Telephone: (617) 347-3313. Accommodations: twenty rooms with twin, double and queen-size beds; private baths with tub/shower; telephones; television in Chamberlain House and Country Motor Lodge. Rates: moderate to expensive, depending on the season and package. Children welcome. No pets. Cards: AE, CB, DC, MC, VISA. Open all year.

Getting there: From Hartford, take I-84, which becomes I-86, to Exit 3 (Sturbridge). From Massachusetts Turnpike, get off at Exit 9. The Publick House is on Route 131 in Sturbridge.

Gourmet Fare and Lovely Victoriana
THE VICTORIAN
Whitinsville

The Victorian is aptly named. But then, everything about this fastidiously maintained inn is apt, from the exquisitely furnished period rooms to the maintenance of the stately old house, now painted salmon pink to bring out its many fine architectural details.

The twenty-three room house was built in 1871 by James Fletcher Whitin, whose thriving textile machinery business made him the mill town's leading citizen. His sons owned a cotton weaving mill across the road from the family house, for living across from, or next to, the family business was common in industrial age. Massachusetts. In its prime, the Whitin house was a showplace of gilded mirrors and chandeliers and Louis XV furniture.

But the house's second owner, Albert Whitin—nicknamed Lord Albert because of his patrician tastes—virtually abandoned the house when he went abroad, never to return. The story goes that he suffered such *mal de mer* on his Atlantic crossing to France that he couldn't bring himself to come home again. Martha Flint, who bought the house in the early 1970s, believes, to paraphrase an old song, "How're you going to keep him in Whitinsville after he's seen Paree?" As bustling as Whitinsville was in the late nineteenth and early twentieth centuries, it could hardly have compared to Paris.

The Victorian

When the Flints saw the house in 1974, it was love at first sight. It was empty and hadn't been lived in for decades, but structurally, it was in perfect shape. Martha says, "We knew nothing about Victorian furnishings, but we knew we needed them to fulfill the spirit of the house." Fortunately, Victorian antiques were not then the rage, so the Flints were able to buy, at modest prices, furniture and accouterments that have become priceless treasures.

Each of the eight guest rooms is as meticulously furnished as the public areas. Of particular interest is the Queen Anne highboy in the oversized Master Bedroom, which has its own dressing room. In the Pond Room another delight is the plum-colored loveseat with a triple-medallion back. And the Armor Room on the third floor is unique. The armor once displayed there is long gone, but there is a fireplace and most unusual tooled leather wainscoting with triple-tiered bas relief wallpaper. The names of the rooms are carry-overs from Whitin days, assigned by Martha when she discovered old keys with the room names attached.

Exquisite as the furnishings are, the Victorian's major claim to fame are the dining rooms. Enthusiastic gourmets have been known to drive down from Boston, up from Hartford or over from Providence or Springfield to experience the exquisite dishes created by chef Claudia Hinsley. You might dine in the small parlor, with pale blue, watermarked silk covering its walls and deep blue napery to match. There is also the more formal room with white marble fireplace and damask draperies and the large Library Room, whose wood-paneled and book-lined walls evoke as much warmth in feeling as its fireplace does in actuality. Among the special delights at table are veal soubisoise, rabbit with basil sauce, and shelled lobster in a brandy-accented mousseline sauce. Desserts, along with everything else, are homemade and delicious.

THE VICTORIAN, 583 Linwood Avenue, Whitinsville, MA 01588. Telephone: (617) 234-2500. Accommodations: eight rooms with twin, double and king-size beds; private baths with tub/shower; no telephones; no television. Rates: moderate. Children welcome. Pets accepted. Cards: AE, MC, VISA. Open all year, except for two weeks in March.

Getting there: From Providence, take Route 146 north. Turn right (northeast) on Route 16. At Uxbridge turn north on Route 122. Whitinsville is just a couple of miles north. From Boston take Route 16 south to Uxbridge, then north onto Route 122 to Whitinsville.

EASTERN MASSACHUSETTS

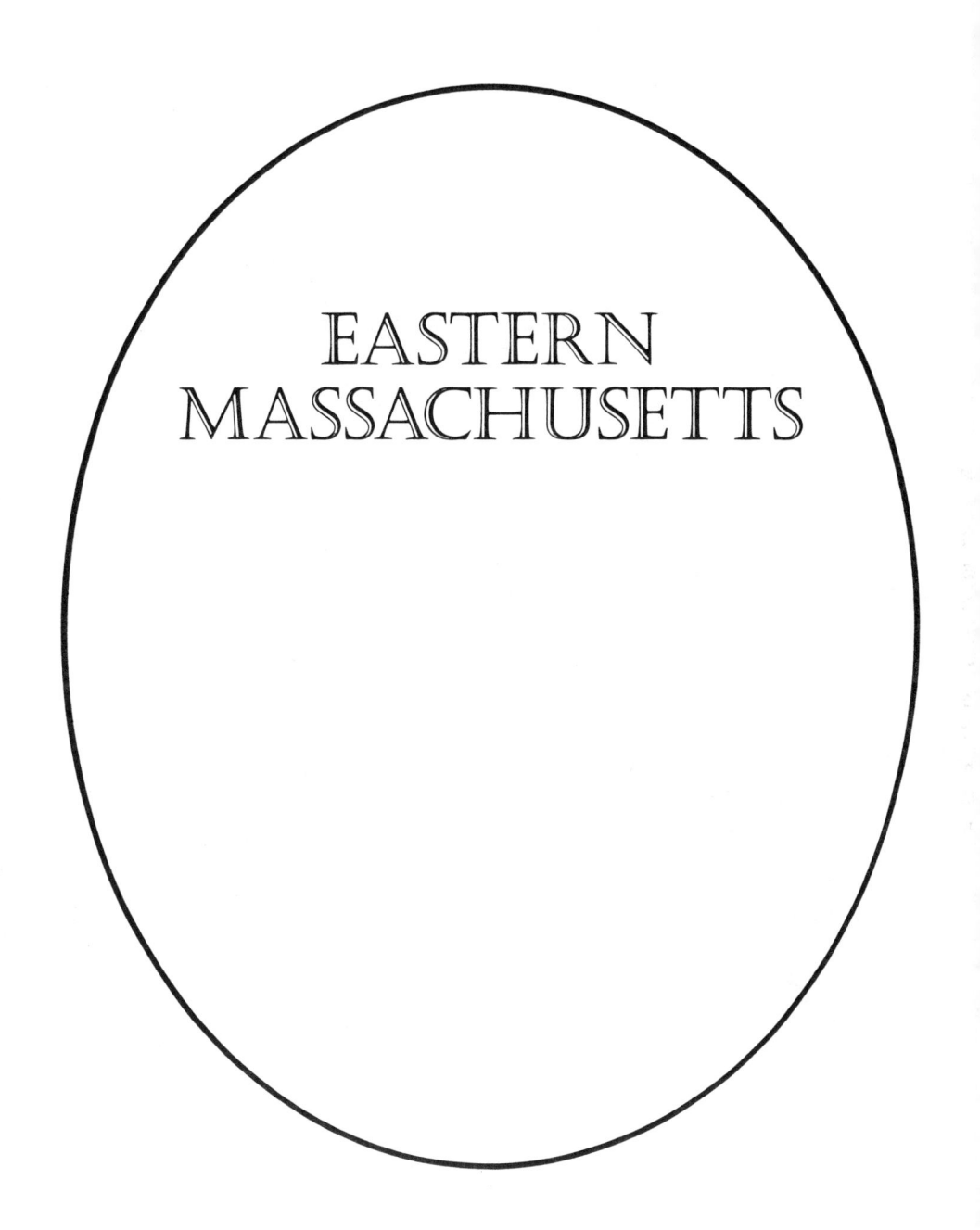

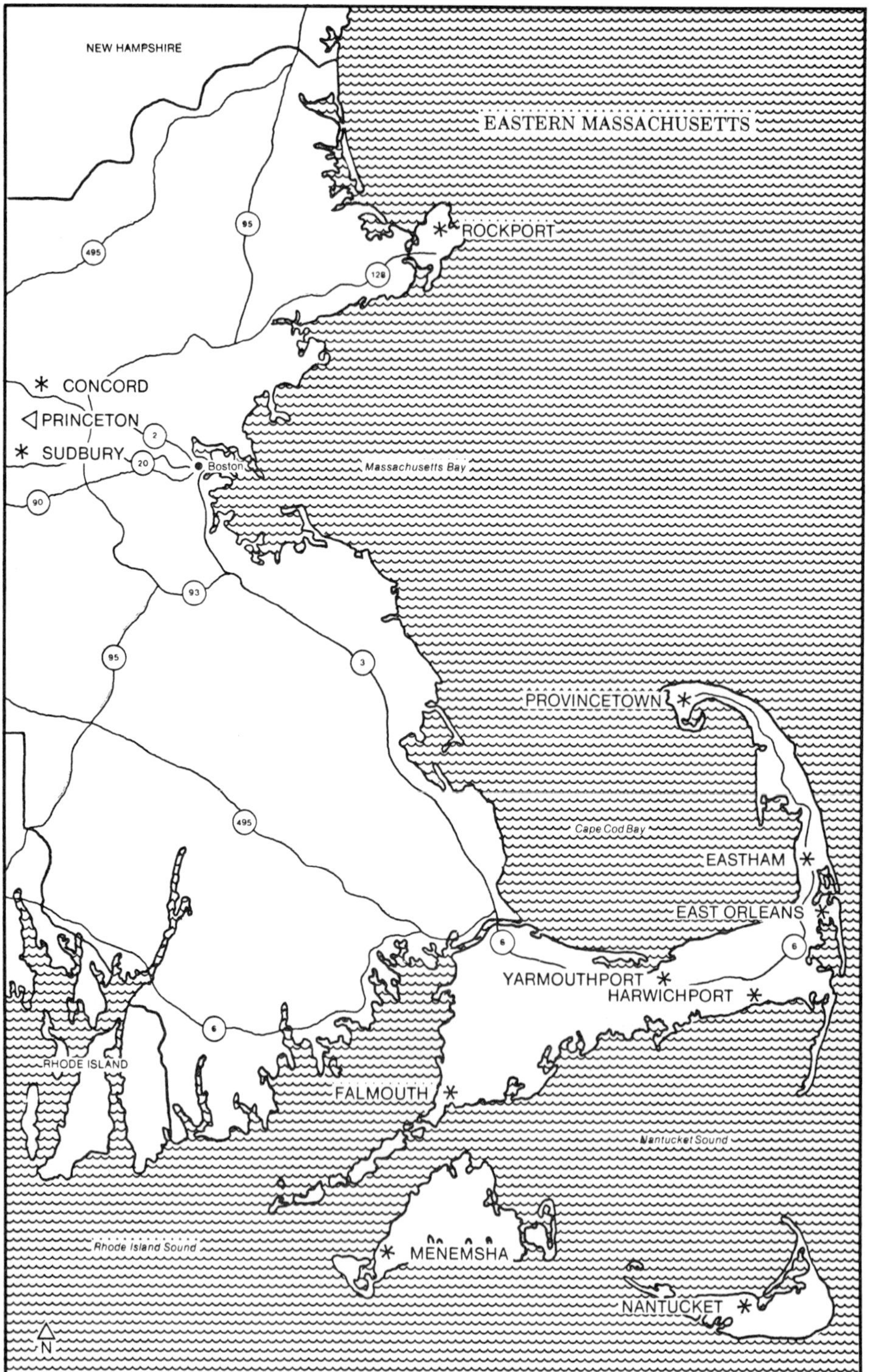
NEW HAMPSHIRE
EASTERN MASSACHUSETTS
95
495
ROCKPORT
128
CONCORD
PRINCETON
2
SUDBURY
20
Boston
Massachusetts Bay
90
93
95
3
PROVINCETOWN
495
Cape Cod Bay
EASTHAM
EAST ORLEANS
6
6
YARMOUTHPORT
HARWICHPORT
6
RHODE ISLAND
FALMOUTH
Nantucket Sound
Rhode Island Sound
MENEMSHA
NANTUCKET
N

Mountainside Grandeur
COUNTRY INN AT PRINCETON
Princeton

Unlike neighboring Concord and Lexington, Princeton has escaped fame, although this tiny mountainside village was a summer resort in the early part of this century. Little evidence of its history remains now, however, and the town is transforming into a bedroom community. But fortunately, the town's grand old inn preserves a bit of the town's romantic past.

The Country Inn at Princeton is a Queen Anne-style country home that once belonged to industrialist Charles Washburn. Built around the turn of the century, this many-gabled inn has known guests such as Theodore Roosevelt and has long been a landmark on the Mountain Road, a steady three-mile incline from village to the base of Mt. Wachusett, the only bona fide peak in eastern Massachusetts. The view from the inn itself is breathtaking, for the building's location takes full advantage of its ridgetop setting. Local authorities claim to be able to see the skyline of Boston on a clear night—perhaps if you squint, you'll be able to see it too.

Inn guests may take advantage of the clear mountain air for skiing in winter at the recently expanded state-owned ski area. There is swimming, bicycling, hiking and fishing in the summer and tennis games are easy to come by on the town tennis courts, though you may prefer to lounge about your rooms. Princeton is also just far enough away from Boston to seem like a vacation spot—about a one and one-half hour drive—so the inn is popular year-round with in-state guests as well as travelers from afar.

The Country Inn at Princeton is one of the most well-respected restaurants in central Massachusetts. The dining areas are gracious and reflect the Victorian atmosphere of the building, and the management, headed by chef Tom Emerick, is very sensitive to the needs and comforts of restaurant guests. It may be possible, for instance, to have a private dinner in the flower-decked solarium on a summer night and watch the light fade from the mountainside.

Restaurant guests are often suprised to learn that the inn even *has* guest rooms. But what guest rooms these are! Each of the six rooms is actually a suite, with a sitting area, formal Victorian furnishings and lovely views from every window. Ceilings are high, most of the beds are massive antiques, all rooms have private baths and once the last restaurant guest has departed, the inn feels like a

Country Inn at Princeton

private home. In the morning, a Continental breakfast is served, usually in the solarium where you might see a deer emerge from the woods or a troop of hardy cross-country skiiers.

COUNTRY INN AT PRINCETON, 30 Mountain Road, Princeton, MA 01541. Telephone: (617) 464-2030. Accommodations: six suites with twin or double beds; private baths with tubs or tub/showers; no telephones; no television. Rates: very expensive, Continental breakfast included. No children. No pets. Cards: AE, MC, VISA. Open all year.

Getting there: From Route 2 west of Boston, take Route 31 south and follow into Princeton. Turn right onto Mountain Road.

Welcome to History's Home
CONCORD AREA

Few towns in the United States can compare to Concord in terms of historical significance. The town was settled in the mid-1600s, the first battle of the Revolutionary War was fought here in the 1700s, and in the 1800s, one of America's greatest literary colonies gathered here to write, think and create. Now, in the 1900s, Concord exemplifies sensible small town success. It is beautiful, it is civilized and it is accessible, without being spoiled.

Bone up on your history before you come to Concord. Otherwise, you'll be overwhelmed by the myriad of museums, battlegrounds, historic homes, and historical drives and tours. And that's not even counting just plain browsing about the back roads. A must-see list would include the Concord Antiquarian Society, the Old North Bridge (where the "shot heard 'round the world" was fired), Walden Pond (although Thoreau would hardly recognize it now), and the Old Manse, for starters. The homes of Alcott, Thoreau, Emerson and Hawthorne are open to the public too. The Concord Bookshop has an outstanding reputation as one of New England's finest and offers an excellent selection of regional books.

Concord boasts several good restaurants too: the Colonial Inn, the Different Drummer, Ephraim's in Sudbury and the Bellecoeur in Lexington for elegant dining. For more informal meals, try the Willow Pond Lounge on Route 2A for seafood and steaks or the Olympian in West Concord for Greek food.

A Homelike Feeling in a Literary House
THE HAWTHORNE INN
Concord

The Hawthorne Inn is a relative newcomer to a town where most everything seems to have been there forever. The house itself is on historically significant property, having been owned at one time or another by Emerson, Alcott and Hawthorne. Each left his mark and provided more stories for innkeepers Marilyn and Allen Mudry to share with you. The couple came to the house in 1976 and began renovating, transforming it into an inn, although for all intents and purposes this is a house, not an inn, and the homelike feeling has been played to full advantage.

Rooms at the Hawthorne are simply furnished. Hardwood floors gleam under braided rugs and beds are brightly splashed with intricate handmade quilts which are made by Marilyn. Bathrooms are shared and the furniture may seem spare until you realize that it is carefully arranged, punctuated by pieces of Allen's or Marilyn's artwork or sculpture. There is a lovely collection of antiquarian books from the house's former owners in the dining room and a decanter of sherry twinkles a welcome in the late afternoon.

Outside, you can stroll among trees planted by Hawthorne or sit in the tiny paved garden area, where flowers bloom profusely from April to October. The large house is a stucco neo-Colonial structure with black shutters and sits far enough back from the busy highway for you to be separated from the rush of passing tourists.

Reserve rooms at the Hawthorne well in advance and don't be surprised if you cannot get a room on a weekend. For the handicapped, there is a lovely room on the first floor, a rarity in country inns. Concord is accessible from Boston by bus or train and most historical sites are within walking or hiking distance of the inn.

THE HAWTHORNE INN, 462 Lexington Road, Concord, MA 01742. Telephone: (617) 369-5610. Accommodations: five rooms with twin, double, twin and double or two double beds; shared baths with tub/showers; no telephones; no television. Rates: very expensive, Continental breakfast included. Children permitted. No pets. No cards. Closed during winter; closing dates vary from year to year.

Getting there: From I-95 (Route 128) take Exit 45 west (Route 2A). Follow signs to Concord, bearing right at blinking light. Inn is on the left about 2 miles past Battle Park on Route 2A.

A Luxurious Spot in American History
THE COLONIAL INN
Concord

So The Colonial Inn is really more like a small hotel than a country inn, per se. But the inn has so much charm, so much history and such a comfortable feeling it's easy to forget that there are sixty rooms and an excellent restaurant under the rambling, many-gabled roof, and that the rooms have conveniences like telephones and televisions. Staying at The Colonial Inn, in the center of a town like Concord is convenient—you can walk to many of the historical attractions, all of the town's fascinating little shops, as well as several restaurants.

Although Concord is clogged year-round with throngs of tourists, the town has never developed a resort-style strip of motels and in fact, it only has two country inns. Visitors stay in Lexington or Bedford, or if being in Concord is important, at the Colonial or the Hawthorne. Three private boarding schools in Concord create a constant demand for rooms.

Staying at the Colonial Inn can be an adventure in itself. You might get lost in the maze of hallways on the first floor, for the building is a bridge of roofs linking several old houses and newer wings into one rambling octopus of a hotel. Just getting to the front office to check in may be a challenge. Finding your room may be the next.

You have three choices of accommodations: the Main Inn, the Prescott Wing and the Keyes House. The Main Inn is the building that faces the town green and from the entrance, looks like it *is* the inn. Built in the early 1700s by Captain James Minot, the Main Inn's spacious rooms are comfortably furnished and many have fireplaces. Walls are hung with old prints of nearby landscapes and the bathrooms, while luxuriously private, may not have the most modern fixtures—but what do you expect in a room that is over 250 years old?

The motel-like Prescott Wing might be the best choice during July and August, when the sea breeze from Boston has a hard time making it all the way out to Concord. These rooms are air-conditioned, modern and functional. If you are looking for the country inn feeling, you won't find it in these rooms, but on a hot summer night, an air-conditioned room can be quite a blessing.

The John Keyes House is separate from the inn, and features several double rooms that have kitchenettes. If you're in town for an extended period, you will be very comfortable here and you'll be out of the main traffic of the inn. Rooms are simply furnished.

At dinner time, plan to spruce up a bit and enjoy a seafood dinner in the dining room. Visit the John Anthony Shop in the inn basement for fine and unusual pewter gifts, then go next door to the Concord

Country Store and stock up on tweeds. Things in Concord don't change much—there's no reason to mess with success.

THE COLONIAL INN, 48 Monument Square, Concord, MA 01742. Telephone: (617) 369-9200. Accommodations: sixty rooms with twin, double or two double beds; private baths with showers or tub/showers; telephones; televisions. Rates: expensive. Children allowed. No pets. Cards: AE, CB, DC, MC, VISA. Open all year

Getting there: Take Route 2A west from Route 128. Follow 2A toward Concord, bearing right at blinking light. The inn is on town green.

The Classic American Inn
WAYSIDE INN
Sudbury

If there is a hall of fame of country inns, the Wayside Inn would be at the top of the list. Immortalized by Henry Wadsworth Longfellow in his *Tales of a Wayside Inn,* it is the oldest continuously operating inn in America. Longfellow's words, written over one hundred years ago, set the standard for what we dream of under antique quilts in New England country inns and what we hear in legends as we sit beside wide hearths. Longfellow created an image of fascinating travelers sharing news and tall tales in the firelight, of hooves clopping in the courtyard, and of weary travelers who gulped their meals, thinking only of their destinations.

The Wayside Inn is still open, still accepting weary travelers, still encouraging tale-telling by the hearth. The difference is that it is a historical monument now, almost a living theatre of its own legendary past. If you are lucky enough to get a room here, do. You will find museum-perfect surroundings and the food is wonderful.

Sudbury was once a frontier outpost of Colonial Boston but has since become a bustling, affluent suburb. Its center is still one of the loveliest in New England, and the proximity to Concord makes this an ideal location for travelers who want to visit the local attractions. The Wayside Inn is just off Route 20, a very busy local highway, and is easy to reach from the Massachusetts Turnpike or I-95.

Route 20 fades to a distant hum as you drive into the Wayside Inn compound, however. The complex of buildings on the grounds include the inn itself, the Wayside Grist Mill, the Redstone School and a chapel. All the buildings and the grounds are maintained by the inn, which is owned and operated by a private foundation. Luckily, the foundation sees the value of keeping the inn open to travelers instead of turning it into a museum.

Although the inn was built in 1702, the Wayside's rooms are graciously equipped with private bathrooms and air conditioning for muggy summer nights. Other things, though, have not been updated. Doors still have latches, not doorknobs, and there are very few ceiling light fixtures in the building. Modernization has taken place only where and when necessary.

Mealtime at the Wayside is a classic experience in American cuisine. The inn's traditional fare has changed little in over two hundred years, yet this is one of the best and most fun restaurants in the Boston area. The food is not haute cuisine, but the seafood is fresh and delicious, the breads are home-baked and include a variety of fruit breads, and the atmosphere, including the constant creaking of floorboards and the crackle of fires, is unbeatable. This is plain and simple food, but you will probably be impressed enough to take home a recipe book and some stone-ground flour from the mill.

Get up early to beat the crowds and explore the buildings and the five thousand-acre reservation. The Grist Mill is one of the most picturesque buildings in the area, an imposing granite structure complete with a waterfall and water wheel to turn the grinding stones. The Redstone School building was moved to the grounds from nearby Sterling. It is the same schoolhouse, built in 1798, described in the nursery rhyme, "Mary Had a Little Lamb."

Inside the inn, you can visit Longfellow's parlor room where he wrote "Paul Revere's Ride," along with many other poems from his *Tales of the Wayside Inn*. The inn, by the way, started out as a tavern, then began accepting guests under the name of the Red Horse Tavern. When Longfellow's book was published in 1863 and met with immediate literary success, the name was changed to the Wayside Inn.

There is plenty to do in the Sudbury area besides visit historical sites. The Sudbury and Concord rivers are ideal for canoeing, and you can re-create Thoreau's lazy days on the local rivers or visit his cabin at nearby Walden Pond. Boston is only a half-hour drive from Sudbury, making this a good headquarters for city sightseeing without the problems of staying in the city. A mile-long string of shopping malls is in nearby Framingham on Route 9 and the area abounds with factory outlets of all types of clothing, luggage and giftware. Antiquing in this neighborhood is for the specialist only, however.

Don't expect bargains, but do expect beautiful displays and some very knowledgeable dealers.

"Food, drink, lodging for man and beast" is still the motto of the Wayside Inn, and the world is still beating a path to its door. Gone are the stagecoaches, the drovers, the drivers and most of their tales, but their memories are here enshrined and their spirits roam a sanctuary that we can share, for a night.

WAYSIDE INN, Wayside Inn Road, South Sudbury, MA 01776. Telephone: (617) 443-8846. Accommodations: ten rooms with twin or double beds; private baths with tubs and showers; no telephones; no television. Rates: moderate. Children allowed. No pets. Cards: AE, CB, DC, MC, VISA. Open all year except Christmas Day.

Getting there: From I-495 in Marlboro take Route 20 exit east. About seven miles east, turn onto Wayside Inn Road after the Wayside Country Store. From I-90 and Boston, take I-95 (Route 128) north to Exit 49. Drive west on Route 20 for about twelve miles to Wayside Inn Road.

CAPE ANN

Cape Ann is the rocky peninsula that juts eastward off the edge of the Bay State. With Boston only about an hour to the south, Cape Ann is an exciting and romantic place to vacation or to live, since it is an excellent place to visit year-round. Route 127, the main street here, sweeps around for over thirty miles in its circuit of Cape Ann. This simple two-lane road joins the twin cities of Gloucester and Rockport and rambles through a half dozen picturesque fishing villages and scenic coves. Although an ideal route for cyclists and motorists, it could easily take a whole day to wind around the Cape, succumbing to the temptations of the clam shacks, antiques shops and beaches along the way.

Both Rockport and Gloucester offer a plethora of places to stay and eat, and many are open year-round. Rooms in Cape Ann's little inns and motels may all be booked during July and August years in advance, so be sure to make reservations before you leave home.

The list of things to see and do on Cape Ann is virtually endless and if you feel the need, Marblehead and Boston are nearby, offering a livelier nightlife. However, most people come to the Cape to rest, paint, bicycle or shop for antiques and art, for some of the best galleries outside New York can be found in the artists' colonies of Rocky Neck in Gloucester and Bear Skin Neck in Rockport. Restaurants equaling the White Rainbow, the Raven and Rhumb Line in Gloucester are hard to find anywhere and the Firehouse, in tiny Lanesville, provides one of the best breakfasts around, serving Finnish breads and pastries spiced with the flavor of the sea outside the steamy windows.

A Step Back in Time at an Old Cape Farm
OLD FARM INN
Rockport

A farm on Cape Ann? Yes, of course, even on Cape Ann there were farms, for even fishermen need milk and eggs. The Old Farm Inn, which was one of the last farms on the Cape, has been converted to an inn and restaurant, although it still retains a country air in the midst of the salt spray and sea gulls.

The Old Farm Inn is a cluster of red buildings set back from Route 127 near Pigeon Cove, a suburb, so to speak, of Rockport. The highway sweeps by the inn so that few passersby note more than the sign. They often fail to note the Halibut Point Reservation beyond the inn as well, a conservation land trust designed to preserve open space and a tidal environment. Over one hundred acres of the reservation abut the acreage of the Old Farm Inn, making this one of the most private places to stay on Cape Ann. Guest accommodations comprise only seven rooms in a converted barn that is adjacent to the main house, now a restaurant, on a five-acre parcel of land.

The Balzarini family has been running the Old Farm Inn since 1964, which is when they bought the farm that had originally belonged to John Balzarini's father. The family has earned an international reputation for fine New England dining and comfortable accommodations. All the rooms have separate entrances, providing a great deal of privacy.

The Halibut Point Reservation is the northernmost tip of Cape Ann, from which you can theoretically be the first person to see the sun rise, if you manage to hike there before daybreak. It doesn't take long after this for the put-put of lobster and fishing boats to fill the air. The granite boulders along the shore make excellent vantage points for watching the parade of ships and boats. Likewise, Halibut Point is the place to be during yacht races, since many races are "to Halibut and back."

Old Farm Inn

Rockport is only a few miles from the Old Farm Inn, a healthy bike ride and a day's hike. Folly Cove is the nearest settlement on the way to Gloucester, where you can eat lobster outside right on the rocks, plus several artists' studios and antiques shops.

In the evening, plan to have dinner in Bill Balzarini's dining room. The restaurant rambles around the front of the old farmhouse, which is filled with delightful fresh ocean breezes and serves excellent seafood and lamb, with duck being the house specialty. Don't forget to bring your own wine, though, since Rockport is a dry town. In the summer after dinner the gardens beckon for an evening stroll. Flowers bloom everywhere, filling the air with their fragrance. On foggy nights, the lighthouse beacons slice through the darkness and fog horns moan—it's nice not to have to drive anywhere.

Guest rooms as neat and clean as these are a pleasure to find. They are filled with oak and maple furniture, have lovely flowered walls and sparkling modern baths. Steep stairs to the second story may be difficult for some, however.

OLD FARM INN, 291 Granite Street (Route 127), Rockport, MA 01966. Telephone: (617) 546-3237. Accommodations: seven rooms with twin, double or two double beds; private and shared baths with tub/showers; no telephones; televisions in most rooms. Rates: moderate, Continental breakfast included. Children allowed. No pets. No cards. Open November through March.

Getting there: Follow I-95 north to Danvers, then continue toward Gloucester on Route 128. Follow 128 to Gloucester. After crossing the Annisquam River, take Route 127 and follow to Rockport.

In a World of its Own
ADDISON CHOATE HOUSE
Rockport

Rockport is a clutter of art galleries, restaurants and gift shops surrounded by fishing piers, docks and crowded roads. By staying at the Addison Choate House, you can walk or bicycle anywhere you need to go. This homelike inn is a large rambling house set sideways to the street, providing a quiet, much-needed reprieve from the bustling town. In the summer, flowers cascade profusely from windowboxes and hanging planters and trail along stone walks.

Everyone feels at home at this inn, which actually is the home of innkeepers Brad and Mary Sweet. They have decorated the Addison Choate with period oak furnishings and patchwork quilts which work beautifully with the polished hardwood floors, sunny windows and airy guest rooms. There is a magnificent sunny breakfast area filled with tiny tables where you can sit and watch the townspeople walk by on their way to work.

Guests who prefer privacy will find the cottage behind the inn perfect. This secluded home-away-from-home has two bedrooms, a kitchen, a private yard and a barbeque area and features leaded windows, some even with stained glass. Overhanging trees camouflage the darkly stained building, making this a magic place, just steps away from the inn's lovely pool area.

The only drawback at the Addison Choate is the cramped parking which is the case in all of Rockport. Traffic jams are the rule rather than the exception on weekends, but the inn is easy to find and you can depend on the inn for quiet, friendly accommodations and a perfect introduction to the magic world of Rockport.

ADDISON CHOATE HOUSE, 49 Broadway (Route 127), Rockport, MA 01966. Telephone: (617) 546-7543. Accommodations: seven rooms with twin, double or queen-size beds; private baths with showers or tub/showers; no telephone; television in public area. Rates: moderate, Continental breakfast included. Children not allowed. No pets. No cards. Open all year.

Getting there: From Route 128 north of Danvers, follow 127 out of Gloucester toward Rockport. The inn is on Broadway (Route 127A), just past the intersection of 127, about a quarter mile from the public wharf in Rockport.

Elegance by the Sea
YANKEE CLIPPER INN
Rockport

The Yankee Clipper Inn, which comprises three separate buildings, is actually three inns, each with its own atmosphere and type of accommodations. The Inn and the Quarterdeck are on the ocean side of Route 127 and offer spectacular views of the sea from almost every window. The Bulfinch House, on the Rockport side of Route 127, is a little quieter and more suitable for independent guests. The latter was designed by New England's premier architect, John Bulfinch, early in the nineteenth century. A nautical atmosphere and a delightful awareness of the community's long association with the ocean pervades all three of the Yankee Clipper's buildings. The doors to the rooms bear little wooden signs carved like clipper ships, identifying each with the name of a famous Chinese trader. The three buildings are all decorated with antique and period furniture.

Deciding which building to stay in often comes down to what sort of meal service you desire. If you plan to stay put, opt for the Quarterdeck or the Inn, for your meals will be included in the room fare. If you'd like to splurge on a rustic lobster feast outdoors or explore local gourmet eateries at night, the Bulfinch House would be a better choice, for meals are not included. It also has more of a country inn feel than the other two buildings, which may seem more like a resort.

In the Bulfinch House, a few of the best rooms are the "Empress of the Sea" on the first floor, which has a king-size bed and a view of the sea; the "Great Republic," and, at the top of the stairs, "Rainbow," where the ocean can be seen from the queen-size bed. Rooms are a bit more formal at the Inn across the street. Favorites are the "Flying Cloud" and the "Sea Witch," which seems to hang out over the ocean. Both have little porches with sleeping couches in addition to beautifully appointed sleeping quarters, full-length mirrors and telephones. If you can live without a view of the sea, "Lightning" has a canopy bed, a modern shower and romantic period wallpaper and furnishings.

The grounds of the Yankee Clipper are carefully manicured and landscaped to take full advantage of sea breezes and views. The heated saltwater pool is a popular place in warm weather, since many find the ocean here too cold for swimming on any but the hottest days. The inn has a small boat for sightseeing trips, and whale-watching or deep-sea fishing trips can be arranged for guests at a moment's

Yankee Clipper Inn

notice. Once you see the Yankee Clipper, however, you may be perfectly content to stroll the granite-strewn shore or curl up with a book on one of the many terraces. This is a comfortable place, in an unequaled setting.

One note about night life in Rockport: This is a dry town and no liquor is sold or served. It is a short hop down Route 127 to Lanesville, which has two liquor stores that are open until 11:00 p.m. Liquor purchased elsewhere by guests may be served at your table at dinner at most of the restaurants in town.

YANKEE CLIPPER INN, Route 127, Rockport, MA 01966. Telephone: (617) 546-3407. Accommodations: twenty-eight rooms with twin, double, queen- or king-size beds, two rooms with double beds and convertible sofa beds; private baths with showers and tub/showers; telephones; television in lounge. Rates: very expensive, meal plan available. Two-night minimum stay on summer weekends. Children welcome. No pets. No cards. Inn and Quarterdeck open year-round, Bulfinch House open May to November.

Getting there: Follow I-95 north to Danvers, then continue toward Gloucester on Route 128. Follow 128 to Gloucester. After crossing the Annisquam River, take Route 127 and follow to Rockport. The main office of the Yankee Clipper is in the Bulfinch House, which is just west of Rockport.

The Playground of New England
CAPE COD

"You're sure to fall in love with old Cape Cod," croons the old song, and in truth, few people can resist the charm of this crooked little peninsula of sand extending from Massachusetts. Tourists beware, though: There are some important things to know about the Cape before you go.

The first lesson of survival on Cape Cod is one of seasons. Summer is high season on the Cape and rooms are scarce. Don't expect to get a room in a country inn on a whim in August. Call in December for summer reservations, or even a year in advance for the best rooms in the best inns. September and October are exquisitely beautiful on the Cape and you might find better rates and less crowds then. Likewise with May and June, although April is still pretty cold and windy.

The second lesson to learn is that Cape Cod has many faces, and several distinct regions in its narrow area. First, there is the ocean side, from Hyannis to Orleans along route 28. This is the lively side of the Cape, chock-full of restaurants, bars, nightclubs, shopping malls, flea markets and motels. Also traffic jams, college students and fast food. Then there is the bay side, along Route 6, from Sandwich to Eastham in the crook of the elbow. Here are the old houses, the shady streets, the antiques shops, the essence of Cape Cod to many people. Then there is the base of the Cape, from Bourne to Woods Hole and up to Falmouth, that is really a combination of the two. Finally, there is the Outer Cape, a sweep of dunes, marsh and magic from Orleans to Provincetown, where the Cape ends in a swirl of poetry, art, music and madness. The Key West of New England.

Always allow extra time when driving to and from Cape Cod, if not for traffic, for stops along the way. If you are flying to Hyannis Airport, don't be surprised if the airport is socked in by fog on either end of your trip. Hyannis is an hour's flight from Boston, and there is regular commuter service. There is also a ferry from Boston's waterfront district directly to Provincetown; its schedule is designed for an overnight stay however, as there is no ferry returning to Boston after dark.

Most people drive to Cape Cod and the recent construction of the Mid-Cape Highway has done a lot to improve driving conditions and times, especially if you are headed to the Outer Cape.

The main attraction to Cape Cod is, of course, the ocean and the beaches. The ocean is everywhere, but nowhere more dramatic and beautiful than along the Cape Cod National Seashore—bring your bicycle, your binoculars and your wildflower and waterfowl identification books. People have been doing it for centuries, now it's your turn.

Getting there: From Boston, take Route 3 south from the Southeast Expressway to the Sagamore Bridge. Take either 6A along the northern shore, the Mid-Cape Highway (Route 6), or continue southwest on 28 to Falmouth.

Privacy and Excellent Dining
COONAMESSETT INN
Falmouth

Falmouth is one of the most accessible towns on Cape Cod. It is a quick sixty miles—in the off season, little more than an hour's drive—from downtown Boston. It is a hustling, bustling kind of place with several neighborhoods offering everything from palacial estates to baudy college nightclubs. This is the starting point for those headed to Martha's Vineyard and Nantucket Islands and ferries come and go from Wood's Hole, only about five miles from downtown Falmouth. Martha's Vineyard is clearly visible from Falmouth's beaches on a clear day.

The Coonamessett Inn is one of many country inn and bed-and-breakfast places in Falmouth. It stands out from the rest, though, by offering an off-the-beaten track atmosphere, an excellent restaurant and a colony of cottages and apartments for unequalled privacy. With Falmouth at your fingertips, make this your headquarters for exploring the Cape and Islands, or just relax day after day. Early reservations are strongly recommended.

Coonamessett hospitality is expressed in many ways. The guest is king here and there is less of a transient feeling than at many Cape inns. The inn is located on lovely Jones Pond which glistens underneath the sun. The grounds surrounding the inn are always impeccable and fresh flowers fill the inn.

The weather-shingled look is popular on Cape Cod and the Coonamessett is an excellent example of how local architecture complements the silvery greens of summer. The house and barn were built in 1796 by Thomas Jones, the inn's name deriving from an Indian expression meaning "place of large fish," perhaps for the bass in local waters. If you're curious about early American architecture, you'll have a field day here. The house is framed with peg joints, nails are headless slivers and the bricks in the fireplace supposedly came over as ballast on British ships.

Rooms here are comfortably furnished, often with antiques or reproductions and paneling is abundant. Paintings by primitive artist James Cahoon are a popular conversation topic, second only to the menu for dinner at the excellent restaurant or what someone just bought at the gift shops on the inn grounds. With its suites and apartments, the Coonamessett Inn makes an ideal place for a small family or for two couples traveling together.

COONAMESSETT INN, Jones and Gifford (P.O. Box 707), Falmouth, MA 02541. Telephone: (617) 548-2300. Accommodations: twenty-five suites, including seven apartments, with twin, queen- or king-size beds; private baths with tubs, showers or tub/showers; telephones; television. Rates: very expensive July to Labor Day, expensive in off-season. Kitchenettes available in some units. Children allowed. No pets. Cards: AE, MC, VISA. Open all year except Christmas week.

Getting there: After Sagamore or Bourne bridges, follow signs for The Islands on Route 28 south and west. Turn left on Jones Road in Falmouth. Follow Jones Road to intersection of Gifford Street; inn is at this intersection.

A Romantic Interlude in the Perfect Cape Cod Inn
THE WEDGEWOOD INN
Yarmouthport

The Wedgewood Inn, on the historic northern bay side of Cape Cod, was first opened to the public in 1983. It has been completely renovated, every detail reflecting the flawless taste of the innkeepers, who have created the perfect Cape Cod inn. Considering the scale of this grand old house, it is hard to believe that it was never an inn before. The stately neoclassic white brick, black-shuttered hostelry is set far back from the traffic of Route 6A and is reached by a meandering brick pathway through lawns and formal plantings. The peace and quiet of the Wedgewood is broken by the bird song floating through wide open window screens.

Decorating a country inn can be done by observing the antiques-and-quilt formula of most other inns, but Jeff and Jill Jackson have gone far beyond this. Much of the furniture is handcrafted reproductions of period pieces, and the inn's symbol might be the graceful Windsor armchairs, which sit before the front windows and in the sunny breakfast room. These chairs invite you to sit and talk awhile, blending beautifully with the deeply oiled wood of pencil post beds and glossy hardwood floors.

The rooms at the inn are all spacious, and all have private baths. The cosy attic room on the third floor has a view of the ocean, rooms on the first floor have access to a private porch, and the front rooms on both floors have working fireplaces.

Out behind the inn, the Jacksons run a little gallery which features imported sporting and landscape prints from England and Jill's own needlework. Many guests enjoy wandering under the shade

The Wedgewood Inn

trees or settling down on a patch of soft, freshly mown grass in summer.

Yarmouthport is centrally located on the Cape and boasts some of the loveliest Cape homes. The Parnassus Bookshop is a browser's delight, as well as the countless antiques shops and galleries. Roads crisscross over to the busier side of the Cape through miles of cranberry bogs and sometimes the Jacksons have extra bicycles for guests to use.

A Continental-plus breakfast is included in the night's fare. Look forward to a sunny breakfast in a room framed with French doors and a wide bay window. Breakfast often includes freshly baked croissants, homemade preserves and herbal tea in delicate china teapots. This room captures the essence of the Wedgewood: the wallpaper and many of the collections of china displayed in the hutches are blue, matching the sky outside the window. Although the huge fireplace is no longer used, it is the perfect complement to this morning scene.

THE WEDGEWOOD INN, 83 Main Street, Yarmouthport, MA 02675. Telephone: (617) 362-5157. Accommodations: six rooms, including one suite with twin or double beds; private baths with showers, tubs or tub/showers; no telephones; no television. Rates: very expensive, Continental breakfast included. No children under ten. No pets. Cards: MC, VISA. Open all year.

Getting there: Take Exit 7 off the Mid-Cape Highway (Route 6). Turn right onto Willow Street. Follow Willow Street to Route 6A (Main Street).

Comfort and Cosiness off the Beaten Track
THE COUNTRY INN
Harwichport

Harwichport is just about the geographical and cultural center of Cape Cod. Everything, except perhaps Provincetown, is less than an hour's drive away. The Country Inn is a classic Cape Cod home, once a guest house on the estate of the founders of Jordan Marsh, New England's largest department store. It has grown, with little porches and wings and a bright picket fence, into a home-away-from-home for hundreds of travelers each year, in an area where motels and camper parks are the fate of the masses.

It's hard to tell which sections of The Country Inn are the original building, but it is probably a safe bet that the rooms with fireplaces are the oldest. There are eleven fireplaces in all, including the public rooms, and although guests are not allowed to use those in the guest rooms, the downstairs hearths usually glow warmly on cool evenings.

There are only six guest rooms at the inn, but all are quiet, have private baths, and have a lovely country feeling. The restaurant downstairs can get pretty busy, but you won't hear the commotion upstairs. One room in the back wing is accessible only by passing through another and these two rooms are ideal for a family or two couples traveling together.

Restaurants at country inns can be a gamble sometimes, but there's no better gauge for a restaurant than the number of outsiders who frequent it. And if you do dine at another establishment, you'll find the inn's parking lot jammed with cars when you return. Why go anywhere else? There is excellent seafood, fresh-baked bread, and the timbered tavern is a pleasant place to while away a night.

All of the rooms at the inn are comfortably furnished with antique beds, lovely prints and old-fashioned quilts and coverlets. There are three hard-surface tennis courts for guests and a swimming pool. Access to a local private beach is included with a night's stay and Dave Van Gelder will take you out for a day's cruise to Monomoy Point, if you like. For extra fun, see if you can accompany him on a fish-buying expedition.

THE COUNTRY INN, Sisson Road, Harwichport, MA 02646. Telephone: (617) 432-2769. Accommodations: six rooms with twin or double beds; private baths with tubs and showers; no telephones; television in public room. Rates: expensive, breakfast included. Children allowed. Inquire about pets in advance. Cards: MC, VISA. Open all year.

Getting there: From Route 5 (Mid-Cape Highway) take Exit 10 to Route 124 and follow to Route 39. Inn is on the right on Route 39, also called Sisson Road, about one mile form Harwich Center.

Elegance by the Sand Dunes
NAUSET HOUSE INN
East Orleans

For location and interior design, the Nauset House Inn should get five stars on a four-star system. The Nauset House is quite simply beautiful, a flawlessly decorated structure set at the edge of the sand dunes on the windswept elbow of Cape Cod. Innkeepers Jack and Lucille Schwarz are antiques dealers as well and operate the White Elephant Shop on the inn's grounds. They are experts at interior design and you will want to spend hours examining all the fascinating pieces of local and American history that are prominently displayed.

Save the antiques for a rainy day, though, because the Nauset House Inn, isolated as it seems by a great salt marsh, is at the edge of world-famous Nauset Beach, the long arm of sand dunes stretching from Orleans southward to Dennis and Eastham. You can walk for hours along the shore, fish in the surf and bicycle on paved pathways, exploring an expanse of uncluttered sea, sand and sky. But it can be windy and chilly, even in the summer, so remember to bring warm clothes for strolling on the beach.

The Nauset House Inn is designed to accommodate travelers who are independent. Breakfast is served at the inn—and what a breakfast!—but you are on your own for the other meals. There are a few good fish eateries in Orleans, or try the Barley Neck Inn down at the end of Main Street for an elegant dinner. The Schwarzes will do what they can to recommend places for you to go and things to see, but they are graciously low key and you may wish to spend some time simply loafing about the inn, which can be surprisingly private.

One of the special features of the inn is a greenhouse sitting room, which was moved piece by piece from an old Victorian mansion in Connecticut. It is filled with plants, small trees, an abundance of flowers and comfortable wicker furniture. Hide yourself behind a cheffalera tree and enjoy a bottle of wine with friends. You'll feel right at home.

The inn started out as a simple farmhouse, but the innkeepers' ambitions and imaginations have transformed it into a dramatic architectural wonderland. There are three buildings housing fourteen guest rooms on the property, all a neutral dark, weathered brown. Details are accented with brick, including a sun patio and some floors in the house. Rooms are attractively designed with a combination of antiques and excellent beds and one room even has its own fireplace for romantic nights in the spring and fall.

For a combination of antique decor and contemporary sophistication, the Nauset House Inn is the jewel of the Outer Cape. Make reservations early, bring your own liquor and plan to enjoy your inn and what will seem, off-season, like your own private ten miles of beach.

NAUSET HOUSE INN, Beach Road, East Orleans, MA 02642. Telephone: (617) 255-2195. Accommodations: fourteen guest rooms with twin or double beds; nine private baths with tubs, showers or tub/showers; no telephones; television in lounge. Rates: moderate, breakfast included. No children under 12. No pets. Cards: MC, VISA. Open April to November.

Getting there: From Mid-Cape Highway (Route 6), take Exit 12 into Orleans. Follow signs to Nauset Beach; inn is located about one-half mile before the beach on Beach Road.

Luxury in a Sea Captain's Mansion
WHALEWALK INN
Eastham

If you picture Cape Cod scattered with low weather-shingled cottages covered with rambling roses and an upturned dory in the front yard, add another dimension to your vision: the ship captain's house. When you stay at the Whalewalk Inn, you can see for yourself what luxury and subtly exotic pleasures the old sea captains enjoyed.

The Whalewalk Inn is a Georgian mansion set back behind a shady lawn on a wide street full of shady lawns. This is a green, soft corner of the Cape, worlds away from the windswept dunes and the rocky pastures of other sections. Tourists buzz by en route to Provincetown, but it is quiet here.. You can stroll around tiny Rock Harbor or head for the sunny beaches.

The Whalewalk Inn is named for its widow's walk, a little balcony-like terrace on the house's roof, used by sea captains' wives to scan the horizon for returning ships. In this case, it was also used for spotting whales as they surfaced off the shore and the inn's name comes from the whaling ship tradition of the Eastham area.

Ginny and Norm DeLaChapelle bought the 150-year-old mansion in 1983 and started tearing it apart. They have redecorated

Whalewalk Inn

several rooms in the main section of the house, adding private bathrooms, Laura Ashley fabrics and wallpapers, and some interesting windows. These rooms are sunny and attractive although sometimes a little bit noisy when guests on the outdoor patio get up early or stay up late.

The rooms at the inn ramble about the grounds to include several housekeeping units in separate cottages and more rooms in the converted barn. The house is still headquarters, though, and you will be delighted by the excellent collection of old prints, books and nautical antiques. No corner of the inn has escaped the De-LaChapelle's touch and the overall effect is classic but comfortable.

The only meal served at the Whalewalk is breakfast, so be prepared to travel a bit in the evening, usually to Orleans, for dinner. But the inn does have a cocktail area with a wet bar where guests may keep alcohol and where ice is always available. Hors d'oeuvres are served at cocktail hour.

The Whalewalk Inn provides elegance, antiques and heartfelt hospitality. This is an excellent base for exploring the Outer Cape, and a lovely place to come home to.

WHALEWALK INN, Bridge Road, Eastham, MA 02642. Telephone: (617) 255-0617. Accommodations: six rooms with twin, double or queen-size beds, five housekeeping cottages also available; private baths with showers or tub/showers; no telephones; television in lounge downstairs. Rates: moderate to expensive, breakfast included with guest rooms, not with cottages. Children over 12 allowed. No pets. No cards. Closed January and February.

Getting there: Take Route 6 (Mid-Cape Highway) east to Orleans Rotary. Take Route 28 to Harbor Road. Follow to Bridge Road; turn right onto Bridge Road.

Artistically Yours
BRADFORD GARDENS
Provincetown

Provincetown is the end of the line, the end of the earth in New England at least. Here at the end of Cape Cod sits a little town that tries—and often succeeds—to be all things to all people. Artists, poets, playwrites, actors, musicians, restaurateurs, the rich and famous, the poor and curious, and all the rest flock to Provincetown.

Sidewalks and restaurants are crowded and no matter how chaotic it gets, one never wants to leave. It's that kind of place.

Provincetown is the unofficial property of the artists among us, for they seem to outnumber the non-artistic four to one. However, Provincetown was once a fishing town, populated by Portuguese immigrants whose flavorful cooking is still a trademark of the town's restaurants. As fishing faded, the arts arrived and now on Provincetown's narrow streets the ghosts of Eugene O'Neill and Tennessee Williams walk past studios and galleries where the famous and the not-so-famous have stretched canvases or written masterpieces for almost one hundred years.

All of the guest rooms at Bradford Gardens are unique, mainly because they are all living art galleries, with paintings on display by local artists. The artwork blends beautifully with the antique furniture and the inn's easy-going atmosphere.

The Bradford Gardens is designed for people who wish to make an extended stay, but overnight guests are welcome too. All the rooms have private baths and color television sets, although the technicolor sunsets at the end of Cape Cod are perhaps more colorful than anything you can get on rabbit ears out here. The rooms have names that describe their characters: the Chimney Nook, the Sun Gallery, the Jenny Lind room, the Yesteryear Room. There's even a Honeymoon Suite! Most rooms have fireplaces and the inn supplies you with a stack of firewood and then leaves you alone.

Everyone talks about the light in Provincetown, and you'll see why on your first morning at the Bradford Gardens. The Morning Room overlooks the garden and is flooded with sun rays that have a different slant, casting a certain light that makes you feel, well...like you're looking at a painting. Not long after arriving, you may feel like marching down to Commercial Street to buy a set of water colors or getting out your camera to try to capture the atmosphere yourself. Join the crowd.

Provincetown is steeped in history. The Pilgrims made the Mayflower Compact here before heading on to Plymouth. Explorers like Smith, Gosnold and Champlain plied the waters in the seventeenth century. In recent years, tourism has replaced fishing as the town's main industry, but there is still the flavor of a seagoing town here.

BRADFORD GARDENS, 178 Bradford Street, Provincetown, MA 02657. Telephone: (617) 487-1616. Accommodations: five guest rooms and three suites, with twin or double beds; private baths with rooms, shared baths with suites, showers or tub/showers; no telephones; television. Rates: moderate to expensive. Children under 12 allowed in outside suites only. No pets. Cards: AE, MC, VISA. Open April to December.

Getting there: Take Route 6 (Mid-Cape Highway) east and north, following signs to Provincetown. Take second Provincetown exit, follow to Bradford Street and turn left. There is also ferry service from Long Wharf in Boston.

Everyone's Favorite Islands
MARTHA'S VINEYARD AND NANTUCKET

Almost everyone you meet on the highway in New England seems headed to or from the islands of Martha's Vineyard and Nantucket, and those who aren't wish they were. These two little sun-speckled spots on the map are everyone's favorite destinations. A few years ago, Vermont even tried to annex the islands, arguing that the easy-going populace had more in common with the rural folks of the Green Mountain State than the hard-nosed hustlers of Beacon Hill. The plan almost worked.

No one knows for sure how many people visit these islands each year, but the ferries that crisscross the water here often practically overflow with passengers. People come for the day, the weekend, the season. Some never go back. It is not easy to get a car to the islands, so many opt for bicycles, motorcycles or hitchhiking. Nothing is out of the ordinary on the islands—people just do what they must to get by.

Martha's Vineyard is larger and more highly populated and is only seven miles off the coast of Cape Cod. The island has several distinct geographical and social regions, known locally as Down Island and Up Island, while the rest of the world is Off Island. Down Island includes Vineyard Haven, with a ferry dock, little shops, guest houses and supermarkets; Oak Bluffs, a seaside shanty town which grew up around a Methodist Revival campground; and Edgartown, a staunch upper crust community of yacht club colors and ship captains' homes. Up Island is the farmland and coastal regions, with towns like West Tisbury and Chilmark and the Indian reservation at Gay Head. It is all beautiful.

Nantucket is quite different from the Vineyard. The town of Nantucket, filled with inns and guest houses, is the center of interest here, and in fact, few accommodations are to be found elsewhere on

Nantucket Windmill

this island. The beaches are not far, and what beaches they are! Miles and miles of sand and pounding surf, including Surfside and Sconset beaches, await your arrival.

Both Nantucket and Martha's Vineyard out-Cape Cape Cod. The relative isolation here in the summer is like a drug, and landowners are careful to preserve the feeling and look of the traditional farms of the area. Many more recently designed homes dot the landscape these days too, as more people are seeking real estate investments here.

When making arrangements to get to the islands, plan well in advance. Reserve a space on the ferry for your car, for if you don't, you most likely will end up in a stand-by line for hours on the hot pavement in either Woods Hole or Vineyard Haven. You may want to leave the car on the mainland, for in Nantucket you can get along perfectly well without a car. On the Vineyard, a car is not necessary if you stay Down Island and use cabs. If you're flying in, expect fog, but if you're lucky, you'll see the islands from the air, a breathtaking sight.

Hear Seagulls Screech Outside Your Window
THE BEACH PLUM INN
Menemsha

There are over a dozen perfectly good places to stay in Edgartown, but they cannot really be called country inns. The Beach Plum Inn, out in the remote fishing village on Menemsha Pond, however, is every bit a country inn and highly commendable. If you don't mind not being in the midst of shopping and restaurants, this place is for you.

Menemsha is a jumble of fishermen's shacks on wobbly wharves at a spot called Menemsha Bight where the pond opens out into the sea and where the only really protected harbor for the fishing fleet can be found. There are a few gift shops, a marine supply store, a few fish markets and Captain Poole's, which is the most famous fish market on the island, and may be the most famous in New England. There's nothing special about it except that there are many, many kinds of fish and shellfish available, along with frozen specialty items. Beware, though: With fish as with almost everything, the prices on the islands are very inflated.

The Beach Plum Inn is set on a rise above the fishing shanties. Inn lore attributes the construction of the inn to the rescue of a shipwrecked timber shipment following a hurricane, and when you've walked along the beach at Menemsha and you've seen what the sea washes up, that story will become more believable. The inn is simply furnished so as not to distract guests from the lovely solitude and sweeping views. Many rooms look out over the ocean and a few face the cliffs at nearby Gay Head.

Dinner at the Beach Plum Inn is one of the delights of visiting the island and should be on everyone's list—if they can get a reservation. Dinner and breakfast are included with the room at the inn, and you'll be thrilled at the fine cuisine and the breathtaking view from the dinner room—if it's not foggy! Dining at the inn also cuts down on your need to have a car with you on the island.

The inn leaves guests to provide their own entertainment, with the exception of a tennis court and the designation of a private beach section for inn guests. Bicycling is the best way to get around the island and you will want to visit the cliffs at Gay Head no matter how you get there. Shopping in Edgartown is very crowded but fun; the Bunch of Grapes Bookshop in Vineyard Haven is one of the best rainy-day havens in New England. For children, there is the Flying Horses Carousel in Oak Bluffs, the oldest merry-go-round in America—though adults have fun trying for the brass ring too. Fried seafood at the sidewalk eateries is a good inexpensive dinner, especially the calamari. The island has four movie theatres, with four different movies every night. And don't leave the Beach Plum without taking an early morning walk. Wander about the docks, observing the boats coming and going and watch the giant crates being loaded and unloaded, with colorful buoy balloons in the background.

The Beach Plum Inn is probably one of the most desirable country inns in America. Most anyone would want to be in this beautiful, secluded spot on the Vineyard with an abundance of fine foods. This is the Vineyard, first class and unforgettable.

THE BEACH PLUM INN, North Road, Menemsha, MA 02552. Telephone: (617) 645-9454. Accommodations: twelve rooms with twin or double beds; private and shared baths with tub/showers; no telephones; no television. Rates: very expensive, breakfast and dinner included. Children allowed but not encouraged. No pets. No cards. Open June to September.

Getting there: It is possible to fly from New York or Newark; take cab from the airport to the inn. If driving, take the ferry and drive west (Up Island) on North Road about seven miles.

The Crown Jewel of Country Inns
JARED COFFIN HOUSE
Nantucket

The Jared Coffin House is one of the most famous inns in all New England and is worth a visit, if not a stay, during any trip to Nantucket. The Coffin House is the sun around which the solar system of Nantucket inn life revolves. Most people try to squeeze in a meal at the inn, especially one of the famous brunches and buffets.

Now owned and operated by the Nantucket Historical Commission, the Jared Coffin House has been an inn for well over one hundred years. However, this imposing three-story brick mansion was restored to its original neoclassic splendor only in the 1960s. No detail has been overlooked here: all the rooms are decorated with period themes and lovely antiques, most of the beds are four-posters and often have canopies, and a few rooms feature beautiful crewel work.

Not all of the inn's forty-six rooms are located in the main house, however. Although it is fun to stay in the main building, so you can rise and descend the lovely curved stairway, equally lovely rooms are available in the Eben Allen Wing, the Daniel Webster House and the Federal House across the street. All rooms have private baths.

Mealtime at the Jared Coffin House is an elegant experience if you choose the main dining room, which requires "proper" dress for dinner, or fun informality in the Tap Room. This is one of several excellent restaurants on the island, but be sure to include several meals at the inn to take advantage of changing specials and daily additions.

The public areas of the inn are breathtaking. A soft silence envelopes the antiques and the feeling is that you are in a home, not an inn. No detail of nineteenth-century life seems to have been overlooked, and all the antiques wear a patina of lived-with feeling. You can sit in the chairs, you can walk across the oriental rugs, and outside, you walk on cobblestone streets and hear old church bells ringing.

Built in 1845, the inn was the first three-story building on the island. The Coffins were—and are—one of the oldest families on both Nantucket and Martha's Vineyard, but their home here has been magnified by the historical society to become an image of the whole island's historical heritage, not just the Coffin family's. Keeping it open and operating and preserved at the same time is a staggering undertaking. Dozens of people work behind the scenes at a hundred little tasks that make inn experiences like this one memorable. Out on the street, passersby pause to snap a picture and gaze in wonderment at the beautiful building.

JARED COFFIN HOUSE, 29 Broad Street, Nantucket, MA 02554. Telephone: (617) 228-2400. Accommodations: forty-six rooms, with twin or double beds; private baths with showers or tub/showers; telephones; televisions. Rates: moderate to expensive. Children welcome. Inquire in advance about pets. Credit cards: AE, DC, MC, VISA. Open all year.

Getting there: Take Main Street from ferry dock to Broad Street.

Thar She Blows!
SHIPS INN
Nantucket

Harpoons, whale oil, stowaways, and the woman left behind are the nautical heritage of the little seaport of Nantucket. Nowhere is the tie to the sea stronger than at the Ships Inn, the home of Captain Starbuck, a romantic name from the pages of Melville's *Moby Dick*.

Starbuck built this lovely three-story home on Fair Street in 1812, when the whaling industry in New England was in full swing. Nantucket was one of a handful of whaling ports, but Melville's poetic imagery has made it synonymous with gutsy whaling captains and fearless harpoonists. You can almost see them now, swaggering up Main Street, bow-legged and awkward on the cobblestone street. Little did Melville know that kerosene would replace whale oil as lamp fuel, or that whales would become so over-hunted that New Englanders would unite to save them from extinction. Nor could he have known that a sand would gradually build up and block the mouth of Nantucket Harbor, making it impossible for big ships to dock here in the twentieth century.

The ferry can still get through, though, so guests can easily book a passage to the island for a stay at the Ships Inn, where little seems to have changed from Starbuck's day. Most of the inn's furnishings are American, from the early nineteenth century, and few inns succeed as this one has in evoking a period flavor. The old captain would feel right at home here, and spooky stories told in the inn's Dory Bar suggest that he may sometimes visit his former home, in spirit at least.

Expect comfortable accommodations, a convenient location, and an excellent restaurant when you choose the Ships Inn as your home-away-from-home on Nantucket. You'll never miss the car you left on the mainland when you stay in the village, for every restaurant, crafts shop, and art gallery is less than five minutes from the inn. You'll want to ask your waitress for tips on the best place to buy a lightship basket or for directions out to Sconset or Surfside for the ultimate in New England beaches.

Even the rooms in this inn are named for ships that once sailed from Nantucket Harbor. Nautical prints decorate the walls, and the Dory Bar really is made from a dory (a small boat used to row out to a larger ship).

The Ships Inn has a popular restaurant, featuring a varied menu of seafood, veal and lamb. The atmosphere here is relaxed and comfortable, and the room is decked with healthy green plants and lit by a sparkling fireplace.

Many a new friendship has been born, and many tales of adventures swapped over dart games in the pub. Don't believe *everything* you hear, but be willing to suspend your mainland suspicions just a little bit, and enjoy the might-be fantasies of island life.

SHIPS INN, 13 Fair Street, Nantucket, MA 02554. Telephone: (617) 228-0040. Accommodations: twelve rooms with twin or double beds; private and shared baths with showers or tub/showers; no telephones; no television. Rates: moderate, Continental breakfast included. Children welcome. No pets. Cards: AE, MC, VISA. Open Easter to Thanksgiving.

Getting there: Take Broad Street from ferry dock, turn left on Center Street and continue to Main Street. Take the first left, Fair Street.

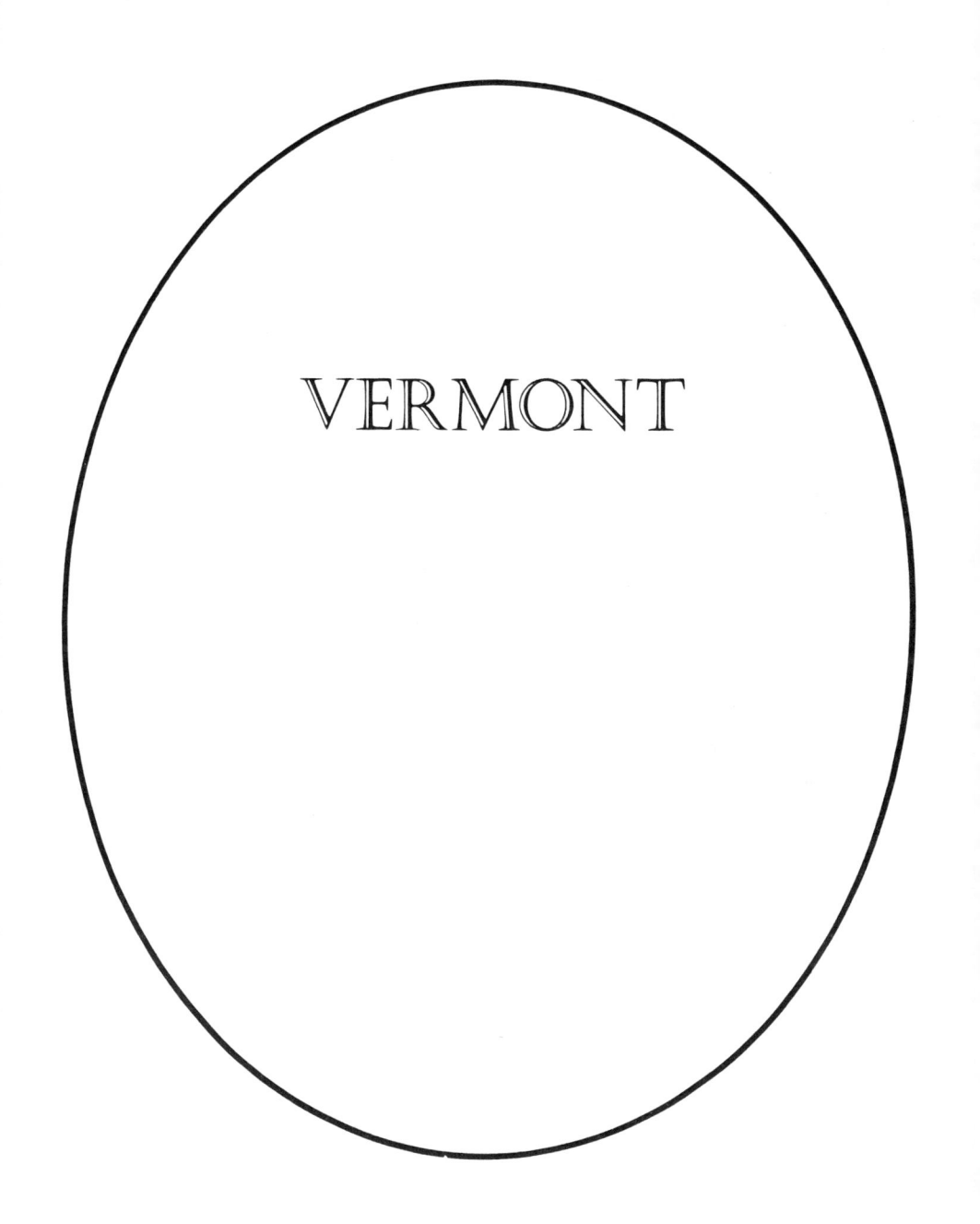

VERMONT

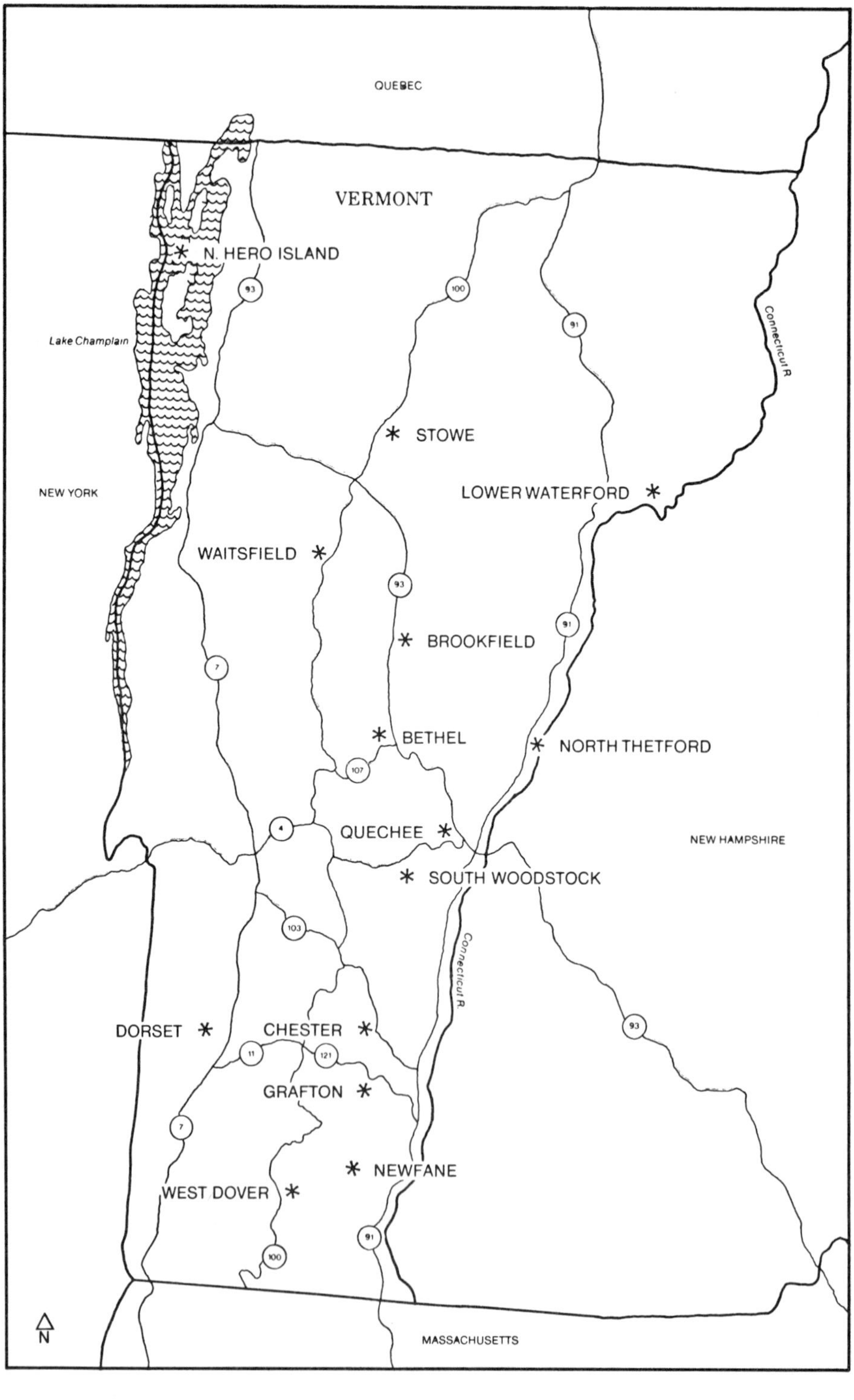
QUEBEC
VERMONT
N. HERO ISLAND
Lake Champlain
93
100
91
Connecticut R.
STOWE
NEW YORK
LOWER WATERFORD
WAITSFIELD
93
91
BROOKFIELD
7
BETHEL
NORTH THETFORD
107
4
QUECHEE
NEW HAMPSHIRE
SOUTH WOODSTOCK
103
Connecticut R.
93
DORSET
CHESTER
11
121
GRAFTON
7
NEWFANE
WEST DOVER
91
100
N
MASSACHUSETTS

VERMONT

Vermont feels like home to most Americans. The Green Mountain State has managed to survive more than two hundred years of statehood while retaining the flavor and spirit of a tiny independent republic. Vermont, in fact, was a republic for a few years after the Revolutionary War before it became a state, and there is still a sense of rugged self-reliance in the modern residents. Since the early 1900s, out-of-staters have flocked to Vermont for peace, relaxation and recreation. The quiet hills are soothing medicine to outsiders and a good dose of Vermont humor and sensibility can go a long way toward restoring your faith in mankind.

Vermont's boundary on the east is the Connecticut River and on the west, Lake Champlain. To the north is Quebec and the grand cities of Montreal and Quebec City. To the south is Massachusetts and the Berkshires, cousins of Vermont's own Green Mountains.

Highways in Vermont tend to run north and south, with only a very few cutting across the mountains. Route 5 follows the Connecticut from Brattleboro to Quebec; Route 7 is a busy commercial road on the western side. Lovely Route 100 winds up a valley for more than two hundred miles through the center of the state and is *the* road for unspoiled scenery and sightseeing. The new interstates, I-91 along the Connecticut and I-89 from White River Junction to Montreal, make traveling faster, but unless you get off and meander through villages and towns, you'll miss Vermont.

Many roads in Vermont are unpaved, but don't let that stop you from exploring and enjoying the wonderful back roads scenery. People from the Midwest often express fear of the steep, hilly byways, but you will find that they are usually well maintained. In winter, the dirt roads tend to withstand the ravages of plowing and frost heaves better than pavement, which buckles under temperature changes, so Vermonters figure it's best to leave well enough alone.

You should plan to spend a day exploring Burlington, the Queen City on the Lake. The University of Vermont is right in downtown Burlington, and the Market Street area has recently been developed into a pedestrian mall lined with specialty shops and fine restaurants—the Deja Vu Cafe is a very special place. It would be hard to call any of Vermont's large towns *cities*, but major services like auto repair, hospitals and restaurants can be found in Brattleboro, Bennington, St. Johnsbury, White River Junction and Montpelier.

Montpelier is the state capital and has to be the smallest and loveliest capital city in the country.

Resort areas cling to the sides of mountains and to the shores of Lake Champlain. Stowe, Killington and the Mt. Snow area (Dover and Wilmington) are the most commercial, but don't let the miles of condominiums bother you—these are just pockets of development that will fade from your rear view mirror and your memory very quickly as the patchwork farms reclaim the landscape.

There is no best time of year to visit Vermont, but the wise tourist would avoid Vermont from March to early May, when mud season is likely to be in full swing. Spring skiing is worth wallowing in mud for, though, so decide for yourself. September and October are by far the most popular months and country inns may be booked for years in advance. Columbus Day weekend is a nightmare of traffic jams but if you can find one place and stay put you will be able to enjoy the spectacular orange and yellow and red of the the flaming maple trees. Make sure you have a place to stay before you leave home—tourists have been known to sleep in their cars, although the chambers of commerce in small towns like Woodstock will often help stranded motorists by offering accommodations in local homes.

Remember that there are more cows than people in Vermont and that almost anything goes in this rugged country. Country stores are the core of all the little villages and the very best way to see the countryside is on foot down a winding back road. Watch out for deer on the road at night and if you happen to be in Vermont during hunting season, stay out of the woods and wear bright colors. Stock up on maple syrup, cheddar cheese and handmade items, especially wood products and furniture, while you are here.

An Antiques Lover's Paradise
INN AT SAWMILL FARM
West Dover

The Inn at Sawmill Farm is an antiques-lover's paradise, for the inn is filled with beautiful period furniture. It is fun to try to guess the origins and uses of the many farm tools and copper pieces hanging throughout this wonderful hostelry, although some seem to have no logical use at all.

Tiny West Dover is just a stone's throw from the thriving metropolis of Mount Snow, a very fine ski resort. The inn, however, is much more than a ski lodge. It is a destination in itself. Built in 1779,

The Inn at Sawmill Farm

Sawmill Farm is easy to pick out on winding Route 100 with its columned facade looking for all the world like a country inn should. There is much more to the inn than faces Route 100, however. Stretching back from the road are tennis courts, swimming pools and lovely little gardens and slate walks, along with the rambling building. The inn's owners, Rodney and Ione Williams and their son, Brill, are responsible for much of the inn's charm. Brill runs the kitchen, Ione is an interior decorator and Rodney is an architect.

The common rooms, with exposed beams and real barnboard siding, are filled with antiques. The formal dining room is decorated with Victorian armchairs and suspended ceiling fans. There are primitive portraits in gilded frames, old hayforks on the barnboard and an old player piano sitting near a solid copper bar.

The rooms are no less perfect. Thick, thirsty bath towels in the private bathrooms, matching wallpaper and fabric in the bedrooms, most of which have king-size beds and, in the ten tiny cottages on the grounds, working fireplaces and a plentiful supply of dry wood.

Nearby Mt. Snow should not make you associate this inn only with winter vacations, however. Scenic Route 100 is a beautiful road, and the many trails in the area are good for biking or hiking. West Dover is about halfway between the large towns of Bennington, a historical center, and Brattleboro, a growing young community with fine theaters and restaurants. Brattleboro also has some excellent factory-outlets and Williams College, just over the border in Massachusetts, is not far.

Dinner is included in the bill for hotel guests, many of whom actually discovered the Inn at Sawmill Farm through its restaurant. Brill Williams, an engineer by training but artist by nature, prepares wonderful meals, featuring dishes such as medallions of veal, beef Wellington, roast duck and rack of lamb.

THE INN AT SAWMILL FARM, Route 100, West Dover, VT 05356. Telephone: (802) 464-8131. Accommodations: twenty-three rooms with twin, double or king-size beds; private baths; telephones; public television. Rates: expensive, meals included. Children over 12 welcome. No pets. No cards. Open all year.

Getting there: From I-91, proceed west on Route 9 through Brattleboro to Wilmington; turn right onto Route 100. Proceed north on 100 to West Dover, about five miles. The inn is on the left, just north of the village center.

A Classic Colonial Vacation
OLD NEWFANE INN
Newfane

It is hard to say what is best about the Old Newfane Inn, the guest rooms or the dining rooms. Both are excellent and very popular, evidenced by the difficulty one has obtaining room and meal reservations. Guests inevitably become devotees after just one visit.

The Old Newfane Inn is a classic Colonial structure in the center of a classic Colonial village. The guest rooms are pristine and charming, some with antique four-poster beds. The inn is blissfully quiet, although don't be surprised if you are awakened to the sound of a marching band (Vermonters love parades and holidays) or a chorus of lawn mowers in summer. But usually there is hardly a sound except for the slam of a screen door or footsteps crunching in the snow.

Whatever happens, don't miss dinner at the Old Newfane. The chef and hostess, owners Eric and Gundy Weindl, provide unforgettable meals. Eric, a graduate of one of the finest hotel schools in Switzerland, presents an excellent French-Swiss cuisine that has been featured in *Gourmet*, *Bon Appetit* and *The New York Times*, to name a few. The menu is suprisingly varied for a Vermont country inn and draws a large number of non-hotel guests.

When you're not eating or sleeping at the Old Newfane, take a walk or drive through the beautiful countryside, perhaps a trip to Dummerston, a lovely mountaintop village, or stroll through the bookshops and gourmet stores of Brattleboro. The music series at nearby Marlboro College is worth checking into as well. Just remember to take a nap and rest up for the next meal that Eric is busy prerparing for you.

OLD NEWFANE INN, Route 30 (P.O. Box 101), Newfane, VT 05345. Telephone: (802) 365-4427. Accommodations: ten rooms with twin or double beds; eight private, two shared baths; no telephones; public television. Rates: expensive. Children over seven welcome. No pets. No cards. Open all year.

Getting there: From I-91, take Exit 2 in Brattleboro. Follow signs towards Manchester and Route 30. Newfane is a very small village on Route 30 about ten miles from Brattleboro. The inn is opposite the general store in the center of town, on your left as you proceed northwest on 30.

Gourmet Food in a Majestic Colonial Mansion
OLD TAVERN AT GRAFTON
Grafton

The Old Tavern at Grafton is perhaps the ultimate country inn. It is a majestic Colonial mansion with rolling lawns, a first-rate riding stable, a gourmet restaurant, and impeccable accommodations, all set in a picture-perfect village by a roaring river. The Old Tavern and all the lovely buildings in Grafton are owned and operated by the Windham Foundation, a non-profit historical preservation organization which bought the town in 1963. The restored town is actually a small resort, although this resort atmosphere is not emphasized.

During peak periods, especially August to October, reservations are hard to get. Repeat guests know the importance of asking far ahead of time, sometimes years in advance. As you wait to check in (once you do get a reservation), you can study the names of the famous people who have stayed at the inn which are painted above the front desk—the likes of Woodrow Wilson, Teddy Roosevelt, Emerson, Thoreau and Hawthorne. The management asks to know your eating plans at check-in time. Although few people are sure of their plans on arrival, there is so much to see and do in Grafton that you might be advised to reserve space at all the meals, using the inn as a base for your adventures.

The Old Tavern has an air of quiet, understated luxury, furnished with English antiques for the most part. You will be comfortable whether you stay in one of the main building's twelve rooms, the New England Cottage across the street or any of the six individual houses about the village that are available for rent.

Old Tavern at Grafton

The grounds of the Old Tavern are beautifully landscaped. Whitewashed buildings are accented in summer by banks of red geraniums, in fall by flame-colored maples and in winter by a stark, clear, sky. The only distraction outside is the roaring of the restaurant's air conditioning plant, an unfortunate necessity. A huge converted barn is attached to the Tavern, containing a multi-level lounge with attractive barn-like decor and comfortable couches.

Horse lovers will be especially fond of the Old Tavern, for you can either rent one of the inn's horses or rent a stall and bring your own. The Tavern has a collection of sleighs and carriages and the clip-clop of hooves can be heard throughout the day. One rental house, White Gates, is right by the stables and is perfect for a family horseback outing.

In winter, Grafton bustles with activity as the town fills with cross-country skiiers. You can glide down the hill from the Old Tavern right up to the leaded glass lampposts that light the town bridge. And no matter what time of year you visit Grafton, you can always delight in the beautifully preserved architecture of this scenic New England hideaway.

OLD TAVERN AT GRAFTON, Main Street, Grafton, VT 05146. Telephone: (802) 843-2231. Accommodations: thirty-seven rooms with twin or double beds, house rentals also available; private baths with showers and tub/showers; no telephones or televisions. Rates: expensive. Children and pets welcome in some accommodations. No cards. Closed Christmas Eve, Christmas Day and the month of April.

Getting there: From I-91, take Exit 5 in Bellows Falls. Follow signs to Route 121 and proceed west on 121 to Saxtons River. Grafton is the next village on 121. The inn is in the center of town, just past the bridge.

On the Main Street of Vermont
CHESTER INN
Chester

In the center of Chester, a town filled with beautiful examples of every period of nineteenth-century architecture, is the lovely old Chester Inn. Banners fly from the wide front porch and the huge balcony and, in the summer, a path of golden marigolds leads up to the inn. The lobby might seem like a lobby from a hotel of a more glamorous era, with its twenty-foot wooden counter where guests check into the tan and brown Victorian.

The Chester Inn is not the typical Vermont country inn where one goes to curl up with a book in an old flannel shirt to watch the maple leaves change color. Guests are welcome to do so, but the inn offers a great deal more: a heated pool, a sauna and a fabulous restaurant, along with an interesting clientele from all over the world.

Every June, Chester comes alive for a holiday weekend unique to Vermont's small towns called Alumni Day. Chester hosts a race which attracts runners from all over New England and there is a parade that passes directly in front of the inn's veranda. Hotel guests are encouraged to join in the fun as friendships are renewed and graduates of the local school celebrate their return.

Another popular time at the Chester Inn is Christmas. Many of the inns in Vermont close over the two-day holiday, or at least shut down their restaurants, but the Chester celebrates in grand style. Owners Tom and Betsy Guido decorate an eleven-foot Christmas tree by the fireside in the main lobby with red bows and white lights and set out a punchbowl. A caroling outing is a must, for the weather usually obliges with a generous coating of snow. "Some people make a point of returning for Christmas year after year," says Betsy. "To them, Christmas means the Chester Inn." Even without Christmas, the Chester is a wonderful place to stay. Any of the thirty-one rooms is a fine place for a peaceful rest, since rarely will you hear more than a lonesome dog's bark after dark in Chester.

Don't miss the excellent international cuisine served at the Chester Inn's fine restaurant. Each page of the beautiful leather-bound menu is dedicated to an entree, featuring a lovely woodcut and description of the meal. Duck and veal are house specialties, although everything is delicious and carefully prepared.

CHESTER INN, Main Street, Chester, VT 05143. Telephone: (802) 875-2444. Accommodations: twenty-nine rooms with twin, bunk, double or queen-size beds, two three-room suites with twin, double or queen-size beds; private baths; no telephones; television in game room. Rates: moderate, breakfast included. Children welcome. No pets. Cards: MC, VISA. Closed from Easter to Mother's Day.

Getting there: From I-91 northbound, take Exit 6. Take Route 103 to Chester. Turn left onto Route 11. The inn is on the left, in the middle of town. Park on the street.

Fine Food and Dutch Hospitality
VILLAGE AUBERGE
Dorset

Just northwest six miles or so from lively Manchester Center is the tiny town of Dorset. And right here in this little town is the Village Auberge, a warm and hospitable inn with an excellent restaurant. Although it sounds French, the owners of Village Auberge are Dutch. Alex and Hanneke Koks are not newcomers, however, to innkeeping or to Vermont. They once owned the Silver Skates Inn (as in Hans Brinker) in Marlboro, but they sold it to return home to the Netherlands. There they discovered that, "Home was really here in Vermont," as Alex smilingly will tell you.

They returned to Vermont and in 1977 found a typical Vermont farmhouse in Dorset, complete with front veranda for rocking on in summer. With considerable effort they have turned its many small rooms into a cosy inn. The name may sound French, but the Koks hope that it conveys the general sense of a European establishment and all that that entails. This basically means an impeccably clean, scrubbed, tidy environment, with seven neat and cheery bedrooms, a comfortable suite that sleeps four, beds made snug with antique quilts and an accommodating staff eager to make your stay pleasant. The Kokses themselves live on the premises, and treat you like welcome guests—it's Dutch hospitality at its warmest!

The dining room dominates here, and the menu, in chef Alex's capable hands, is decidedly, though unostentatiously, French.

Though the Manchester area boasts a number of good restaurants, you'll be tempted to spend most of your dining time right here at the inn—and with good reason. When you can feast on superbly prepared breast of duck in a raspberry vinaigrette, Cornish hen forestiere with a chestnut stuffing, filet mignon with mousse de volaille or sweetbreads aux morilles, why travel elsewhere? Each meal begins with a lightly browned, piping hot cheese fritter. Appetizer choices might be cream of mustard soup (far subtler than it sounds), coquilles St. Jacques, proscuitto with an innovative stewed prune relish or escargots in garlic butter. Desserts, the work of Hanneke Koks, range from creme brulee laced with preserved ginger to mocha cheesecake to a Grand Marnier tartlette. The Kokses have just bought the old Dorset Inn, but they will continue to live in and run Village Auberge.

Dorset's handy location near the Green Mountains, Mother Myrick and Big Equinox peaks; near good ski slopes, Stratton, Big Bromley, Mount Snow; and near the Emerald Lake State Park makes it a magnet for skiers, hikers, vacationers and foliage watchers. In short, a spot for each and every season.

VILLAGE AUBERGE, Route 30, Dorset, VT 05251. Telephone: (802) 867-5715. Accommodations: six rooms with twin, queen- or king-size beds; private baths with tub/showers; no telephones; television in suite only. Rates: moderate. Children and pets welcome. Cards: MC, VISA. Closed part of November and part of April.

Getting there: From Manchester Center, take Route 30 north. The inn is on the right side of the road as you pass through Dorset.

Awaken to a Coaching Horn
THE KEDRON VALLEY INN
South Woodstock

Where else but at the Kedron Valley Inn could you wake up on a Sunday morning to the sound of a coaching horn and the thunder of hooves on pavement? From your window here, you can see a coach and four-in-hand charge through the village and screech to a halt in front of the South Woodstock Country Store, and then watch the whip jump down and run inside for Sunday's *New York Times*.

The Kedron Valley Inn is situated at the heart of South Woodstock. Next to this grand brick structure is a tidy little brick building that was once the village store but is now the inn's pub. Next to the pub is the new store, a great place to pick up a wedge of cheese and catch up on the local gossip. These three buildings are the village center. The whole thing.

You don't really need a car when you stay at the Kedron. There is a swimming pond, private tennis courts and a riding stable. In addition, there are excellent cross-country skiing and hiking trails in South Woodstock. No doubt you'll meet some interesting people during your stay at the Kedron. Many horsemen come to take advantage of the well-maintained trails, while others are in town for the Country School of Photography, a well-established institute on a hill overlooking the village. And too, the town is home to many noted celebrities and literary figures. You never can tell who you might find challenging you for a game of darts in the pub at night.

Some country inn purists may object to the inn's motel-like addition. The rooms, however, are comfortable and tidy with private baths and firm beds and will appeal to those who seek more privacy than the simple rooms most inns offer. The rooms in the inn are homey and the view from the windows is wonderful. Listen for sleighbells in the winter.

Meals at the Kedron are simple and inexpensive. Red flannel hash, blueberry pancakes or a Basque omelet for Sunday brunch, hot oatmeal with maple syrup (gathered and boiled on the premises) for breakfast, and Vermont ham for dinner. This is real New England cuisine.

THE KEDRON VALLEY INN, Route 106, South Woodstock, VT 05071. Telephone: (802) 457-1473. Accommodations: thirty-one rooms with twin or double beds, one three-room family suite; private baths with tubs, showers and tub/showers; no telephones; public television. Rates: expensive. Children and pets welcome, inquire first. Cards: DC, MC, VISA. Open all year; dining room closed in April.

Getting there: From I-91, take Exit 8 (Route 131) west. Follow 131 to Route 106 north, about eight miles. The inn is on Route 106 about ten miles north in the center of South Woodstock, just after the South Woodstock Country Store.

The Kedron Valley Inn

A Palatial New England Farm
THE QUECHEE INN AT MARSHLAND FARM
Quechee

Before Quechee became a resort, it was a farming and mill town on the banks of the Ottauquechee. The roaring river has cut a gap of more than 150 feet through the rocky terrain, forming the Quechee Gorge. And almost as long as there has been a Quechee, there has been Marshland Farm, a grand, palatial New England farm built in 1793 as the homestead of Colonel Joseph Marsh, the first Lieutenant Governor of Vermont.

Colonel Marsh would be amazed to see his home—and his town—nearly two hundred years later. Quechee has been developed into the perfect Vermont village, with hundreds of condominium units and single family houses tucked out of sight in the hills. This resort has gained international fame and praise as a family recreation center, but before you sign on the dotted line for a condominium, come stay a night or two at Marshland Farm.

The inn is one of the largest in Vermont. A recent addition for the large new restaurant added more guest rooms as well, bringing the total up to twenty-two. All rooms are furnished with Queen Anne antiques or reproductions, including brass and four-poster beds, braided rugs and early American style fabrics. Each room has a full private bath and rooms here seem more private than at other inns.

One of the delights of Marshland Farm is that you can set up a vacation for yourself as country- or as resort-like as you please. There is hiking and cross-country skiing, horses graze in white fenced pastures on the grounds and an antiques store is housed in the barn. Inn guests also have privileges at the Quechee Club, which includes golf, tennis and skiing. Quechee has its own polo team which plays on the fields down by the river —a lovely hike from the inn—on Sunday afternoons and there are rafting expeditions through the gorge for the more independent and daring guests. One may also join the many thousands of tourists who pass through neighboring Woodstock each day. Be sure to see the draft horses and oxen at work at the new Billings Farm Museum, a ten-minute drive from Quechee. Ask one of the innkeepers, the Yaroschuks, for directions to Billings Farm on the Quechee side of the river in order to avoid the traffic on Route 4. It is a lovely semi-paved road through beautiful farmland.

The Quechee Inn shines at mealtime. Begin with a drink and friendly conversation in the common room adjoining the restaurant, which is thoughtfully equipped with games, comfortable couches and a fireplace. The restaurant is one of the best in the area, serving superbly prepared fresh native foods. Watch for fiddlehead ferns in the spring—they grow abundantly along the banks of the Ottauquechee. Breads and breakfast muffins are a house specialty.

QUECHEE INN AT MARSHLAND FARM, Clubhouse Road (P.O. Box 47B), Quechee, VT 05059. Telephone: (802) 295-3133. Accommodations: twenty-two rooms with twin, double or twin double beds; private baths with showers and tub/showers; no telephones; no televisions. Rates: expensive, Continental breakfast included. Rates vary with the season. Children welcome. No pets. Cards: MC, VISA. Open all year.

Getting there: From I-89, take Exit 1 (Route 4) west toward Woodstock and Rutland. Take first road on right, Clubhouse Road; the inn is on the right about one mile down Clubhouse Road.

A Granite Palace on the River's Shores
STONE HOUSE INN
North Thetford

Bring your canoe when you stay at the Stone House Inn. In fact, you might even want to arrive at the Stone House Inn *in* your canoe. This relatively new inn on the shores of the Connecticut River is part of a unique inn-to-inn canoeing arrangement. Four inns, each approximately one day's canoe from the other on the mighty Connecticut, have joined to offer a package deal for canoers. You sleep and dine at an inn, they pack you a lunch and you paddle off in the morning for the next one.

Even non-canoeists will find the Stone House Inn a relaxing, rejuvenating stopover. Art and Dianne Sharkey have refurbished one of the great stone houses of the Connecticut Valley, creating a six-room country inn with all the finest trimmings, offering comfortable, country-style accommodations in a lovely rural area.

The Stone House can be the base for many interesting excursions. The inn is only minutes away from Hanover, New Hampshire, and the road to Topsham from Thetford is one of the loveliest in all Vermont. Don't let the Thetfords confuse you—there is East Thetford, Thetford Center, Thetford, Thetford Hill and finally, North Thetford. Be sure to visit them all, for each offers something different. Don't miss Thetford Hill, the site of Thetford Academy, where beautiful New England homesteads perch in a village set higher than the surrounding farmland.

The granite exterior of the Stone House Inn is surrounded by a gracious sweeping veranda with a gazebo-like curve at one corner—just the spot for a quiet evening conversation or a planning session with your road map for the next day's activities. Inside, the inn is filled with antiques, lovely carpets and six sunny rooms, each with a lovely view.

Behind the inn is a picturesque little pond with a little log bench to sit upon while watching lazy water bugs crisscross the peaceful surface. Just beyond the inn, the road dead ends and leads into a wildlife management zone. The peace and quiet at the inn is broken only when the Dartmouth crew strokes by on the river, the coxswain shouting his commands to the crew.

The Stone House Inn is off the beaten path for the average tourist—all the better for you to relax and get to see the real Vermont. Request Room 6 in the summer. This unheated room is lovely, although it is simply furnished with a double bed that almost completely fills it. But what a room! It projects from the back of the house and seems to hang over the pond. Small-paned windows encircle three sides and in the daytime, sunlight plays on the walls and floors. Waking up in this room is waking up in heaven. There is no sound but the rustling leaves outside—bring your coffee upstairs, fall into one of the overstuffed chairs and enjoy.

The Stone House Inn is open all year and offers an excellent setting for cross-country skiing as well as summer sports. The heated rooms are always warm and cosy, even in the deepest February blizzard, and the downstairs fireplaces are always blazing.

STONE HOUSE INN, P.O. Box 47, North Thetford, VT 05054. Telephone: (802) 333-9124. Accommodations: six rooms with twin or double beds; shared baths; no telephones; public television. Rates: inexpensive, Continental breakfast included. Children allowed. No pets. Cards: MC, VISA. Open all year.

Getting there: From I-89, take Exit 14 and turn right on Route 113, then left on Route 5. Follow Route 5 for about two miles. In North Thetford, there is a very sharp turn in Route 5, with a large red barn on the curve. The inn is at the end of a little dirt road behind the barn.

A Pocket of Victoriana
THE GREENHURST INN
Bethel

The Greenhurst Inn is perched on a sweeping curve in U.S. Route 12 along the White River. This inn is not one of the Colonial or Federalist country inns that one usually thinks of as a Vermont inn, but is instead a monument to another equally important facet of Vermont tradition, the Victorian period. Turrets of Victorian mansions reaching into the sky along with the mountain peaks are reminders of the time when mill towns like Bethel came into their own, when a certain elegance previously unknown prevailed in these beautiful valleys.

Located in the middle of Vermont, the Greenhurst is surrounded by many different recreation areas. The inn is at the junction of two roads, U.S. Route 12 and an unpaved local road, called simply the Bethel North Road. The latter offers incredible panoramas of mountains and fields stretching to the west of the White River Valley. Local recreation includes river rafting, best in the spring when the rivers are full; the hang-gliding center in nearby Gaysville; shopping in nearby Woodstock; skiing at Killington, a quick twenty-three miles south; or the fall fair in Tunbridge, only a few miles up the road. An excellent restaurant is the Barnard Inn, only twelve miles south on Route 12 on the shores of Silver Lake.

The Greenhurst's gazebo and clay tennis courts are clues to the romantic past of the lovely building. Built in 1891 by the Harringtons of Philadelphia, it is one of the finest examples of Victorian architecture in the region, embellished with porches and turrets and gingerbread trim.

Lyle and Barbara Wolf, refugees from the busy pace of Los Angeles, moved to Vermont and the Greenhurst in 1982. Although the inn had been open to the public since the 1930s, the Wolfs decided to take the business one step further and restore the inn to its Victorian splendor. After only a few years, the Wolfs have succeeded. When you arrive at the inn, you are greeted by a beautiful etched window in the front door, a fine example of the etched glass which once abounded in Vermont, but is so scarce today.

Each room has its own personality and unique furnishings. A front room, washed with sunlight, is decorated in white wicker, while others have tiny Victorian fireplaces with Italian tilework or hand-crocheted coverlets. No need to fear winter here, for most rooms are equipped with electric blankets. All have antiques and a selection of books in case you forgot your own. Strains of Mozart and Haydn waft up the stairway to your room from the common rooms below.

The public rooms of the Greenhurst are beautiful and antiques dominate the high-ceilinged ones in the front of the house. Doors have lovely floral glass knobs and heavy, polished brass hinges and one room features a chandelier with seven concentric circles of crystal prisms.

Muffins, coffee and homemade jams are featured at breakfast here. Afterwards, either curl up in the bentwood rocker in the living room or head out on an adventure through the mountains. The Greenhurst makes a relaxed and pleasurable vacation headquarters.

THE GREENHURST INN, U.S. Route 12, Bethel, VT 05032. Telephone: (802) 234-9474. Accommodations: ten rooms with twin, double, or queen-size beds; two rooms have private baths, others share; no telephones; television in parlor. Rates: moderate to expensive, Continental breakfast included; dinner available family style with advance reservation. Children welcome. Pets allowed. Cards: AE, MC, VISA.

Getting there: From I-89, take the Bethel-Royalton Exit, marked Route 103. Follow it past the State Police Headquarters to Bethel. At the fork of Route 12, bear left onto Route 12 south, crossing the bridge. The inn is at the fork of the road about a quarter mile south.

The Greenhurst Inn

A Homey Retreat by the Floating Bridge
GREEN TRAILS INN
Brookfield

The Green Trails Inn is a homey enclave in a quiet little village, surrounded by miles of rolling farmland and rushing rivers. Once an early New England farm, the Green Trails now provides peace and quiet amidst a beautiful countryside. The approach to Brookfield and the Green Trails from Interstate 89 in Randolph is a most beautiful and scenic drive. From the exit, the road climbs to Randolph Center, the highest town in Vermont. The Vermont Technical College fronts the main street, which is lined with beautiful houses. Behind these buildings, expansive views of the mountains open in either direction—sunrise and sunset are spectacular here. After Randolph Center, the road winds down through some of Vermont's best dairy country. The steep hillsides provide acres and acres of open pasture which are covered with sheep and cattle clinging to the vertical grasslands.

Brookfield's citizens have resisted change and the opportunity to grow, keeping the town much as it was a hundred years ago. When I-89 was designed, Brookfield's citizens rejected the proposal for an interchange that would have given them easy access to the route, preferring to be off the beaten track. The interstate now charges through town without letting anyone off. Likewise, they politely turned down proposals to pave the town's main streets and "improve" the town by building a suspension bridge to replace their famous Floating Bridge.

The Floating Bridge is Brookfield's claim to fame and must be crossed to reach the Green Trails Inn. Those who fear bridges need not fear this one, for it is supported by over eight hundred floating barrels, so that instead of going over the water, you cross it on the surface. When the wind blows or when several cars are on the bridge at once, water washes over the structure, although never covering more than a few inches. Brookfield's town center straddles the bridge so that recent renovations kept the townspeople isolated from each other. Given their druthers, no doubt, most would have been happy to be stranded on the Green Trails side, where they could enjoy the inn's pub and its fine food.

The Green Trails Inn comprises the main house and the general store, which were built in 1790 and 1840, respectively. Both have been well preserved. The decor is Victorian, although the rooms vary in

Green Trails Inn

style and accommodations. The rooms over the general store are efficiencies with kitchen facilities.

The Fork Shop, once a factory where pitchforks were made for the endless haying of fields in the area, is a good place for drinks and dinner. The menu, which attracts a variety of local patrons as well as inn guests, features daily specials of simple, hearty and delicious fare, just what you would expect in a town like Brookfield.

If you have a choice, ask to stay in the Stencil Room, which features basket-patterned stenciling on the walls. All rooms are delightfully old-fashioned, with flowered wallpapers and interesting old furniture that not only looks great but is comfortable as well. Most rooms have double beds covered with patchwork quilts and most have private baths.

What to do in Brookfield? The inn's recently opened stable makes possible riding through the incomparable countryside. Allis State Park is a few minutes up the road, and you're never far from spectacular scenery, great antiquing prospects and some of the most friendly and interesting people in the state.

The Green Trails Inn is open year-round. Winter is beautiful here, for the riding trails of summer make excellent cross-country ski trails and Brookfield hosts an annual ice harvesting festival. All the major ski areas are close by—try Sugarbush Valley in Warren/Waitsfield, an hour away across high mountain roads and passes, or a less precarious ninety minutes by interstate.

GREEN TRAILS INN, Pond Village, Brookfield, VT 05036. Telephone: (802) 276-3412. Accommodations: fifteen rooms with twin or double beds, efficiency with kitchen or apartment with kitchen; private and shared baths with tubs, showers and tub/showers; telephones; public television. Rates: inexpensive to moderate, available with breakfast or with breakfast and dinner. Children welcome. Some pets. No cards. Open all year.

Getting there: From I-89, take Exit 4 (Route 66). Proceed to Randolph Center and join Route 14, following it north to Brookfield; cross the Floating Bridge; the inn is on the left across the bridge.

Isolated yet Sophisticated
TUCKER HILL LODGE
Waitsfield

The Tucker Hill Lodge is just up the road from the highly developed, dynamic Mad River Valley, an indentation in the Green Mountains running south from near Stowe. The Mad River is hardly that at all, however, except when the spring rains cause a torrential run-off and the boulder strewn creekbed is filled with a raging current. Along the Mad River's shores, developers have created one of the most sophisticated yet liveable resort communities in America, although the Tucker Hill Lodge is far enough away to be isolated and seem far from civilization.

This small inn caters mostly to adults who seek privacy, quiet and fine food. However, there is a hiking service in the snowless months and a cross-country ski touring center on the grounds in the winter. It is up to you to choose how much—or how little—you wish to do here.

It is never easy to get a reservation at the Tucker Hill Lodge, for it has many regulars. Many guests return every season or stay for an entire week, taking advantage of the inn's reduced rate for long-term guests (a ten per cent discount is available if you stay Sunday through Friday in the summer). The inn does not encourage one-nighters or drop-ins, so be sure to plan far in advance when you make a trip to the Mad River Valley.

The rooms at the inn are simple yet comfortable. Many have private baths which, after a day on the slopes or on the trail, are comforting to return to for a steamy, hot shower. Fresh flowers brighten every room and each bed is covered with a quilt made by a local craftsman.

The Tucker Hill Lodge attracts a diverse and interesting clientele. For many, staying in the inn is close enough to nature, while for others the inn is headquarters for ambitious mountain-climbing adventures on nearby Camel's Hump, Vermont's second highest peak. Many fascinating conversations develop around the fireplace in the living room where guests gather to knit, read and talk.

The Tucker Hill Lodge is synonymous with good food in Vermont and dinner is included in the room rate. Many outsiders head for the inn at dinner time as well. The menu changes nightly, often offering excellent fish which is delivered from Maine every day or wonderful

Tucker Hill Lodge

homemade pasta, to name a few. Breads and desserts are delicious and the service is helpful and pleasant.

Tucker Hill Lodge is affiliated with several of the inn-to-inn adventure plans in Vermont, including those for hikers and bicyclists. Check with the inn or with the service headquarters for more information. You can also enjoy tennis on the inn's popular clay courts during your stay.

Don't miss the Mad River Valley's local galleries, boutiques and the many excellent restaurants. A trip to The Store in Warren is a must as well. Although it looks like a charming Vermont country store, you can buy fine French wine, gourmet foods, homemade desserts and designer clothes here, in addition to fly dope, a fishing license or the Sunday newspaper.

TUCKER HILL LODGE, Route 17, Waitsfield, VT 05673. Telephone: (802) 496-3983 or (800) 451-4580, outside Vermont. Accommodations: twenty rooms with twin, three twin, twin and bunk, twin and double, double and bunk or queen-size beds; fourteen rooms with private baths; no telephones; television in living room. Rates: moderate, dinner included. Well-behaved children welcome, discount possible on some meals for small children. No pets. Cards: AE, MC, VISA. Open all year.

Getting there: From I-89, take Route 100 south. Follow signs to Warren and Waitsfield. Past center of Waitsfield Village, take a right onto Route 17 toward Middlebury. The inn is about one and one-half miles farther on the left.

A Classic Inn at a Classic Resort
GREEN MOUNTAIN INN
Stowe

If your idea of a vacation at a ski resort is clouded by the gloomy expectation of yet another faceless condominium rental, head to the Green Mountain Inn. Here, in the heart of New England's largest and most famous ski resort, you can combine the best of New England charm and tradition with the convenience of an in-town location that is only a short hop to the lifts. In non-ski season, Stowe is no less lively, for world class tennis matches, hiking, mountain climbing, bicycling, antiques shows and sales and plenty of fine shops, along with many excellent restaurants and pubs, will keep you busy. Stowe is, quite simply, the recreation capital of inland New England.

The Green Mountain Inn is located in the center of the town at the intersection of Route 100 and Mountain Road, which leads to two ski areas, Mt. Mansfield and Spruce Peak. The rambling old inn looks much as it must have 150 years ago when it was built as a stage stop in the tiny village. Stowe's ski industry has grown up around the village, but the picturesque center has remained unspoiled.

Inside, there are several small sitting rooms, perfect for family gatherings or intimate conversations. Colonial and English antiques and fabrics complemented by milk-painted woodwork and soft carpeting set the mood for casual luxury. The dining room, recently redecorated and expanded, features glossy polished hardwood floors that slope and creak due to the age of the great wide boards, and there is an old dumbwaiter in the dining room, still used by bartenders to send drinks up from the lounge below. The menu is studded with traditional Yankee entrees. Breakfast is irresistable, when the delicious aroma of fresh-baked muffins fills the inn.

Innkeeper Lewis Kiesler has overseen the renovation and redecoration of the inn, furnishing each of the fifty-nine guest rooms with reproduction Colonial furniture designed especially for the building. Thirty-six of the rooms feature romantic canopy beds crowned with arches of crisp fabric and complemented by milk-painted wainscoting. Each one has the modern convenience of a full private bath, a television and a telephone. Rooms in both the main inn and in the addition are comfortable and convenient to the inn's many guest services, which include a Nautilus-equipped health spa, heated pool and rooms for busines meetings.

GREEN MOUNTAIN INN, Route 100, Stowe Village, VT 05672. Telephone: (802) 253-7301. Accommodations: fifty-seven rooms with double or twin beds; private baths with tub/showers; telephones; television. Rates: moderate to expensive, modified American plan optional. Children welcome. Some pets allowed, inquire ahead. Cards: AE, CB, DC, MC, VISA. Open all year.

Getting there: From I-89 take Route 100 north to Waterbury. Proceed north on Route 100 through Waterbury Center to Stowe. The inn is at the intersection of Route 100 and the Mountain Road, opposite the bookshop.

Landmark on the West Coast of New England
NORTH HERO HOUSE
North Hero Island

The rolling hills and rushing brooks of Vermont come to a halt at Lake Champlain, a wide stretch of water separating Vermont from New York for more than half the state's western border. In the past few years, Lake Champlain's Vermont shores have come to be known as the "West Coast of New England." Boating and other water sports take over during the summer on Champlain and people come from all over the world to soak up the sun and relax along its shores.

Strung out in the northern quadrant of the lake are a dozen or more islands known as the Champlain Islands, all connected by a winding highway. There are ferries to New York State and this is a most scenic route to Montreal and Quebec, for old-fashioned farms with split-rail fences and haystacks line the road.

North Hero is one of two islands granted to Revolutionary War hero Ethan Allen, leader of the famed Green Mountain Boys, and islanders are still proud of their link with Vermont's most famous native. In Allen's day, though, there was no highway linking the islands, of course, and great schooners plied the waters between the mainland and the islands. These were isolated outposts, and you can still get the feeling of remoteness when you relax at this wonderful country inn, leaving the rest of the world behind.

North Hero House is actually several houses. There are four buildings with a total of twenty-three guest rooms. The inn itself is a grand building across the street from the lake. The restaurants, lounges and offices are here, along with six lovely rooms, each with private bath and double beds. The lakeview rooms have private screened porches for relaxing on summer nights and the front porch of the main inn is lined with high-backed rocking chairs. You may also stay in the Cove House, Southwind House (formerly the general store) and Homestead. Each of these buildings is a short walk across the road from the main inn and all are right on the water. Watch for loons—and listen for them at night. Accommodations here are simple and designed for active guests. You'll find lots of towels in your room

North Hero House

along with plenty of beach chairs for relaxing outside. Meals are arranged around the best swimming and boating hours of the day.

Expect some unusual treats at mealtime, especially the soups and fish entrees, and plan to be around for one of the sumptuous Sunday evening buffets outdoors. Innkeeper Caroline Sorg does the cooking and there is always a surprise.

North Hero Island is practically the farthest corner of the state. But it is a magic corner and not to be missed. Make the North Hero House your destination or a night-over stop between visits to Burlington and Montreal. Both Stowe and the museum at Shelburne on lower Lake Champlain are quick drives.

NORTH HERO HOUSE, Champlain Islands, North Hero, VT 05474. Telephone: (802) 372-8237. Accommodations: twenty-three rooms with twin and double beds; private baths; no telephones; public television. Rates: moderate. Children welcome. No pets. No cards. Open mid-June to Labor Day.

Getting there: From the New York shore of Lake Champlain, take ferry from Plattsburgh. From Vermont side, follow I-89 north from Burlington to Exit 17. Follow Route 2 through the Champlain Islands to North Hero.

The Stuff That New England Legends Are Made Of
RABBIT HILL INN
Lower Waterford

Lower Waterford began as a crossroads of sorts in the road between St. Johnsbury and Portland, Maine. In the early 1800s, there was an active trade route through the village, although it never grew to be much larger than its current eight or ten houses. The Briar Patch, the small building next to the Rabbit Hill Inn, was actually the town's first inn, an early hostelry for teamsters who delivered goods from the seaports to the interior. In 1834, what is now the main building was built as a larger inn. As many as one hundred wagons a day passed through Lower Waterford year-round, and it is easy to imagine the little village humming with activity.

Lower Waterford is tiny, but on a Friday evening in almost any time of the year, dinner guests create a mini-traffic jam as they jockey for parking spaces outside the inn's restaurant. In this quiet, undeveloped Northeast corner of Vermont, the restaurant of the Rabbit

Hill Inn is a mecca, the overall tempo upbeat and festive. The restaurant at the Rabbit Hill Inn is excellent. The food, served simply and in hearty portions, is a well-presented Continental cuisine with a home-cooked touch.

If possible, ask to stay in the main building. The room to the right at the top of the stairs is particularly large and nice—it even has its own organ! Each room has a private bath and you will enjoy your accommodations no matter where you stay. If you prefer absolute privacy, opt for the rooms in the motel-like wing of the main building, all of which have separate exits to the outdoors. Most rooms have panoramic views of the White Mountains and the Connecticut River, a view that has remained unchanged in 150 years. Many of the rooms have working fireplaces, and the hotel staff will be glad to help you with your fire. To be snowbound in front of a fireplace at the Rabbit Hill is the stuff that New England legends are made of.

When not relaxing at the inn, you will want to drive through the miles of farmland around Lower Waterford or head for the ski trails at nearby Burke Mountain. There is also the maple museum at St. Johnsbury and numerous covered bridges cross the Connecticut River in this area. Hanover and Dartmouth College are about an hour's drive south in New Hampshire and an interesting afternoon can be found in the historical society of neighboring village, Concord, where there is a wonderful museum which focuses on life in the Northeast Kingdom, both past and present.

RABBIT HILL INN, Route 18, Lower Waterford, VT 05848. Telephone: (802) 748-5168. Accommodations: twenty rooms with twin, double, twin double or queen-size beds; private baths with tub/showers; no telephones; television in five rooms. Rates: expensive. Children and pets welcome. Cards: MC, VISA. Closed November and April.

Getting there: The inn is on Route 18, about seven miles south of the intersection of I-93 and I-91.

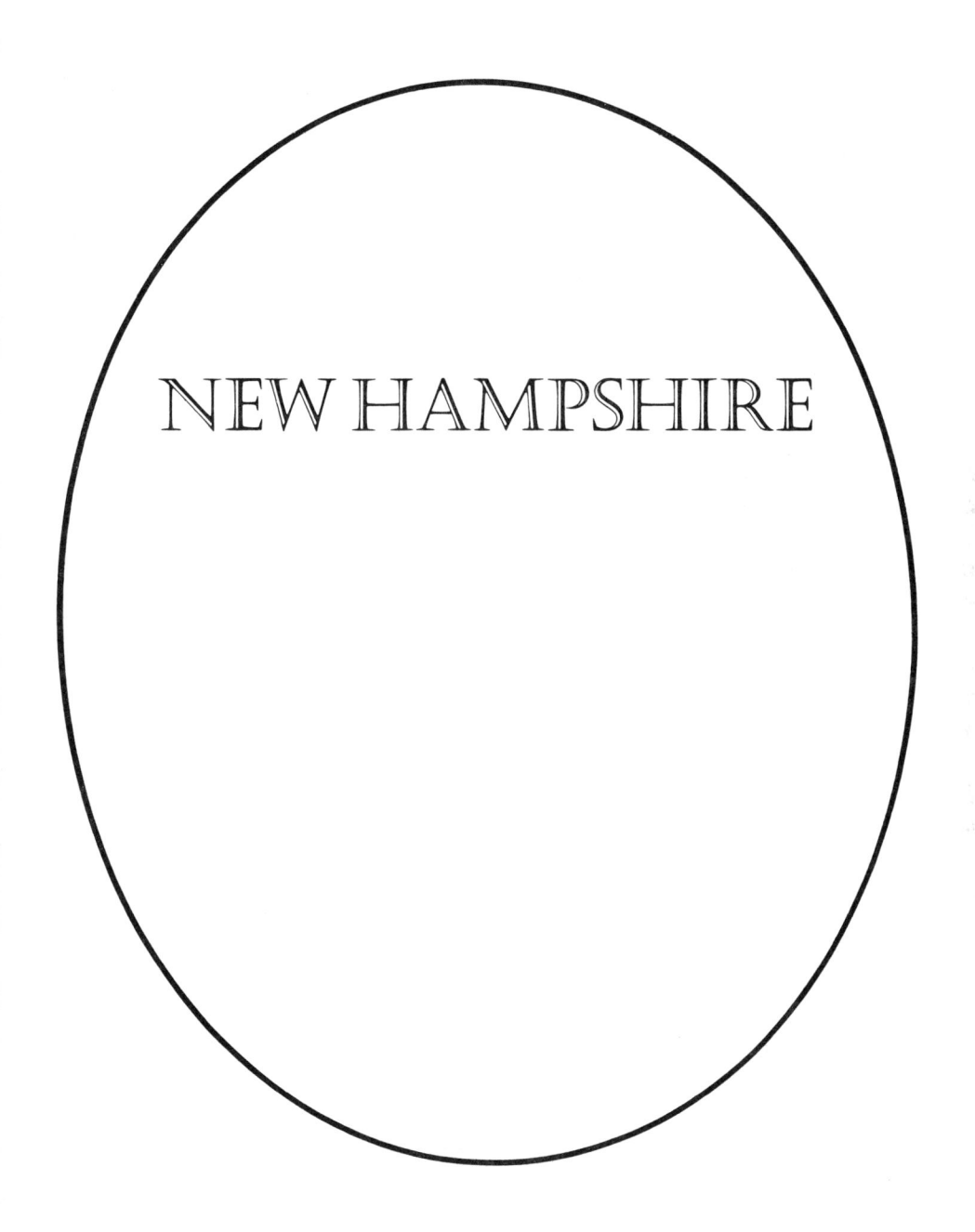

NEW HAMPSHIRE

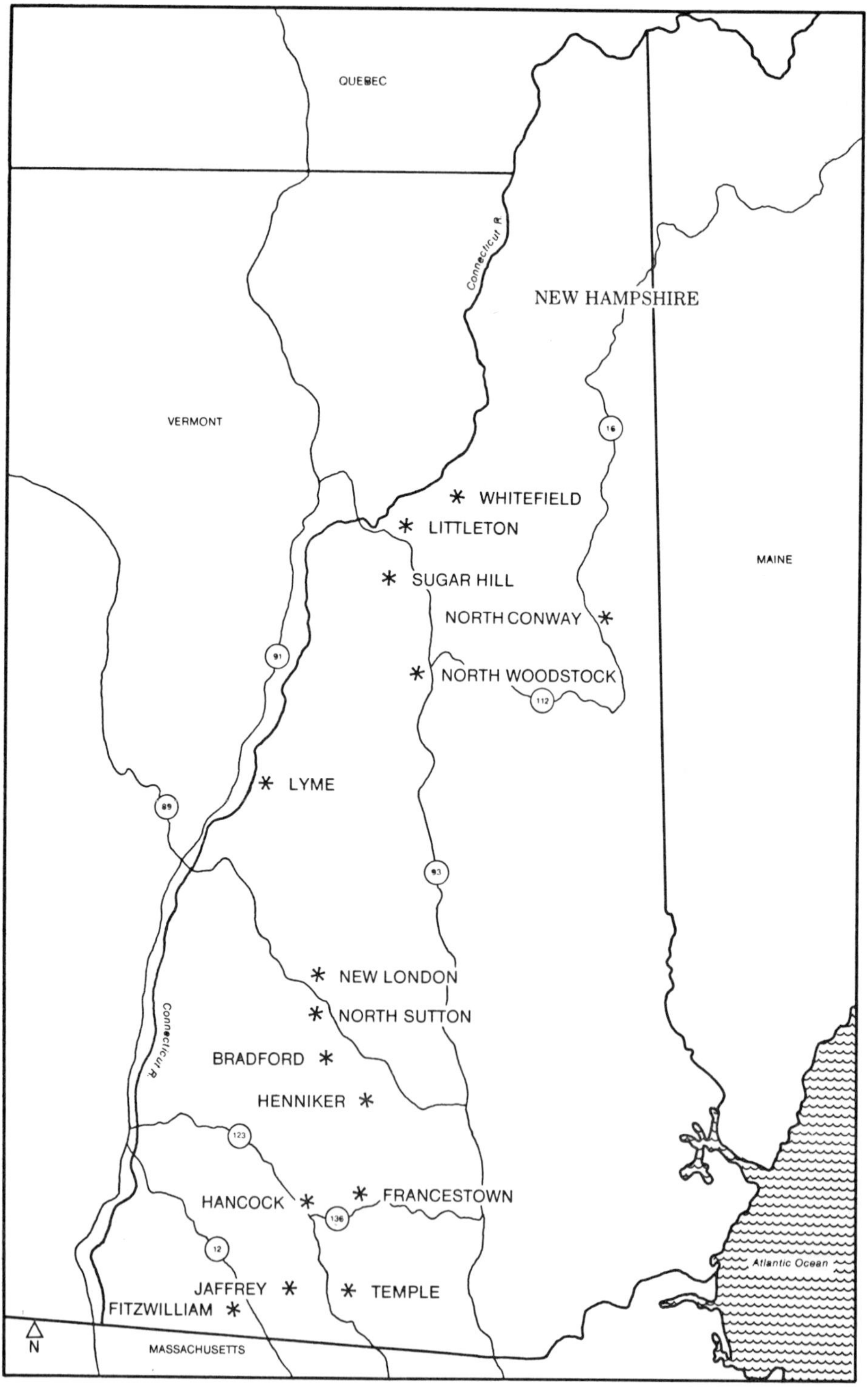
QUEBEC
VERMONT
NEW HAMPSHIRE
MAINE
MASSACHUSETTS
Connecticut R.
Atlantic Ocean
N
16
91
89
93
112
123
136
12
WHITEFIELD
LITTLETON
SUGAR HILL
NORTH CONWAY
NORTH WOODSTOCK
LYME
NEW LONDON
NORTH SUTTON
BRADFORD
HENNIKER
HANCOCK
FRANCESTOWN
JAFFREY
TEMPLE
FITZWILLIAM

The Heartbeat of New England Inns
THE NEW ENGLAND INN
Intervale

It's 1809. You're a teamster who has spent a long day with a load of goods along the Boston-Montreal road. You've just made your way through Pinkham Notch and you can feel your horses stepping a little bit lighter, as if they too sense that the Bloodgood Farm and its warm fire are nearing. A warm supper and dry bed awaits.

Not much has changed around Intervale since 1809 in terms of hospitality. Thousands of travelers pass through the eastern slopes of the White Mountains each day, and a few lucky ones have booked rooms at the old Bloodgood Farm, now called the New England Inn. A warm welcome is still top priority here, and a pleasant stay is guaranteed.

Calling one's inn The New England Inn takes a lot of confidence, but the Johnstons, your innkeepers, have always felt that their inn was something special, a landmark of the region. Slowly but surely, they have built the inn into a self-sufficient center for vacationers and passers-by. The restaurant is superb, the list of inn activities endless, and the decor looks like a set designed for the ultimate country inn.

This is truly a four-season resort. Skiing in the Cranmore-Jackson-Conway area lasts through three seasons in good years and none of the eastern slope's major ski areas is more than a half hour away. This inn was at the forefront of the cross-country craze, and you'll find a complete ski touring center offering lessons and rentals.

In summer, bicycling and hiking replace skiing as the main activities. You'll want to make at least one day hike up Mt. Washington, New England's highest mountain, though it takes more than a day to get to the top. Head instead for an interim destination like Tuckerman's Ravine, where skiiers brave "The Headwall" as late as Memorial Day, just to say that they have skiied one of the great vertical challenges of the world. No lifts here—skiiers backpack up a two-mile trail and then climb with handholds up to "The Lip" where they put their skis on. Scary stuff, but fun to watch.

Of course, there's no need to even leave The New England Inn. It is a comfortable, homey place. The entrance is dominated by the ancient hearth and cooking cranes of the house's original kitchen, and the smells wafting from the new kitchen will make you want to pull up to the nearest table and wait for the next meal.

The restaurant menu is New England cuisine elevated to a new culinary art. Pumpkin bisque is a result of the melding of local foods with a great chef's imagination. For breakfast, there may be a fresh fruit buffet or baked apples served with whipped creamn and maple syrup. At dinner, expect simple splendor: baked ham with a rich rum raisin sauce, chops, or a beef stew. No one has ever left the New England hungry or cold. With fireplaces blazing against the chill and the reflective sparkle of cut glass vases and stemware, this elegant corner of the inn will stay in your memory for years to come.

There is a variety of accommodations to choose from here, ranging from a standard room in the main house or a single remote cottage, complete with fireplace and a stack of dry wood. All rooms are comfortably furnished with country fabrics, wallpapers, and antique or reproduction furniture.

In summer, the front yard of the inn becomes a bevy of activity as guests head for the four-tee golf course or the clay tennis courts. You can watch the shadows cross the mountains or walk out to the stables where the Mallets keep their horses used for sleigh and hay rides for inn guests. At the end of a long, hard day of play, there is a pleasant piano bar and the promise of an excellent meal to come.

THE NEW ENGLAND INN, Route 16A, Intervale, NH 03845. Telephone: (603) 356-5541. Accommodations: forty-eight rooms with twin or double beds, ten in one-bedroom cottages; private and shared baths with tub/showers; no telephones; no television. Rates: moderate, breakfast included. Children allowed. Pets allowed only in cottages and subject to surcharge. Cards: AE, MC, VISA. Closed in April.

Getting there: From I-93 north, take Woodstock Exit. Drive east on Route 112 to Route 16 and follow to the resort loup, Route 16A.

FRANCONIA NOTCH REGION

"The Rocky Mountains of the East" will seem an appropriate description of the White Mountains as you crane your neck to catch the view on the drive through Franconia Notch. The Notch is the gateway to the White Mountains, a parkway that winds through dramatic scenery, dominated by the Old Man of the Mountains, a chillingly realistic rock formation hanging off a granite cliff and reflected in Profile Lake.

Once through the Notch, the region opens up and offers a variety of terrain and atmospheres. There is Sugar Hill, a community of farms and summer homes set in rolling hills against the stark panorama of the nearby mountain ranges. There is Littleton, the folksy downtown of the region, where you can buy jeans with flannel linings and stop by the diner and feel right at home no matter what you say, do, or wear. There is Bethlehem, quiet, sleepy and jammed with traffic on a summer's day with people eager to view the mountains and see the grand old inns. Whitefield is the central hub of the region's highways and Woodstock, at the entrance to the Notch, is a blazing strip of neon signs amidst a wilderness where moose and bear roam the shores of the Pemigewasset River.

When you head for the Franconia region, come prepared for dramatic scenery and a tradition of tourism. Bring an extra jacket, a pair of field glasses and your walking or hiking shoes. A camera is a must, although you will wish there was a lens that could capture the 180-degree—sometimes 360-degree—views around you.

Farmhouse Warmth in a Stark Landscapes
KIMBALL HILL INN
Whitefield

Whitefield is one of the most charming towns in the White Mountains. Its village square is surrounded by shops and gas stations with mechanics on duty, a rare find in the mountains. Charles Cooley's rambling bookshop on the green, specializing in rare and out-of-print books, is one of the largest in New England. There are also several excellent restaurants nearby, such as the Cafe des Artists and the Playhouse Inn north of town.

The Kimball Hill Inn's driveway climbs straight up a mountainside for a mile before reaching the inn, formerly a farm, which is perched on the side of the mountain, surrounded by meticulously groomed lawns and hay fields. Although many inns in this region were part of a larger resort from the grand turn-of-the-century tourist boom in the White Mountins, Kimball Hill is not. Instead, it is a home, and a simple New England home at that. However, the stark white farmhouse with its steeply pitched roof is a relief after driving through forty miles of Victorian gingerbread!

It is not the architecture that one first notices at the Kimball Hill Inn, however. Rather, it is the incredible panorama of the Presidential range rising above the sloping hay fields. The peaks—Adams, Jeffer-

Kimball Hill Inn

son, Madison, Washington, et al—seem to constantly change with the sun, clouds and leaves. Pull up a rocking chair on the porch and watch nature perform. Inside, the inn is furnished mostly with Victorian antiques. All rooms have private baths and comfortable beds and most have a view of the mountain. Some have sitting areas and one of these has a sofa bed for larger parties. Cots and cribs will be supplied if needed.

KIMBALL HILL INN, P.O. Box 74, Whitefield, NH 03598. Telephone: (603) 837-2284. Accommodations: nine rooms with three twin, double or twin and double beds; three cottages with three double or two double beds and queen-size sofa bed; private and shared baths in inn, cottages have private baths with showers and tub/showers. Rates: moderate, Continental breakfast included; no telephones; no television. Children welcome. Pets welcome with advance notice. Cards: AE, MC, VISA. Closed in April.

Getting there: Take I-93 north to Whitefield; proceed southeast on Route 116 and follow sign uphill to Kimball Hill Inn.

The Country Store of Country Inns
THE BEAL HOUSE INN
Littleton

Have you ever wandered through an antiques store and longed to move right in? Have you ever wondered just what it would be like to live surrounded by antiques, far from the twentieth century? If so, head for the Beal House Inn. If you really do fall in love with that little hutch in the corner of your room, buy it. Everything at the Beal House is for sale. In fact, when you walk in the door of this rambling old house, it is hard to tell if you're in an antiques shop or a country inn. Sitting right in the middle of a display of primitive folk art are two inn guests having lunch and discussing their plans for the afternoon, the waitress is pouring coffee from an old enamel pot that has a price tag dangling from the handle, and all the lovely old advertising art on the walls is marked with little price stickers. The only thing in sight that is modern is the luggage of the people checking out—and even they are carting off antiques they purchased during their stay!

The Beal House Inn, a good central location for a vacation in the White Mountains, has survived the many phases of the tourist industry in northern New Hampshire. The main house was built in 1833, near the center of the busy little burg of Littleton, one of the main shopping centers of the area. In the late 1800s and early part of this century, tourism flourished as trainloads of vacationers were brought to the great resort hotels, now empty, of nearby Bethlehem. When cars replaced the railroads, tourist cabins replaced the resorts and then the motels replaced the little cabins. Now another wave, the return of the country inn, looks to be the wave of the future for this part of New Hampshire.

The Beal House Inn has been open to guests for about fifty years. Its colorful history includes a stint as the town's poor farm. Slowly but surely, the development of downtown Littleton has crept closer to the old house, but the town does not menace. It is a pleasant, peaceful place to stroll, shop and lunch. Logging trucks barrel through town on their way to the sawmills as the river makes its circuitous route through the town's dams and locks, originally built to power the shoe factories which once comprised the major industry of the town. The ski areas of Cannon and Loon are close, making for convenient wintertime fun.

The Beal House Inn has fourteen rooms and, if you wish, you can buy your room's entire furnishings after you've tried them out for a night or two—guests have been known to! Innkeepers Doug and Brenda Clickenger carry on the tradition started by the first antiquer to live in the house, a Mrs. Grady, who supplemented her income from boarders with sales of antiques.

But although the Beal House is filled with exquisite old furnishings, do not be intimidated by them, for they are meant to be used and enjoyed. The beds are comfortable, the plumbing works well, all the modern conveniences are present and the food is great.

Breakfast is one of the most enjoyable times of day at the Beal House Inn. The Clickengers serve you in a large beamed dining room with antique (of course) china, serving dishes and silver. As you sink your teeth into a buttery popover, you get a view of the beautiful mountainsides, a preview of the the wonderful scenery outdoors.

THE BEAL HOUSE INN, Main Street, Littleton, NH 03561. Telephone: (603) 444-2661. Accommodations: fourteen guest rooms with twin or double beds; nine with private baths; telephones; no television. Rates: moderate, breakfast included. Inquire about children. No pets. Cards: AE, CB, DC, MC, VISA. Open all year.

Getting there: From I-91, take Exit 42 into Littleton. Proceed to the intersection of Routes 18 and 302; turn onto Route 302 (Main Street).

A Sampler of New England Tradition
THE HOMESTEAD
Sugar Hill

Sugar Hill may be just what the doctor ordered if you need to get away, step back in time and get some wide open space around you. This mountain ridge community is hardly more than a cluster of houses along the roadside, each one looking more like a Currier and Ives model than the last. Sugar Hill, still a relatively undeveloped area, is set in the middle of spectacular scenery, surrounded by beautiful mountain peaks and meadows which provide cross-country skiing in winter. And best of all, the Homestead Inn is in Sugar Hill, along with some of the best dining to be found in the White Mountains.

Sugar Hill is on the ridge above the more developed town of Franconia. You must pass through the famed Franconia Notch, a dramatic pass through the entrance to the White Mountain Region, to reach both Franconia and Sugar Hill. Count on Franconia for ski shops, lunch restaurants and a lively night life. Count on Sugar Hill for a classic New England vacation. The Homestead Inn dates back to the 1880s when the Bowles family began to take in travelers in this house. The current innkeepers, the Serafinis, are the seventh generation of the same family to operate the inn.

Accommodations at the inn are as varied as the guests. The main house has ten guest rooms with shared baths and gorgeous views from every window. The rooms in the Family Cottage, a farmhouse-style building across the street from the inn, all have private baths. One of the inn's most popular rooms, the Parker Room is located here. The Orchard House, a private building available for groups, has two bedrooms with private baths and a kitchen, living room and dining room of its own. The Chalet is a rustic log building with a beautiful fieldstone foundation that rents as a package as well.

A glance at the register in the entry of the Homestead shows how this inn's reputation has traveled. Many people come from California, Texas and the Midwest. This is a quiet inn, however, and the average guest here may be a bit older than at some of the livelier inns near the ski resorts.

Dinners at the Homestead are excellent. Served in the pine-paneled dining room lined with the family's impressive china and glass collections, the delicious food is served in a simple, elegant country New England style. And although the Homestead provides complimentary breakfast, plan at least one pancake feast at Polly's Pancake Parlor. Neither the food nor the view can be beat.

After breakfast, put on your walking shoes and stroll up towards Sunset Hill, past the lovely old summer homes reminiscent of the Gatsby era which line the road. The view across the rolling golf courses from the top seems to go on forever, providing one of the best opportunities to learn the names of the Presidential Range peaks—Washington, Adams, Jefferson, Madison et al.

THE HOMESTEAD, Route 117, Sugar Hill, NH 03585. Telephone: (603) 823-5564. Accommodations: seventeen rooms with twin or double beds; seven with private baths; telephones in Chalet and Orchard House only; no television. Rates: inexpensive, breakfast and dinner included. No children. No pets. No cards. Open end of May to November 1; Thanksgiving weekend; December 23 through the ski season.

Getting there: From I-93, take Franconia exit. Turn left onto Route 117 after Franconia and follow uphill for about two miles. The Homestead is on the left after Polly's Pancake Parlor.

The Inn at the Top of the World
SUNSET HILL HOUSE
Sunset Hill

One of the main attractions of the Sunset Hill House in Sugar Hill is the food. It also has the advantage of an incredible view, for it is set atop a ridge with views of jagged mountain peaks and dramatic skies. Every room has a view at this inn and the changing skies, the landscapes and the play of light and dark on the mountains and valleys make the Sunset Hill House memorable. A camera is a necessity here.

Sunset Hill House was once only one of a number of buildings servicing a huge inn that was on the property, the Sugar Hill House, which was destroyed many years ago. The old golf course remains, along with the Sunset Hill House, which may have been an annex to the original inn or used to house employees. All thirty-five guest rooms are pleasantly decorated, with comfortable beds and fluffy pillows and each has a private bath. And when you return from dinner, you will find that a maid has slipped in and turned down your bed for you.

Dinner at Sunset Hill is a treat. The veal is outstanding, although all of the food is excellent. There is a long chain of dining rooms along the back wall, each one giving a different perspective on the view. Make sure to be seated in time for the glorious sunset show.

Sunset Hill House is just up the road from the Homestead and behind the Homestead is the Sugar Hill Sampler, a huge barnlike gift shop with a wide selection of merchandise. Down the hill toward Franconia is Polly's Pancake Parlor, a must for at least one of your breakfasts.

SUNSET HILL HOUSE, Sunset Hill Road, Sugar Hill, NH 03585. Telephone: (603) 823-5522. Accommodations: thirty-five rooms with twin, double or queen-size beds; private baths with tubs, showers and tub/showers; no telephones; television in tavern. Rates: very expensive, breakfast and dinner included. Children welcome. Pets welcome. Cards: AE, MC, VISA. Open all year.

Getting there: From I-93, take exit marked for Franconia village. Drive through the village and turn left onto Route 117 and follow for about two miles. Turn left at the Homestead, just after Polly's Pancake Parlor. The Sunset Hill House is about one-half mile farther on the left. Park on the road.

A Peaceful Weekend in the Country
THE WOODSTOCK INN
North Woodstock

This is not *the* Woodstock Inn in the middle of Woodstock, Vermont. This is the other one, perhaps the best-kept secret in New England, It is located in New Hampshire and is marked by a beautiful sign painted with a sunrise hanging alongside Route 3. Here you will be greeted by Mrs. O'Toole, eager to regale you with tales of the old days in Boston.

Not too many years ago, a huge interstate highway, I-93, cut a wedge through the White Mountains, by-passing all the little villages that used to make their livelihoods from the tourist traffic. North Woodstock was one of those towns, and although things have slowed down, the people are proud and the town survives.

Scott and Eileen Rice bought an old Victorian here a few years ago and restored it, creating a jewel of a country inn. It had been empty for twenty years and there was a lot of work to be done, but much of the beautiful Victorian trim was still intact. Today, their inn is a charming combination of old and new, accented by delicious food and a friendly staff. The public rooms of the inn are homelike and comfortable and, except for the television in the living room, it seems like one hundred years ago. There are only six guest rooms at the Woodstock Inn, and all share bathrooms upstairs. The rooms are large and each has both a double and a twin bed with down comforters with lovely appliqued covers. Old wallpapers, big bay windows and decorative moldings are everywhere. Each bedroom is named for a mountain peak in the area. One of the locals' favorite peaks, Osceola, is easy to spot because of a scar from a huge landslide many years ago. The locals have some interesting legends which explain how the scar got there.

North Woodstock is at the entrance to the Franconia Notch State Park and the White Mountain National Forest, so there is no shortage of things to do in this area. There are a dozen tourist attractions and twice as many natural or scenic spots in the area, all within ten or fifteen minutes' drive of the inn. The Kancamangus Highway begins in North Woodstock, cutting through the mountains to the resort town of North Conway, excellent for shopping and sightseeing. It is a beautiful drive, although the highway is closed in winter past the Loon Mountain Ski Area. Skiing is just minutes away in Loon or a half hour's drive to Waterville Valley or Cannon Mountain.

Meals are served in the house in the winter, while in the summer the center of activity is the large screened porch that runs along two sides of the house. The seats at the romantic little tables are old theatre seats and candlelight plays on the walls long into the night. The prix fixe dinner is served only on weekends and reservations are required. A hearty breakfast is included with the room price.

WOODSTOCK INN, Route 3, North Woodstock, NH 03262. Telephone: (603) 745-3951. Accommodations: six rooms with double or twin and double beds; three shared baths; no telephones; television in three rooms and downstairs. Rates: inexpensive, breakfast included. Children welcome. No pets. Cards: MC, VISA. Open all year.

Getting there: From I-93 northbound, take Exit 32 to Route 112. Proceed to Route 3 and turn right; the inn is on the right.

NEW LONDON REGION

For over one hundred years, New London's Lake Sunapee has drawn record numbers of summer visitors. First they came by carriage, then by train, and now some even come by private plane. With the development of the major ski areas at Mt. Sunapee and King Ridge, New London has grown into a year-round resort town, while still maintaining its style and charm.

Even with cars parked along its main street, New London feels like a nineteenth-century village. The streets are wide, with only a few side streets. Beyond and behind the shops, the inn and the buildings of Colby-Sawyer College, are wide open fields, post rail fences and beautiful mountain views. No one ever suffered from claustrophobia in New London.

Many of the stately homes in the town belong to part-time residents from New York or Boston, although more and more of the town's residents are sticking around all year, often after retiring. The college keeps a steady flow of young people and a steady level of cultural activity, which are often so rare in remote New England towns.

New London is only five minutes off I-89, about halfway between Concord and Lebanon, the nearest big towns. Plan to spend a few hours just strolling through New London, and have a sandwich at

The Lyme Inn

Peter Christian's Tavern, a friendly pub in the center of town. Roads lead in every direction out of town: toward the activity of Lake Sunapee or toward the tranquility of an outlying region like Kezar Lake. You'll delight in this backroads capital of New England.

Magical Elegance in a Quiet Town
THE LYME INN
Lyme

What are you doing next October? Forget this October, because the Lyme Inn is probably already booked. Rooms at this well-known and well-loved inn can be very hard to reserve, especially on fall weekends when neighboring Dartmouth College is hosting an Ivy League football game. But do hang in there until you can get a room. The Lyme Inn is worth the wait.

Lyme is a lovely town on the Connecticut River, just north of Hanover, a bustling, cosmopolitan college town filled with good restaurants, shops and the host of many cultural activities. Lyme has none of these, but it does have its inn, set just off the town green. The lovely rolling countryside is perfect for bicycling and cross-country skiing, several ski areas such as the Dartmouth Ski Bowl are nearby, and there is often a crew meet on the Connecticut River.

The carefully decorated interior of the Lyme Inn will take your breath away. But although it is awe-inspiring, with its fine antiques and folk and primitive art pieces, the inn is comfortable and inviting, from the three intimate country dining rooms and the fine tavern, lined with deacon's benches and hung with old tools, to the flawlessly decorated guest rooms, several with fireplaces. Much of the artwork is for sale, although the furnishings are not. Room 9, furnished with a stunning bed painted with sea and mountain vignettes, a spinning wheel and a rocking chair by the fireplace, is one of the best. Room 15, which has a day bed along with a double bed, is set off by dark, contrasting colors and is perfect for families. The wide front veranda is a wonderful place to take your morning coffee if the weather is accommodating.

Fred and Judy Siemons set an excellent table, thanks to the work of chef Hans Wickert. Unexcelled in the area, the food is a mix of Continental cooking and traditional New England foods. This is one of the few places in the north country that you can order hasenpfeffer, a delicious rabbit stew.

Before you continue your travels, check the huge antique map of Grafton County which is in one of the dining rooms. You will be amazed at the size of Grafton County, which extends from Lyme on the Connecticut River to Lyman deep in the White Mountains, over an hour's drive to the north. This old map will help you plan your travels through the county, which cuts a huge swath through several geographical and cultural regions of the state.

THE LYME INN, Lyme, NH 03768. Telephone: (603) 795-2222 or 795-4404. Accommodations: fifteen rooms with twin, double or day and double beds; ten with private baths; no telephones; television in sitting room. Rates: moderate to expensive, breakfast included. No children under eight. No pets. Cards: AE, MC, VISA.

Getting there: Take Hanover-Norwich exit from I-91. Cross the Connecticut River and proceed to the center of Hanover. Follow Route 10 to Lyme. The inn is just past the end of the green at a fork in the road. Park in the back.

A Colonial Hotel with Something for Every Season
THE NEW LONDON INN
New London

Tucked away in the west central portion of the state, New London is the home of Colby-Sawyer College, the King Ridge Ski Area and Lake Sunapee. The New London Inn is on the busy main street of the village, surrounded by specialty shops which should provide a whole afternoon of browsing. There is plenty to do here, no matter what time of year you come.

The two-story inn, with its wide veranda and, in the summer, colorful flower garden out front dates back to 1792. It is one of the largest inns in the area, with twenty-four guest rooms upstairs, each differing a little from the rest. Most have lovely flowered wallpapers, four-poster beds, and curtains that rustle in the breeze. You may wish to request a room away from the street for a little more quiet, although there is not much commotion in New London after dark. The public areas of the inn are beautifully decorated with flowered chintz slipcovers on the furniture, tall bookcases and plenty of shaded lamps for reading a good book. The front desk personnel are helpful and courteous and you will find the morning papers out early, a convenience not available at many other inns.

Don't miss breakfast on the sunporch, a good opportunity to meet other inn guests and get helpful hints for sightseeing in the area. The front porch, lined with rockers, is a pleasant place to lounge in the summer. In winter, it is usually filled with skis propped against the wall by guests who have skied right up to the inn's door!

If you need help planning your stay in New London, go across the street to the tourist center and ask. The advice is free and friendly and might make the difference between a day spent enjoying every minute or a day spent meandering aimlessly—although that can be fun too!

THE NEW LONDON INN, Main Street, New London, NH 03257. Telephone: (603) 526-2791. Accommodations: twenty-four rooms with twin, double or twin double beds; private baths with tubs, showers and tub/showers; no telephones; public television. Rates: moderate. Children welcome. No pets. Cards: MC, VISA. Open all year.

Getting there: From I-89 take Exit 11 or 12 and follow to New London. The inn is on Main Street opposite the tourist information booth.

A Jewel in the Wilderness
THE FOLLANSBEE INN
North Sutton

Located in the undeveloped, barely populated west central portion of the Granite State, the Follansbee Inn is the center of attention in the little crossroads of North Sutton. The Follansbee Inn is alive with travelers and dinner guests, the lack of diversion in North Sutton being the inn's main attraction.

The Follansbee Inn is popular both winter and summer. Spring draws fishing aficionados who come for trout season in the local brooks or try for bass or lake trout in the lake. In winter, ice fishing is a major activity in New Hampshire.

All the guest rooms are on the upper floors, the downstairs functioning as a town center of sorts. People are constantly coming and going, stopping at the little gift shop or checking to find out who called to have their car jump-started in the sub-zero temperatures.

Skiers flock to the local slopes at King Ridge, Pat's Peak and Whaleback. Cross-country skiing is excellent as well and, on a clear cold day in January, there may even be skating on the lake.

Be sure to include dinner at the inn in your trip plans. The inn has an excellent reputation across the state for fine dining, with simple yet elegant meals. Rack of lamb and chicken are two specialties.

FOLLANSBEE INN, P.O. Box 92, North Sutton, NH 03260. Telephone: (603) 927-4221. Accommodations: twenty-three rooms with twin or double beds; eleven with private baths; telephones; public television. Rates: inexpensive. Children welcome. No pets. Cards: MC, VISA. Open all year except for two-week periods at Thanksgiving and Easter.

Getting there: Take Exit 10 from I-89 and follow North Road to Route 114. Turn right on 114 and proceed to village of North Sutton. The inn is on the left in the center of town.

THE NORTHERN MONADNOCK

The sun shines on the southern slopes of Mt. Monadnock and the snow falls on the northern. The terrain to the north of the grand mountain is a little rockier and a little steeper and towns seem to be a little bit farther apart. This remoteness gives a feeling of independence in the little towns like Hancock, Henniker and Bradford. There are no big cities in this part of the state; each village seems able to provide for itself.

Skiing and antiquing are two major industries in this part of the state. Your innkeepers can direct you to ideal cross-country or downhill spots or draw a treasure map for a day on the antiques trail. If you're lucky, you might be visiting on the weekend of the New Boston

Fair, officially known as the Hillsborough Country Fair, or the Cheshire Fair in Keene.

For a meal outside the dining room of your inn, you'll have to drive to Concord, Manchester, Keene or another country inn. Beware traveling in this region in November and April—everything seems to close. Locals call April mud season, a month-long siege between winter and the first signs of spring. Unless your favorite colors are gray and brown and your vehicle is equipped with four-wheel drive, plan to visit this region when the mud is dry and the flowers are blooming. You'll be glad you came.

A Grand Old Country Inn with a Bright New Face
THE BRADFORD INN
Bradford

Jim and Mary Jo Snipe thought that they had left innkeeping behind when they sold the Pasquaney Inn in nearby Bridgewater, but when the Bradford Inn came on the market, the Snipes got right back into it and haven't looked back since. The Snipes immediately refurbished the Bradford, giving new wallpaper, furniture and draperies to many of the rooms. This large, spacious inn is distinguished by a grand wide staircase, high ceilings and large guest rooms. Built in 1890, the Bradford has a more ornate exterior than many of the plainer, more sedate Colonial inns in New Hampshire. Shuttered windows crowd the three-storied facade and the columned verandas give the inn a very inviting look.

Concord, the state capital, is a short drive and there are all sorts of recreation facilities in the area, such as Lake Sunapee State Park or Bradford's own Lake Massasecum. In the winter, there is skiing at Sunapee, Pat's Peak, Whaleback, King Ridge or cross-country skiing wherever the local trails may take you.

The Snipes predict that the renovation of their inn will never end. In the meantime, the inn is comfortable, attractive and filled with charming antiques and art of all periods. And not to be missed, the inn's dining room is reason enough alone to make the trip here.

THE BRADFORD INN, Main Street, Bradford, NH 03221. Telephone: (603) 938-5309. Accommodations: twelve rooms with twin or double beds; baths with tubs, showers and tub/showers; no telephones; public television. Rates: inexpensive to moderate, European

The Bradford Inn

plan or modified American plan. Children allowed. No pets. No cards. Open all year.

Getting there: Take Exit 9 from I-89 northbound and follow Route 103 west to Bradford. The Bradford Inn is on the left after the intersection of Routes 103 and 114.

Escape to a Colonial Home
COLBY HILL INN
Henniker

The rolling countryside of central New Hampshire unwinds like a series of picture postcards as you approach the lovely little town of Henniker, home of the independent and proud New England College. Also located in Henniker is one of the area's most charming country inns, the family-run Colby Hill Inn. Off the beaten track and just up the road from the tiny crossroads in the center of town, this rambling old Colonial home is framed by flaming maple colors in the fall, soft greens in summer, and fragrant pink apple blossoms in the spring. In winter, underneath cold, clear blue skies and in the midst of stark white landscape, the warm and cozy Colby Hill Inn waits, ready to melt the chills. One or more of the Glover clan is certain to rise from a rocking chair and greet you as you enter the massive front door of the inn, built 160 years ago.

The spacious layout of the Colby Hill allows guests to spend time as privately or as publicly as they please. There are several sitting rooms for chatting, quiet reading, or working on one of the jigsaw puzzles which always seem to be in progress. The many birds drawn to the outdoor feeders at the large window are a constant source of amusement as well. The serene, well-kept grounds include a swimming pool and skiing and hiking trails. And, although hilly, the countryside around Henniker is wonderful for bicycling and hiking. Good skiing can be found at Pat's Peak and Lake Sunapee. Lake Sunapee is popular for boating in the summer as well.

If you're more interested in pure relaxation, however, you can poke through the old barns and sheds on the inn's grounds, take an antiquing trip to Hillsborough or simply gaze upon the beautiful hills from a lawn chair. Concord, the state capital, makes a good short trip for movies and dinner.

Accommodations at the inn are not luxurious, but furnishings are lovely and the rooms are delightful. Most of the beds are genuine antiques—be sure to ask Don, Jr. for an explanation of how the bed bolts hold together the lovely three-quarter beds in the front room. Braided and hooked rugs adorn the polished pine floors and the rooms are warm and cosy in winter, despite the inn's age or howling wind outside. Downstairs, you can curl up next to the fire for hours with a good book and no one will bother you.

COLBY HILL INN, Western Avenue, Henniker, NH 03242. Telephone: (603) 428-3281. Accommodations: twelve rooms with twin or double beds; private and shared baths with showers and tub/showers. Rates: moderate to expensive, breakfast included. Children over six welcome. No pets. Cards: AE, MC, VISA. Open all year.

Getting there: From I-89, take Route 202 to Henniker. The inn is about one-half mile past the center crossroads on your right.

Spectacular Home Cooking at a Country Farm
THE INN AT CROTCHED MOUNTAIN
Francestown

The Inn at Crotched Mountain is within walking distance of the Crotched Mountain ski area, but keeps the hustle and bustle at an arm's length. Here you will find the homeyness and warmth that you need after a day on the slopes or the cross-country trails with none of the loudness and distraction. The Inn at Crotched Mountain was once a working farm, and now only a small sign warns you that this *is* an inn. The grounds are beautifully maintained and right behind the house the earth drops away, revealing a sweeping panorama of mountains to the north.

From the outside, the inn does not look large enough to have fourteen rooms, but four of them have private baths and some even have fireplaces as well. Every guest room is sunny and decorated with lovely floral patterns and antique or reproduction furnishings. Rooms located in different parts of the house serve the different needs of different guests. Early-to-bed types won't want to sleep over the dining room and tavern, while early-to-swim types might want a room that has easy access to the pool area at the back of the house.

The pool and tennis courts are highlights in the summer months. The comfortable lawn furniture in the back attracts many guests who admire the view, read or play games. The weather changes quickly here and you can watch a thundershower approach in August or a snow squall headed your way in February. Sunsets and sunrises are incredible.

The Inn at Crotched Mountain is only a short drive from Manchester, the state's largest city and just minutes from Milford, which has some fine new restaurants and fun shops. Nearby Mt. Vernon is considered by many to be the antiques capital of New Hampshire. Golf is minutes away at the Tory Pines resort.

Include dinner at the inn on your itinerary. The inn is open to the public for dinner, so the tiny dining room in the center of the house is often jammed with people dining on spectacular home cooking. Innkeepers Rose and John Perry are successful with their difficult task, running both a successful restaurant and a quiet, attractive inn.

THE INN AT CROTCHED MOUNTAIN, Mountain Road, Francestown, NH 03043. Telephone: (603) 588-6840. Accommodations: fourteen rooms with twin or double beds; four private baths; telephones; public television. Rates: moderate. Dinner served Thursday, Friday and Saturday nights during ski season; Tuesday through Sunday in summer; every night in the fall. Children welcome. Pets subject to surcharge. No cards. Open all year except last week of October to Thanksgiving and end of ski season to Memorial Day.

Getting there: From I-91, take Route 9 east to Keene; proceed east on 101 to Peterborough. In Peterborough, take Route 202 north to Bennington, then Route 47 to Francestown. Follow signs to Crotched Mountain Ski Area off Route 47 by turning onto Mountain Road. The inn is about one mile up Mountain Road on the right.

A Window on the Main Street of New England
JOHN HANCOCK INN
Hancock

New Hampshire can be very desolate, especially in the west. You can drive for miles on highways bounded by endless forests of fir trees and boulder-strewn stream beds. There seem to be no houses, no towns along these roads, and on Interstate 89 between Concord and Lebanon, there is a twenty-mile stretch without exits or services. There is nothing but trees. You'd expect it in Wyoming, but this is the East!

Hancock is an oasis in the middle of this no-man's land. As you first drive through the town, you may think that you have stumbled upon a re-created eighteenth-century New England village, for each house is meticulously preserved, with lush gardens in the summer and colorful maples in the fall. There are picket fences, a wide Main Street and a wonderful country inn which revives guests with a wholesome meal and a good night's sleep under a friendly roof. The Hancock is distinguished from the other buildings along the main thoroughfare by its mansard roof and columned facade. An excellent time for a visit is late September to early October, since this is one of the best places for foliage touring in the fall. However, the inn's popularity often makes it difficult to get reservations at peak tourist times.

Although the inn's name is the John Hancock Inn, it is unlikely that John Hancock ever really stayed here. His family did own a large grant of land in southwestern New Hampshire that included what is now the town of Hancock and the inn took its name from the town's famous namesake when it opened its doors to the public in 1789. This is the oldest continuously operating inn in New Hampshre and every effort has been made to preserve the Colonial flavor.

The inn has ten guest rooms, each with its own bath. The rooms are simple, decorated with an eclectic combination of antique and reproduction pieces, bright white spreads and old patterned wallpapers. Be sure to ask to see the inside of the large room upstairs with a mural by itinerant painter Rufus Porter. The primitive scene shows the mills and houses of old Hancock—but it could be any New Hampshire village in the early 1800s.

The public areas of the inn are among the most spacious and gracious of any inn in the region. Wide board floors and stenciled walls, primitive paintings and sloping floors and ceilings all lend to the atmosphere of a cosy, early American winter's day in the company of the friendly locals or your fellow travelers. The tables are constructed with bases of old bellows from a foundry and the booth seats are actually carriage or sleigh seats. The help is friendly and the food is very good. Why travel farther?

There is plenty to do around Hancock besides enjoying the scenery. Ski areas such as Temple Mountain provide winter activities and there is a lovely town pond for swimming in the summer. Nearby Harrisville, another beautiful town, hosts an annual Zucchini Festival when everyone in town, along with thousands of out-of-towners, gather to celebrate this venerable squash. Peterborough, only about ten miles away, is home to a summer theatre and music series.

JOHN HANCOCK INN, Route 123, Hancock, NH 03449. Telephone: (603) 525-3318. Accommodations: ten rooms with twin or double beds; private baths with tubs, showers or tub/showers; no telephones; public television. Rates: inexpensive to moderate. Children welcome. Surcharge for pets. Cards: MC, VISA. Open all year except some holidays and short periods in late fall and early spring.

Getting there: From Route 3 in Bedford (the Spaulding Turnpike), take Route 101 west to Peterborough. Turn right onto Route 202 north. Go about ten miles north of Peterborough to Hancock. Turn onto Route 123 and proceed through town to the inn.

THE SOUTHERN MONADNOCK

Known as "The Currier and Ives Corner of New England," the southern Monadnock region is a far cry from the more rocky, rugged and less populated New Hampshire regions to the north and northeast. This hilly, river-laced countryside is a photographer's paradise, unequaled in New England. Old farms, quaint villages and sweeping views, always domintated by the barren peak of Mt. Monadnock, are the symbols of the area.

There is more to do in the southern Monadnock area than in almost any other part of New Hampshire. Antiques stores, general stores, art galleries and factory outlets vie for the traveler's time and savings. There are state parks for hiking, ski areas for winter sports, and fishing in the many lakes and streams, which is a passion, not just a pastime here.

Country inns seem to be at the heart of the area's activities, often providing the only full-service restaurants around. You can count on the inns recommended here to be the center of life in the villages, where, if you sit still long enough, you'll become absorbed in the daily hubbub of life in these out-of-the-way places. And you thought nothing ever happened in those little towns.

There are no interstate highways in this part of New Hampshire. Roads are winding, often with steep grades and sometimes a cow or a flock of sheep in the middle of the road. Drive slowly. And when someone waves to you as you pass on a back road, know that you have not been mistaken for someone else. They're just saying hello. It's a local custom, and not a bad one at that.

Watch the World Go By from Your Rocker
THE BIRCHWOOD INN
Temple

A massive brick and clapboard building featuring a wide, sloping porch crowded with rocking chairs, the Birchwood Inn looks exactly as you would expect a New England revolutionary era tavern to look. An idyllic setting for a country getaway, the Birchwood is a landmark country inn, known far and wide for dining and accommodations.

Although Temple, with only about seven hundred inhabitants, is not a big town by any means, there is always some sort of event going on that will fit into your vacation or weekend schedule. The countryside is beautiful and the town is close to the Massachusetts border, an easy two-hour drive from Boston. Mt. Monadnock is nearby for hiking and climbing, there are many lakes, and you'll find an abundance of art and antique treasures in the area.

Guests leave the Birchwood Inn feeling a part of the village, for the town and the people of Temple are an integral part of a stay at the Birchwood, perhaps accounting for the attachment that so many guests have to this inn. Temple's citizens eat at the Birchwood, they stop by the inn's little gift shop and they are, all in all, a very friendly group.

The Birchwood's interior is the inn's major attraction for many people. One highlight is the newly restored Rufus Porter mural on the main floor. Porter was a well-known itinerant artist who, in Colonial days, decorated walls and houses all over New England with his artwork. Very few of his works remain, and even fewer are in the excellent condition that this one is in.

The ground floor, with its lovely, sunny breakfast room, is only one small part of the inn's appeal. Upstairs, you will find seven delightful bedrooms, each decorated with a different theme. Antiques abound and you can stare through the curtains out across the town fields to the great mountain and imagine what it must have been like to sleep at the Birchwood two hundred years ago. Things haven't changed much, except that the beds are much more comfortable and the plumbing works well. They say that Henry David Thoreau slept here one night long ago.

Temple is not close to any major entertainment area, but there is no need to worry. The inn serves excellent meals at dinner and breakfast. For lunch, meander down the road to New Ipswich for a bite at the Carriage Stop or pick up picnic ingredients at the general store in Temple. Dinner is a must at the Birchwood, where you have at least two choices, usually one fish and one meat entree. After dinner, you can enjoy a bottle of wine in the public room, if you happened to remember to bring one with you—Temple has no liquor licenses, so the inn can only furnish you with ice and glasses.

THE BIRCHWOOD INN, Route 45, Temple, NH 03084. Telephone: (603) 878-3285. Accommodations: seven rooms with twin, double, twin and double or twin double beds; shared baths; no telephones; public television. Rates: inexpensive, breakfast included. Children welcome. No pets. No cards. Open all year except two weeks in April.

The Birchwood Inn

Getting there: From I-91, take Route 9 east to Keene. In Keene, proceed east on 101 through Peterborough. Turn left onto Route 45, which goes right into the center of Temple. The inn is set back from the town green on the left, just before the village store.

On the Quiet Side of the Mountain
MONADNOCK INN
Jaffrey

Each of New Hampshire's three resort regions, the White Mountains in the north, the Lakes Region in the middle, and the Monadnock in the southwest, has a unique flavor and style. The Monadnock reaches northward far beyond the one mountain, covering the entire area west of Interstate 93 and south of Interstate 89. A casual, friendly region with more than a dozen wonderful country inns, the Monadnock Region was once a quite exclusive vacation area. Today, many farms and summer houses are still maintained by families who have been coming to the area for generations, but most of the hotels are closed now. People who come to the area now seek peace and quiet or good mountain climbing and skiing. Antiques hunting is a popular sport here too.

The Monadnock Inn, located in Jaffrey Center, is one of the most charming inns in this area. Jaffrey Center, a quiet crossroads, is landarked by one of the most spectacular white country churches in New England and is just up the road a few miles from the town of Jaffrey, a bustling little country village with stores and churches and even an occasional traffic jam in foliage season. The Monadnock, an inviting, rambling old inn, is flanked by a wide, screened veranda and topped with a softly curving gambrel roof. In warm months, diners enjoy the mountain breezes at tables on the veranda, while in winter a glowing fire and the tavern provide warmth and comfort. Part of the charm of this inn is its winding stairways and warm, comfortable rooms. No two are alike, but most are filled with nice reproductions of antiques and there are delightful views from every window. Many beds are old four-posters and lovely rugs cover the hardwood floors.

Plan to eat at the Monadnock. The food is excellent and many outsiders join hotel guests for dinner. Be sure to leave room for dessert, however, for the Monadnock offers many delicious house specialties.

Take time out to explore the lakes and the back roads around the Jaffrey area during your stay. Cross the street and visit the little bookshop which specializes in out-of-print books and, in the summer months, take a short drive to the Cathedral of the Pines, a religious retreat. Nearby Fitzwilliam and Peterborough have many interesting antiques shops.

THE MONADNOCK INN, Route 124 (P.O. Box B), Jaffrey Center, NH 03454. Telephone: (603) 532-7001. Accommodations: fourteen rooms with single, twin or double beds; private and shared baths with tubs, showers or tub/showers; no telephones; no television. Rates: moderate. Children welcome. No pets. Cards: MC, VISA. Open all year; no meals available on Christmas Eve, Christmas and New Year's Day.

Getting there: From I-91, take 119 east through Hinsdale and Fitzwilliam to Rindge. Turn left onto Route 137 north. In Jaffrey, turn left onto Route 124. The Monadnock Inn is on the left, just past the church.

A Nineteenth-Century Stage Stop
FITZWILLIAM INN
Fitzwilliam

The sign in front of the Fitzwilliam Inn, featuring two rotund nineteenth-century characters sitting in ladderback armchairs before a roaring fire, enjoying long-stemmed pipes, conversation and cups of grog, captures the essence of this hostelry. These two old fellows would fit right in at the Fitzwilliam even today, for little has changed since the inn opened as a stage stop in 1796.

The inn is on the common right in the middle of the quiet little town of Fitzwilliam, known for its stately summer homes, countless antiques shops—and its inn. In the springtime, nearby Rhododendron State Park bursts with flowers and brings sightseers from all around, while nearby Mt. Monadnock is always available for hiking and mountain climbing. Fitzwilliam is near Keene and Brattleboro, Vermont, which are fun places to explore. There is a harness raceway with night racing a few towns away in Hinsdale as well.

Although embellished with beautiful antiques and stenciled walls, the Fitzwilliam is very comfortable, for the furnishings are not held at an arm's length to be admired but rather, they are used and meant to be enjoyed. A luxurious new swimming pool and sauna brings the twentieth century to the Fitzwilliam, but it has kept to its stage stop tradition, for it is now a stop for the Vermont Transit Bus Line, with direct buses to the inn from New York and Boston.

At dinnertime every window of the Fitzwilliam blazes with light and the little town square fills with cars of people coming to eat at one of the area's finest restaurants. Through a row of little paned windows on one wall of the dining room you can see tiny lanterns glowing above the heads of diners intent upon their meals. The fare at the Fitzwilliam is simple and the prices are reasonable. Homemade breads and desserts are a house specialty, and the entrees—often specials of roast beef or trout or fresh seafood—are all delicious.

Expect the unexpected at the Fitzwilliam Inn, whether it be an impromptu music concert in one of the living rooms after dinner or a celebrity guest in the tavern, always a popular place. Tales are told and travelers revived, just as they have been for almost two hundred years.

FITZWILLIAM INN, Fitzwilliam, NH 03227. Telephone: (603) 585-9000. Accommodations: twenty-five rooms with double or twin double beds; twelve private baths; no telephones; public television. Rates: inexpensive. No meals included. Children welcome. Pets subject to surcharge. Cards: AE, CB, DC, MC, VISA.

Getting there: From I-91, take Route 119 east to Fitzwilliam. The inn is on the green in the center of the little village.

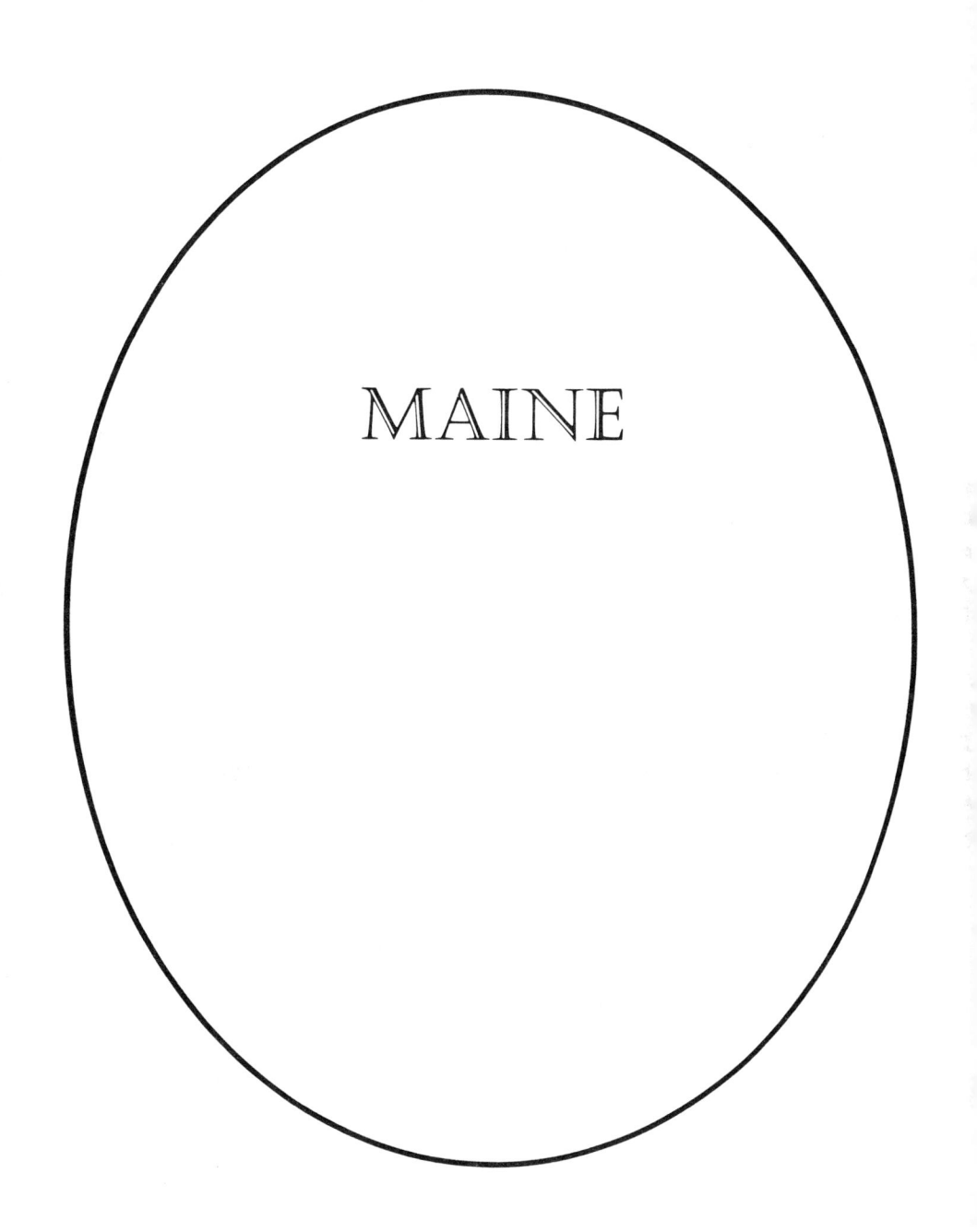

MAINE

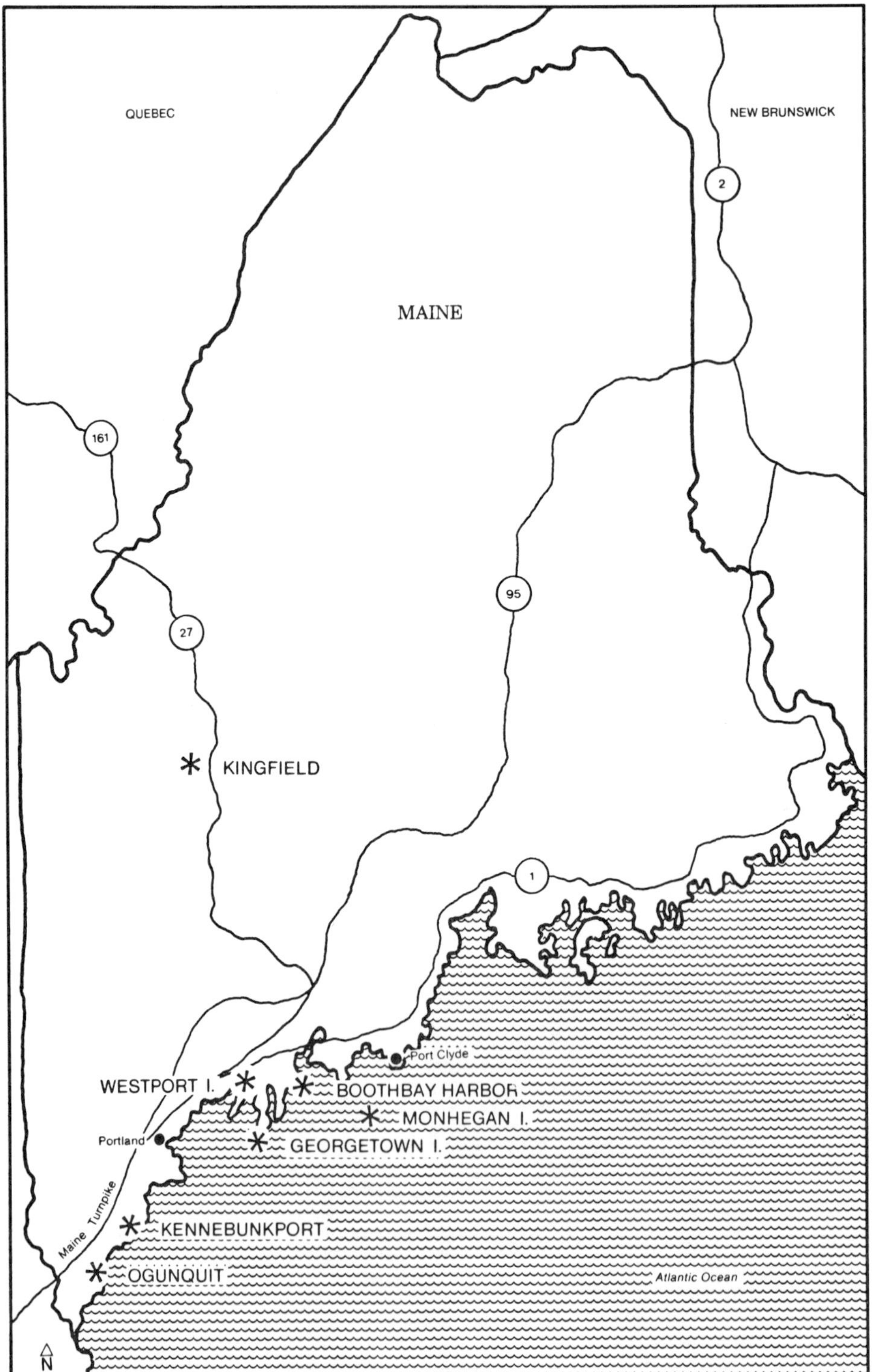
QUEBEC
NEW BRUNSWICK
2
MAINE
161
95
27
KINGFIELD
1
Port Clyde
WESTPORT I.
BOOTHBAY HARBOR
MONHEGAN I.
Portland
GEORGETOWN I.
Maine Turnpike
KENNEBUNKPORT
OGUNQUIT
Atlantic Ocean
N

On the Rocks and in the Sky
THE PERKINS COVE INN
Ogunquit

The Perkins Cove Inn is a simple place. The rooms aren't fancy or loaded with antiques, but a patina of comfortable wear instantly makes you feel at home. Good thing, too. You wouldn't want anything inside the inn to distract you from the incredible scenery that fills every window. The view from the porch of the Perkins Cove Inn is a classic Maine scene, with sloping old docks, rocks covered with sea spray and swooping gulls. The porch at this inn is especially important. The inn is at the end of a little lane, so there is no car traffic. Still, you can get to know the boats in the harbor and watch the low water mark come and go as the hours pass. This is doing nothing—in style.

The inn is behind the wharves at Perkins Cove, one of the most popular tourist attractions in southern Maine. A jetty separates the inn's peninsula from the main wharves, so guests have privacy from the crowds without sacrificing the glorious view. The boutiques and art galleries on the wharves are a short walk across a charming little footbridge. A special treat in this setting is the sounds of the sea. As soon as you get out of your car, you will hear the squawk of sea gulls and the crashing, pounding surf. The hum of puttering lobster boats and the thud of dripping crates as they are heaved onto the wharves complete the symphony as innkeepers Ann-Marie and Bob Johnson rise from their porch rockers to greet you with a hearty welcome.

The inn has several guest rooms in the main part of the rambling house, along with a motel-like ell of rooms with private entrances and a separate cottage. In Maine, it's the basics that count, and this is just what the The Perkins Cove Inn provides: steaming hot showers, sparkling rooms and individually controlled thermostats. These things mean a lot in Maine, especially if you visit in the off-season, when The Perkins Cove Inn offers bargain rates.

In spring and fall, the television room in the main part of the house replaces the windswept porch as the center of inn gatherings. Guests gather here for the late news each night, exchanging stories of the day's adventures deep sea fishing, antiquing or crafts shopping.

Perkins Cove is actually a neighborhood of the seaport Ogunquit, known for its wide sandy beaches and sophisticated hotels and restaurants, which are unusual for Maine. The Perkins Cove Inn offers no meals, but you can stroll over the footbridge for a picnic-style seafood dinner at Barnacle Billy's Restaurant or a gourmet meal at the famous Whistling Oyster. Farther along, past the restaurants and boutiques, there is a pathway, the Marginal Way, which leads through the rocks along the shore to Ontio Beach.

THE PERKINS COVE INN, Woodbury Lane, Ogunquit, ME 03907. Telephone: (207) 646-2232. Accommodations: fourteen rooms with twin, double or two double beds; private and shared baths with showers or tub/showers; no telephones; television in main house common area. Rates: moderate, inexpensive in off season; no meals. Children welcome. Pets allowed if arrangements made in advance. No cards. Open late spring through fall.

Getting there: From Route 1, take Shore Road into Ogunquit village. Follow signs to Perkins Cove past many inns and motels. Turn onto Woodbury Lane on the left. The inn is the large white building on the left at the end of the lane. Do not bear left onto Perkins Cove wharves at the curve at Laura Tanner House restaurant.

KENNEBUNKPORT REGION

Maine is a special place, but one could take a lifetime exploring it and still not know it or its people. It is vast, varied and often quite empty. If you are seeking solitude, almost any place in Maine is ideal. The first-time visitor, especially someone from outside New England, might find Maine baffling, its vast distances disconcerting. There are a few pockets of Maine, however, particularly along the coast, where there is lots to do, lots to see, and explorers can get their feet wet—or could, if the water wasn't so darn cold all year.

Kennebunkport could be called the capital of seacoast Maine, particularly the stretch south of Portland. This village is home to at least a dozen excellent country inns and as many or more bed-and-breakfast hostelries. The village on the wharves is a maze of tangled streets that are little more than paths that always seem to be clogged with people. It is rather disorienting to try to drive around town, so park your car at your inn and walk when possible.

Shopping is one of Kennebunkport's main attractions, where tumble-down wharves and sail lofts have been converted into fashion boutiques and gift shops with surprisingly appealing wares. There are restaurants offering every imaginable rendition of fried, broiled or baked seafood. Sandwiched in between these attractions are glorious views of the harbor, bicycle or hiking expeditions to Cape Porpoise and the open ocean, and a survey of seaside architecture which will leave you wondering why the tiniest puff of wind doesn't blow the whole town down. Special attractions here include the Seashore Trolley Museum, a memorial to the old streetcar line that used to deliver vacationers to the southern Maine seacoast, the St. Anthony Monastery and Shrine, the lovely grounds a delightful escape from the crowds in Dock Square, and the Brick Store Museum in nearby Kennebunk.

A Victorian Night in a Forest of Lilacs
ENGLISH MEADOWS INN
Kennebunkport

On the way from Kennebunk to Kennebunkport is the English Meadows Inn. It lies on the edge of the village, a quiet haven for tourists seeking rest and simple luxury, the name evocative of the inn's ambience. Flowers fill the grounds and the house—and even a wheelbarrow in the front yard. The great orange doors hint at the eclectic mood here.

The English Meadows Inn is the life work of the Kelly family, the innkeepers. The English Meadows has been open to the public since the early part of the century and little has changed, except that the barn and stables are no longer needed to put up drivers and stagecoach horses, so they have been converted into small, comfortable guest rooms. The center of the huge old barn has been opened up into a warm common room with a fireplace—the rooms here are excellent for family gatherings and other group stayovers. According to the Kellys, teenagers especially enjoy staying in the barn's beamed rooms.

Inside the main house, the rooms are classic country inn guest rooms, evidence of the Kellys' expertise and excellent taste in antiques. Each room is individually furnished, often with brass or brass and iron antique beds. Hardwood floors are accented with scattered hooked and braided rugs. Most rooms share a bath and all feature lovely garden or meadow views from dormer windows. Traffic in and out of Kennebunkport settles down after dark, so you can count on blissful quiet for a good night's sleep.

One of the most pleasant aspects of staying at the English Meadows is breakfast in the dining room, which is brightly lit by sunlight streaming through a beautiful multi-paned bow window. At break-

English Meadows Inn

fast, you can count on the Kellys to help you plan sightseeing or shopping expeditions in Kennebunkport or to give you directions on your way back to the rest of Maine.

One last note: Beware this inn in June—the scent of the banks of lilacs, some more than one hundred years old, can be intoxicating!

ENGLISH MEADOWS INN, Route 35, Kennebunkport, ME 04046. Telephone: (207) 967-5766. Accommodations: fourteen rooms with twin, double or two double beds, one efficiency suite with kitchen in the barn; private and shared baths with showers or tub/showers; no telephones; television in TV room. Rates: moderate, full breakfast included. Two-day minimum stay in July and August. No children under 12. No pets. No cards. Open April through October.

Getting there: From I-95, take Exit 3 and follow signs to Kennebunk. Turn left on Route 35 south and follow into village of Kennebunkport.

A Perfectly Proper Place in the Port
THE CHETWYND HOUSE
Kennebunkport

Is blue your favorite color? Then prepare to feast your eyes at the Chetwynd House, a four-bedroom hostelry in the midst of the fun and chaos off Dock Square in Kennebunkport. You will know the inn as soon as you see it—a pristine white clapboard ship captain's house with blue shutters.

Parking your car is a veritable challange here, but fortunately there are usually several spots blocked off in the inn's driveway or on the street. Once you find a spot, however, file away your keys. Chances are you won't need them here. The inn is a minute's walk from everywhere in the middle of this busy little town and you'll get there faster by walking anyway.

Although there are only four guest rooms, the inn always seems to be in the middle of town happenings. Many of the guests here are return visitors and many are artists. You will learn a lot about other guests at innkeeper Susan Chetwynd's unforgettable group breakfasts where fresh fruit, fish dishes and even oyster stew may appear on the table.

The Chetwynd House is one of the most carefully furnished inns anywhere. Each guest room is decorated with a certain style or color, and rooms are designated by names, like Fern Room or Blue Room rather than by numbers. The Gable Room has a private bath and features a cannonball bed, an old favorite New England design, with round "cannonballs" at the tops of the rugged posts. Everywhere, you will see blue carpeting, blue china, and sometimes, even Mrs. Chetwynd dressed in blue.

CHETWYND HOUSE, Chestnut Street, Kennebunkport, ME 04046. Telephone: (207) 967-2235. Accommodations: five rooms with double, queen- or king-size beds; shared baths with showers or tub/showers; no telephones; no television. Rates: expensive, deluxe breakfast included. Children not allowed during summer or Washington's Birthday weekend; call ahead about children the rest of the year. No pets. No cards. Open all year.

Getting there: Take Exit 3 off Maine Turnpike and follow to Route 35. Turn left on 35 and follow into Kennebunkport and Dock Square. Turn right onto Ocean Avenue in Dock Square and then two blocks later, left on Chestnut Street. The inn is on the left, a white house with blue shutters and a small sign hanging outside.

A Shipmaster's Mansion
CAPTAIN LORD MANSION
Kennebunkport

Have you ever wanted to just curl up in one of those bedrooms that are re-created in museums? Did you ever tour a president's home and long to leap over the little barrier and sit down in a rocking chair? At the Captain Lord Mansion, the furnishings and atmosphere befit a museum, but the experience is yours for the asking. Just remember to call at least three months in advance to get a room, as the Captain Lord Mansion is one of the best-known inns in the Kennebunkport area. It was built as the home of Captain Nathaniel Lord in the early 1800s on a parklike parcel of land on the Kennebunk River, just out of the town's busy dock area. Today, the captain's home offers a generous dose of authentic historical atmosphere and a living lesson in architecture, period furnishings and dignified settings.

Legend has it that the house was built by the captain's ship carpenter friends—no doubt boat-building experts who put their expertise into the intricate moldings, veneers, inlays and the graceful, gravity-defying suspended staircase which rises three stories through the heart of the house. Most of the rooms at the inn have fireplaces and all have private baths. Your room may feature a canopy bed or a giant four-poster of massive mahogany. Most rooms have small sitting areas with comfortable upholstered furniture.

Two favorite activities at this inn include breakfast in the warm kitchen with your hosts, Rick Litchfield and Bev Davis. Another favorite is a three-story climb to the widow's walk, an enclosed cupola where townspeople once watched for Captain Lord's ship to be returning. Count on the Captain Lord Mansion for a generous dose of historic elegance. For a boisterous evening, try another inn—this one is for the dignified and the romantic, befitting a sea captain in his own home.

CAPTAIN LORD MANSION, Green and Pleasant (P.O. Box 527), Kennebunkport, ME 04046. Telephone: (207) 967-3141. Accommodations: sixteen rooms with double, queen- or king-size beds; baths with tubs, showers or tub/showers; no telephones; no television. Rates: very expensive, breakfast included. No children under 12. No pets. No cards. Open all year, two-night minimum stay June to October and on all weekends.

Getting there: From Route 35 in Kennebunkport, turn onto Route 9, crossing drawbridge. Turn right onto Ocean Avenue, then take the fourth left to the corner of Green and Pleasant.

All You Can See Is Sea and Sky
GREY HAVENS INN
Georgetown Island

The place for romantics is the Grey Havens Inn, an isolated, romantic, old-fashioned country inn right on the water. You don't have to drive five hours north to Bar Harbor to find "the real Maine." This is it, and how beautiful! A rambling, shingled building built in the turn-of-the-century style, it seems to be held in place by two tall turrets and a sweeping veranda which wraps around the structure. All you can see from any window in this giant inn is sea and sky and pine trees. The only sound is an occasional boat chugging along or the screech of a seagull. No traffic, no noise. The Hardcastles, the Texans who own the inn, are quick to remind guests that only the most well-behaved children need apply for rooms here. Peace and quiet are included in the room fee.

What rooms these are! The turret rooms at the Grey Havens Inn are certainly among the most unusual and most romantic at any inn in New England. Room 17, known as the Bridal Suite, is particularly charming. Walls aren't just walls here, but are smooth veneered ship-style paneling of horizontal lathing and the beds are not ordinary beds but are made of brass or brass and iron. Rooms have little wash basins and multi-colored quilts—not one detail seems to have been overlooked. The rooms are linked by great wide hallways and reached by baronial staircases from the ground floor, which contains a large dining room and a giant living room with fireplace and huge picture window. Every window seems to give a new view of the ocean, making this an especially magical place on a stormy day, when rain pelts the windows and you roll over and go back to sleep, sinking deeper into your antique bedclothes.

In the height of summer, Georgetown is a lively place, with Reid State Park's lovely swimming beach attracting great crowds. It is one of the few sand beaches this far north in Maine, but watch out! The water is very cold. Most people prefer to swim in the fresh water ponds that dot the peninsula and use the beach for sunbathing or a very quick dip. There are also miles of country roads for quiet strolls around the inn, and nearby Wiscasset is a great antiquing spot. Boat watching is a popular sport and just hanging around the inn or your room is a pleasant enough experience.

There is not much night life in Georgetown, so you will have to rely on your own resources or some new-found friends at the inn.

Bath is not far away, and you can tour the restored part of this old shipbuilding capital—a good dinner can be had at the Grapevine. Dinner is served at the inn, as are breakfast and lunch, and you can enjoy good, simple cooking and fresh seafood here.

GREY HAVENS INN, Reid Park Road, Georgetown, ME. Mailing address: Box 82, Five Islands, ME 04546. Telephone: (207) 371-2616. Accommodations: seventeen rooms, including two suites, with twin or double beds; private and shared baths; no telephones; television in den. Rates: expensive, Continental breakfast included. Well-behaved children over 12 only. Make arrangements for pets in advance. No cards. Open June through September.

Getting there: Take Maine Turnpike to I-95 north of Portland. Follow I-95 north until it turns into Route 1 and follow north through Bath. Cross the bridge in Bath and take an almost immediate right onto Route 127 south. Follow signs to Reid State Park. Inn is on the left, on Reid Park Road.

A Formal Farm in a Country Setting
SQUIRE TARBOX INN
Westport Island

The Squire Tarbox Inn is an excellent example of what most people expect a country inn in New England to be. It is steeped in history, restored to a hair's breadth of perfection, and cushioned in comfort with just the right measure of modern conveniences. The food is exemplary, your hosts gracious, and the setting—well, the setting is *real* Maine. You're out in the country now.

There are only six rooms here, but they vary widely in mood and decor. The front rooms are pristine and antique—lovely moldings, white bedspreads and tasteful appointments. But stride across the dining room to the barn, actually an ell of the main house, and you will find a huge wall of authentic barnboards and four charming, romantic rooms in the loft, made cheery with bright curtains and coverlets on the beds.

The inn is on Westport Island, making the lively little town of Wiscasset, with some of the most interesting antiques shops in Maine, "town" for the inn. It is worth a good day's exploring, especially to see the giant rotting hulks of old sailing ships that lurk by the bridge over the Sheepscot River. Try lunch at The Garage, a converted car repair shop, for a good meal and a lovely view of the water.

Westport Island is peopled mainly by long-time residents who work in the local lobster industry or commute to jobs in Wiscasset or Bath, although there is a lively and growing summer population and many new, architecturally interesing vacation retreats. Many locals dine at the Squire Tarbox, evidence that it is one of the best eateries around. There is a simple gourmet elegance here in an antique setting—and you won't have to worry about negotiating the tortuous, endless road back to Wiscasset.

To insure accommodations at the Squire Tarbox, call well in advance. Fall is an especially nice time to visit and it may be easier to get a room then. Bring a sweater for the night chill and comfortable shoes for a walk down to the brook. And don't forget to make those dinner reservations.

THE SQUIRE TARBOX INN, Route 144, Westport Island, ME 04578. Telephone: (207) 882-7693. Accommodations: nine rooms with twin or double beds; private and shared baths with showers or tub/showers; no telephones; no television. Rates: moderate, breakfast and dinner included. Children over 12 welcome. No pets. No cards. Open May through October.

Getting there: Follow I-95 north of Portland to Route 1 and continue through Bath. Turn south on Route 144 and follow 144 for about eight miles. The inn is on the left.

A Bit of Scotland by the Sea
THE THISTLE INN
Boothbay Harbor

Boothbay Harbor is one of the most scenic and one of the most popular tourist regions of Maine. But while this little peninsula seems to be fairly littered with motels, cabins and full-service resorts, there are not many bona fide country inns. There is, however, the popular Thistle Inn.

This inn may sometimes seem to be two completely different places, for by day, it is quiet and serene, a lovely village inn with simple, clean accommodations and a lovely Scottish-accented dining room and menu. After dinner, however, the mood changes abruptly, and the tavern, with its piano and its bar made from an old dory, and the geranium-decked veranda, draw yachtsmen and the town's citizens as well as tourists. Tall tales and sea stories abound during these lively evenings, though it can be tough to sleep in the rooms above the bar before closing hours.

Many great friendships have started and ended in the bar at the Thistle, just as many legends around town begin, "One night at the Thistle...." A great number of these legends are directly attributable to the late Miss Leone, who formerly owned the inn and who was the unofficial social and political leader of the town and a great promoter of the Scottish tradition. Her spirit lives on here, however, in every toast and raised glass.

Either eat in East Boothbay at Lobsterman's Wharf, *the* place to get a fresh lobster meal outside by the water, or join the merriment in the tavern back at the Thistle. You can count on the folks at the bar to give good advice on the best boat to take out to Monhegan or the least expensive lobsters to buy to take home.

The Thistle is right on Route 27 as you come into the harbor area. You can walk from here to anywhere downtown for a movie, a meal or a quick "Brud's hot dog" as Brud rolls by. A stroll across the harbor footbridge at night is glorious, and window shopping is fun after dark when the crowds have abandoned the sidewalks. Enjoy breakfast at the Thistle or join the young and old at Robin's coffee shop on the pier for one of the best blueberry muffins in the world. Don't miss the schooner museum and plan on taking one of the many harbor cruises while you are in town. You can also catch a ferry from Boothbay to Squirrel Island or Monhegan. There are the festive Windjammer Days in July, the Drunken Sailor Races, the visiting celebrities who stroll the streets and, everywhere, there are boats, in every size and every shape.

    Peace and tranquility can be found out of the downtown area. The winding roads are perfect for cycling and hiking. Lobster Cove is a nice destination, only about a mile's hike from the harbor. Ocean Point is popular with cyclists, where pounding waves crash near a tiny chapel made from rocks on the beach, and where a stiff ocean wind will almost sweep you off your feet, a big switch from the calm harbor waters. Out of town in the other direction, the road wanders past field and forest to Southport, perhaps the most scenic area on the whole peninsula. White washed houses are built right on the piers and treacherous old bridges lead to points of land with names like Seal Island and Dogfish Head. Here you can see seals at play and watch giant yachts glide past the lighthouse.

THE THISTLE INN, 53 Oak Street, Boothbay Harbor, ME 04538. Telephone: (207) 633-3541. Accommodations: eight rooms with twin or double beds; shared baths with showers or tub/showers; no telephones; television in the bar. Rates: inexpensive. Children welcome. Pets welcome. Cards: AE, DC, MC, VISA. Open all year.

Getting there: From Route 1, follow Route 27 through Boothbay into Boothbay Harbor. Bear right at the big fork, staying on Route 27. Inn is on the left. Parking may be a problem if you arrive after dark.

Beautiful Surroundings with Just the Basics
MONHEGAN ISLAND

Are you unable to live without television? Do you expect to make important business or personal calls during your trip? Do you drive everywhere? If the answer to any of these questions is yes, then think twice before going to Monhegan Island for a vacation. You might be better off staying in Boothbay Harbor and taking the ferry over for a day trip. Monhegan Island is unique in the 1980s, for it is built on ingenuity and independence rather than modern technology. The roads are designed for foot traffic and must be shared with deer. What electricity there is comes from a generator in the basement of one of the inns. The rest of the island is lit by kerosene.

    This island is a haven for artists. Many who paint here are on leave from the frantic pace of the New York art scene and seek the peace and quiet they know that only Monhegan can provide. You will see many of them painting the beautiful landscapes that the island provides and also see their finished works for sale in the gallery in town.

Monhegan is a place to forget the hubbub of the real world. Hiking is popular here and the cliffs at the end of the island provide good vantage for spotting the spouts of visiting pilot whales. Watch your step, however, for shipwrecks once were common here. The old iron posts implanted in the rocks were used to anchor rescue lines.

Rooms are often booked six months in advance in Monhegan since the island has so few rooms and so many who want to return. Just be patient and prepare to plan your vacation around a room's availability, which may be more likely in spring or fall. If nothing else, visit the island for just a day if you aren't able to spend the night.

Sunrise and Sunset in Rustic Surroundings
THE ISLAND INN
Monhegan Island

More people are staying at the Island Inn on a summer night than live on the entire island in winter. The rambling old inn has forty-five rooms under its old weather-warped roof, and none is fancy by mainland terms. However, by island standards, this is the Ritz. Rooms at the Island Inn provide either a sunset or a sunrise view, for the sun sets over the water and rises over a lovely meadow where island deer graze. The best thing about these rooms is the view, since the inn's furnishings are spare.

The Island Inn and the nearby grocery store/snack bar is the news headquarters of Monhegan because of the constant coming and going of guests who have news—like who's winning the World Series or what plays just opened on Broadway. Despite the simple setting and the rustic amenities, the island has a very sophisticated summer populace.

Meals are served downstairs in the dining room. Breakfast and dinner are included with the room and lunch is optional. Be prepared for simple, wholesome food and remember to bring some snack food with you to stow in your room or knapsack—food prices on the island are even higher than in Boothbay Harbor—which are sky high.

THE ISLAND INN, Monhegan Island, ME 04852. Telephone: (207) 372-9681. Accommodations: forty-five rooms, two suites, and one cottage with double beds; shared and private baths; no telephones; no television. Rates: moderate, breakfast and dinner included. Children welcome. No pets. No cards. Open June through September.

Getting there: Cars are not allowed on Mohegan Island. Take the mail boat from Port Clyde (near Northeast Harbor) or take a passenger ferry in the summer months from Boothbay Harbor; reservations may be necessary. Dress warmly and wear sensible shoes, preferably rubber soled. If you need to plug in any appliance (for instance, a contact lens kit) you will be in trouble here overnight. Frequent power blackouts are common, as is telephone service interruption.

Classic, Friendly and Steeped in History
THE WINTER'S INN
Kingsfield

When people think of Maine, especially country inns in Maine, they generally think of the coast. The great inland of Maine, with its vast wilderness and towering mountains, has traditionally been left to canoers, hikers and campers, and consequently there are only a few inns in this part of Maine. There is one, however, that is like no other in any part of New England: The Winter's Inn.

The Winter's Inn is conveniently located in Kingsfield, home of the prosperous four-season Sugarloaf resort. The area is known as the Carabasset Valley, which has, in the past ten years, grown into one of the premier resort areas in New England. This is quite remarkable, given that it is at least a five or six hours' drive from Boston and that it is so close to the Quebec border. People come to ski the snow fields at the summit, the only deep-powder skiing available on a regular basis in New England, or they come to explore the hiking trails and to canoe the lakes. And some come just to stay at The Winter's Inn.

The Winter's Inn is registered with the National Register of Historic Places. It was designed by the Stanley Brothers, of Stanley Steamer fame, for a valley resident, Mr. A.G. Winter, Jr., whose descendents still live nearby. The inn has been completely restored to its original luxurious state, and is known both for its fine accommodations and its excellent restaurant, which is open to the public.

No architectural element seems to have been omitted from this building, but the Stanley brothers managed to figure out how to link them all together. There is a great deal of curved glass, which gives the front of the building a bow-shaped appearance. A lovely Georgian staircase is now buffed to a glowing oak tone and beautiful pillars support the ceilings and the fireplaces that give the house a warm glow in the winter. During the ski season the top floor of this formal house is a dormitory for skiers. This may be the ideal way for a family to be able to afford to stay here.

The Carabasset Valley is an excellent resort area all year, and the Winter's Inn is only closed in spring and late fall. Howver, be prepared for Maine's legendary "no see 'ums" and black flies if you plan to hike or canoe in the summer. Early fall, the foliage season, is a great time to visit. You can also take in the country fairs at North New Portland or Farmington and share some fun with native Mainers after the hordes of tourists have gone.

THE WINTER'S INN, P.O. Box 44, Kingsfield, ME 04947. Telephone: (207) 265-5421. Accommodations: twelve rooms with twin, double, or king-size beds, one suite; private and shared baths with showers or tub/showers; no telephones; no television. Rates: expensive, breakfast and dinner included; two-day minimum stay. Well-behaved children over six allowed; call ahead to make arrangements. No pets. Cards: AE, DC, MC, VISA. Open Thanksgiving to April and mid-June to the end of October.

Getting there: From Boston area, take I-95 north to the Maine Turnpike. Take Exit 12 (Route 4) in Auburn and follow signs to Farmington. In Farmington, take Route 27 north to Kingsfield. Proceed through the village, then bear left. Inn is on the hill behind the general store.

INDEX

INDEX TO INNS

CONNECTICUT
Bee and Thistle, Old Lyme, 40–41
The Birches Inn, New Preston, 15
Bishops Gate, East Haddam, 32–33
Boulders Inn, New Preston, 16
Butternut Farm, Glastonbury, 30–31
The Copper Beech Inn, Ivoryton, 35
The Elms, Ridgefield, 10–11
Griswold Inn, Essex, 36–38
Homestead Inn, Greenwich, 4–6
The Hopkins Inn, New Preston, 16–17
The Inn at Chester, Chester, 33–34
The Inn at Mystic, Mystic, 43–45
The Inn on Lake Waramaug, New Preston, 18–19
The Litchfield Inn, Litchfield, 19–20
Norwich Inn, Norwich, 45–46
Old Lyme Inn, Old Lyme, 41–42
Old Riverton Inn, Riverton, 27–28
Ragamont Inn, Salisbury, 24–25
Roger Sherman Inn, New Canaan, 8–9
Silvermine Tavern, Norwalk, 6–7
Stonehenge, Ridgefield, 11–13
Toll Gate Hill Inn, Litchfield, 20–21
Under Mountain Inn, Salisbury, 25–26
Wake Robin Inn, Lakeville, 22–24
West Lane Inn, Ridgefield, 13–14
Yankee Pedlar Inn, Torrington, 21

MAINE
Captain Lord Mansion, Kennebunkport, 218–219
The Chetwynd House, Kennebunkport, 217–218
English Meadows Inn, Kennebunkport, 215–217
Grey Havens Inn, Georgetown Island, 220–221
The Island Inn, Monhegan Island, 225–226
The Perkins Cove Inn, Ogunquit, 213–214
Squire Tarbox Inn, Westport Island, 221–222
The Thistle Inn, Boothbay Harbor, 223–224
The Winter's Inn, Kingsfield, 226–227

MASSACHUSETTS
Addison Choate House, Rockport, 126–127
The Beach Plum Inn, Menemsha, 144–145
Bradford Gardens, Provincetown, 140–142
The Candlelight Inn, Lenox, 85–86
Colonel Ebenezer Crafts Inn, Sturbridge, 108
The Colonial Inn, Concord, 119–121
Coonamessett Inn, Falmouth, 132–133
The Country Inn, Harwichport, 135–136

Country Inn at Princeton, Princeton, 115–117
Deerfield Inn, Deerfield, 100–103
Federal House Inn, South Lee, 78
Gateways Inn, Lenox, 86–88
Haus Andreas Inn, Lee, 82–83
The Hawthorne Inn, Concord, 118–119
Hotel Northampton, Northampton, 95–96
The Inn at Stockbridge, Stockbridge, 75–76
Jared Coffin House, Nantucket, 146–147
The Lord Jeffery Inn, Amherst, 96–98
Merrell Tavern Inn, South Lee, 80–82
Nauset House Inn, East Orleans, 137–138
Old Farm Inn, Rockport, 124–126
Publick House, Sturbridge, 109–110
The Red Lion Inn, Stockbridge, 76–77
The 1780 Egremont Inn, South Egremont, 72–73
Ships Inn, Nantucket, 147–148
Stagecoach Hill Inn, Sheffield, 70
The Victorian, Whitinsville, 110–112
Village Inn, Lenox, 88–90
Wayside Inn, Sudbury, 121–123
Wedgewood Inn, Yarmouthport, 133–135
Whale Inn, Goshen, 98–99
Whalewalk Inn, 138–140
Wheatleigh, Lenox, 90–91
The Wildwood Inn, Ware, 104–107
The Williamsville Inn, West Stockbridge, 83–84
Windflower, Great Barrington, 73–74
Yankee Clipper Inn, Rockport, 128–130
Yankee Pedlar Inn, Holyoke, 93–94

NEW HAMPSHIRE
Beal House Inn, Littleton, 187–188
The Birchwood Inn, Temple, 205–208
The Bradford Inn, Bradford, 198–200
Colby Hill Inn, Henniker, 200–201
Fitzwilliam Inn, Fitzwilliam, 209–210
The Follansbee Inn, North Sutton, 196–197
The Homestead, Sugar Hill, 189–190
The Inn at Crotched Mountain, Francestown, 202–203
John Hancock Inn, Hancock, 203–204
Kimball Hill Inn, Whitefield, 185–187
The Lyme Inn, Lyme, 194–195
Monadnock Inn, Jaffrey, 208–209
The New England Inn, Intervale, 183–184
The New London Inn, New London, 195–196
Sunset Hill House, Sunset Hill, 190–191
The Woodstock Inn, North Woodstock, 191–192

RHODE ISLAND
The Admiral Benbow Inn, 58–59
The Atlantic Inn, Block Island, 51–52
Hotel Manisses, Block Island, 52–54
The Inn at Castle Hill, Newport, 59–61
The Innetowne, Newport, 61–62
The Queen Anne Inn, Newport, 62–63
Shelter Harbor Inn, Westerly, 49–50
The 1661 Inn, Block Island, 55–56
Wayside, Newport, 65–66
The Yankee Peddler Inn of Newport, Newport, 63–65

VERMONT
Chester Inn, Chester, 158–160
The Greenhurst Inn, Bethel, 167–168
Green Mountain Inn, Stowe, 175–177
Green Trails Inn, Brookfield, 170–172
Inn at Sawmill Farm, West Dover, 152–154
The Kedron Valley Inn, South Woodstock, 161–162
North Hero House, North Hero Island, 177–179
Old Newfane Inn, Newfane, 155–156
Old Tavern at Grafton, Grafton, 156–158
The Quechee Inn at Marshland Farm, Quechee, 164–165
Rabbit Hill Inn, Lower Waterford, 179–180

Stone House Inn, North Thetford, 165–167
Tucker Hill Lodge, Waitsfield, 173–175
Village Auberge, Dorset, 160–161

INDEX TO AREAS

CONNECTICUT
Chester, 29, 33–34
The Connecticut River, 29, 32–38
Danbury, 3
The Eastern Shore, 39–46
East Haddam, 32–33
Essex, 29, 36–38
Fairfield County, 3–14
Glastonbury, 30–31
Greenwich, 3, 4–6
Guilford, 39
Hartford, 28–31
Ivoryton, 35
Lakeville, 22–24
Lake Waramaug, 14, 15–19
Litchfield, 19–21
The Litchfield Hills, 14–15, 19–21
Mystic, 39, 43–45
New Canaan, 8–9
New Haven, 39
New London, 39
New Preston, 15–19
Northwestern Connecticut, 22–28
Norfolk, 22
Norwalk, 3, 6–7
Norwich, 45–46
Old Lyme, 40–42
Ridgefield, 3, 10–14
Riverton, 27–28
Salisbury, 24–26
Sharon, 22
Stamford, 3
Torrington, 21
Westport, 3
Wethersfield, 29

MAINE
Boothbay Harbor, 223–224
Georgetown Island, 220–221
Kennebunkport Region, 214–219
Kingsfield, 226–227
Monhegan Island, 224–225
Ogunquit, 213–214
Westport Island, 221–222

MASSACHUSSETTS
Amherst, 92, 96–98
The Berkshires, 69–74
Boston, 123
Bourne, 131
Cape Ann, 123–130
Cape Cod, 130–141
The Central College Belt, 92–99
Chilmark, 142
Concord, 118–121
Concord Area, 117–123
Deerfield, 100–102
East Central Massachusetts, 103–107
Eastham, 131, 138–140
East Orleans, 137–138
Edgartown, 142
Falmouth, 131, 132–133
Gloucester, 123
Goshen, 98–99
Great Barrington, 73–74
Harwichport, 135–136
Holyoke, 93–94
Hyannis, 131
Lee, 82–83
Lenox, 69, 84–91
Lexington, 117
Marblehead, 123
Martha's Vineyard, 142, 144–145
Menemsha, 144–145
Nantucket, 142–143, 146–148
Northampton, 92–93, 95–96
Oak Bluffs, 142
Orleans, 131
Pittsfield, 69
Princeton, 115–117
Provincetown, 131, 140–142
The Quabbin Reservoir, 92, 103–107
Rockport, 123–130
Sandwich, 131
Sheffield, 70
South Egremont, 72–73
South Hadley, 92
South Lee, 78–82
Springfield, 92
Stockbridge, 74–84
Sturbridge, 107–112
Sudbury, 117, 121–123
Tanglewood, 69
Ware, 104–107
West Concord, 117
West Springfield, 92
West Stockbridge, 83–84
West Tisbury, 142

Whitinsville, 110–112
Williamstown, 69
Woodshole, 131
Yarmouthport, 133–135

NEW HAMPSHIRE
Bethelem, 185
Bradford, 197, 198–200
Concord, 193, 198
Fitzwilliam, 209–210
Francestown, 202–203
Franconia Notch Region, 184–192
Hancock, 197, 203–204
Henniker, 197, 200–201
Intervale, 183–184
Jaffrey, 208–209
Keene, 198
Lebanon, 193
Littleton, 184, 187–188
Lyme, 194–195
Manchester, 198
New London, 195–196
New London Region, 193–197
Northern Monadnock, 197–204
North Sutton, 196–197
North Woodstock, 191–192
Southern Monadnock, 205–210
Sugar Hill, 184, 189–190
Sunset Hill, 190–191

Temple, 205–208
Whitefield, 185–187
Woodstock, 185

RHODE ISLAND
Block Island, 49, 50–56
The Coastal Route, 49–56
Galilee, 49
Newport, 50, 56–66
Point Judith, 50
Providence, 50
Westerly, 49–50

VERMONT
Bethel, 167–168
Brookfield, 170–172
Chester, 158–160
Dorset, 160–161
Grafton, 156–158
Lower Waterford, 179–180
Newfane, 155–156
North Hero Island, 177–179
North Thetford, 165–167
Quechee, 164–165
South Woodstock, 161–162
Stowe, 175–176
Waitsfield, 173–175
West Dover, 152–154

COUNTRY INNS GUIDEBOOKS
In 101 Productions' Series

Country Inns of the Far West: California $7.95
Country Inns of the Far West: Pacific Northwest $7.95
Country Inns of New England $7.95
Country Inns of New York State $7.95
Country Inns of the Mid-Atlantic $7.95
Country Inns of the Old South $7.95
Country Inns of the Great Lakes $4.95
Country Inns Cookery $6.95

If you cannot find these books in your local bookstore,
they may be ordered from the publisher:
101 Productions, 834 Mission Street, San Francisco CA 94103
Please add $1.00 per copy for postage and handling.
California residents add sales tax.

TO ORDER: Indicate quantity for each title above and fill in form below.
Send with check or money order to 101 Productions.

NAME _____

ADDRESS _____

CITY_____ STATE_____ ZIP_____

PATRICIA BROOKS, a resident of New England for 30 years, is the author of *Best Restaurants Southern New Engand* and a regular restaurant reviewer and columnist for the Connecticut Section of *The New York Times*. Her articles on travel and food in New England have also been published in *Travel and Leisure, Vogue, Bon Appetit, Harpers Bazaar, House & Garden* and *Cuisine*.

FRAN JURGA GARVAN, a free-lance writer specializing in food, is the author of *The Farmers Market Cookbook* and articles for many magazines, including *Yankee*. A lifelong resident of New England, she has more than ten years' experience in the New England restaurant business.

ROY KILLEEN, whose drawings illustrate this book, is an architect, formerly with Anshen and Allen of San Francisco, and a one-time resident of Newport, Rhode Island. He also has designed 101 Productions' "Mini-Mansion" series of historical architectural models and illustrated a number of other 101 books.